Rethinking Sales Management

Rethinking Sales Management

A strategic guide for practitioners

Beth Rogers

John Wiley & Sons, Ltd

Telephone (+44) 1243 779777

Email (for orders and customer service enquiries): cs-books@wiley.co.uk
Visit our Home Page on www.wiley.com

Other Wiley Editorial Offices

John Wiley & Sons Inc., 111 River Street, Hoboken, NJ 07030, USA

Jossey-Bass, 989 Market Street, San Francisco, CA 94103-1741, USA

Wiley-VCH Verlag GmbH, Boschstr. 12, D-69469 Weinheim, Germany

John Wiley & Sons Australia Ltd, 42 McDougall Street, Milton, Queensland 4064, Australia

John Wiley & Sons (Asia) Pte Ltd, 2 Clementi Loop #02-01, Jin Xing Distripark, Singapore 129809

John Wiley & Sons Canada Ltd, 6045 Freemont Blvd, Mississauga, ONT, L5R 4J3, Canada

Wiley also publishes its books in a variety of electronic formats. Some content that appears in print may not be available in electronic books.

Anniversary Logo Design: Richard J. Pacifico

Library of Congress Cataloging-in-Publication Data

Rogers, Beth, 1957-
Rethinking sales management : a strategic guide for practitioners / Beth Rogers.
p. cm.
Includes bibliographical references and index.
ISBN 978-0-470-51305-7 (cloth : alk. paper) 1. Sales management. I. Title.
HF5438.4.R64 2007
658.8'1 – dc22

2007019144

British Library Cataloguing in Publication Data

A catalogue record for this book is available from the British Library

ISBN 978-0-470-51305-7 (HB)

Typeset in 11/15 pt Goudy by SNP Best-set Typesetter Ltd., Hong Kong
Printed and bound in Great Britain by TJ International Ltd, Padstow, Cornwall, UK
This book is printed on acid-free paper responsibly manufactured from sustainable forestry in which at least two trees are planted for each one used for paper production.

Contents

Foreword

The life of a sales manager has never been easy. In the early 1980s, a study inside Xerox Corporation showed that their sales managers would need to work for an average of 29 hours each day to fulfill all the requirements of their job description. Only one-third of the job description items were about selling or managing salespeople; the rest were mostly administrative. But, if you ask anyone who was around in those days, they'll tell you that although sales management was hard work it certainly wasn't intellectually demanding. There was little that was strategic about the sales manager's job. In one of the 10 largest business-to-business salesforces in the United States, new managers were given this advice:

> The sales manager's job is to get more calls, get more demos, get more proposals and get more closes. This means pushing your people hard. Nothing else works. You'll find that using your muscle beats using your brain . . . Selling is a numbers game. Push the more button; push it hard, push it often and keep pushing it.

From the lofty perspective of a new century we can look back at this approach to selling and feel smug about how quaint and naïve it sounds. Yet, at the time, it was probably the best advice available. Where could a new sales manager go for help? Training was hard to find – and even if you found it, it didn't help you much. Even the best companies were teaching questionable techniques. Along with tips on how to dress to impress, IBM's sales training was putting great emphasis on the initial few seconds of the call. "It's what you do in the first 20 seconds that will make or break your success" they assured a generation of salespeople selling multi-million dollar mainframe computers. Managers were advised to rehearse their salespeople's opening "patter". They practiced their teams in how to give a firm handshake, but not ***too*** firm, and a wide smile, but not ***too*** wide. Xerox, generally admired at the time for its sales training, was still teaching its top major account salespeople primitive closing techniques that today even the proverbial used-car salesperson would be ashamed to use. And most other companies were worse. I worked with one salesforce where training taught new salespeople never to allow customers to speak because "if you let customers talk they will create their own doubts".

I don't want to labour the point, but it's clear that selling has come a very long way since those dark ages. Over the last 25 years, selling has evolved into a discipline or, to use a generally misunderstood term, it has become a science. By 'science' I don't mean a cold and calculating impersonal process that is the sworn enemy of art. I mean, specifically, that a science meets five criteria:

- A science is based on a body of tested knowledge that helps us to understand and predict the world.
- A science uses an approach based on facts, not on superstitions or suppositions.
- A science has a set of teachable skills, models and concepts, that can be ***learned*** through education and training.
- A science has developed a means of objectively researching and testing relevant ideas and theories.
- A science has a set of methods for measuring and improving the skill of its practitioners.

Twenty five years ago, nobody could argue that the sales profession did a good job of meeting any of these criteria. At best selling was a partially understood craft; at worst it was a bundle of superstitions – "a blue tie will increase your sales" or "if, during your presentation, the buyer crosses his leg and it points toward the door you have lost". Imperceptibly, year by year, this kind of folklore has been supplanted by fact. Naïve methods have become sophisticated. Nobody today argues that muscle is more important than brains. In short, the sales profession has grown up. Measured against my criteria, sales can, at last, make a claim to be a business science on a level with its great rival, *marketing*. We no longer have to rely on the folklore of old. We now have well-researched and validated models of effective sales behavior that stand up to scientific scrutiny. My own work, which studied 35,000 sales calls in 23 countries, would be one example of how a measured scientific approach has paid dividends. We now know, from the work of researchers, the sales skills that are most effective, and we can teach them, coach them and measure the improvements that result from them.

But it's not just researchers like me who have advanced the sales profession. Technologists and systems designers have played an increasingly important role. We finally have Customer Relationship Management (CRM) systems that are radically changing the way we sell. First-generation CRM, in the 1990s, was a disaster for sales. It was created by programmers, and was cumbersome and time-consuming. In most cases these early CRM systems didn't generate enough extra revenue to pay for their high installation costs. Rightly, they met with resistance and sabotage. "Electronic lies are no better than manual lies" complained one sales manager from an insurance company. CRM built itself a justifiably bad reputation as a time waster that took salespeople away from customers in order to spend hours each week filling in user-hostile electronic forms.

Then came a second generation of CRM with greater utility. These newer systems delivered better salesforce management data, better forecasting and improved ease of use. We're now seeing the emergence of a third generation of CRM systems which allow coordination of complex global accounts and which provide tangible benefits to salespeople and customers alike. These third-generation systems also allow the use of effectiveness analytics – a fancy way to describe the capacity to test hypotheses by interrogating the CRM database. So, for example, many leading companies, particularly those in technology, are building intelligent engines to mine their CRM data for useful correlations that let them build better predictive selling models. For example:

- A software company found from their CRM data that when one of their senior executives made a customer visit at the pre-proposal stage the chances of a contract increased by 18%.

- A control systems supplier discovered that their chances of success almost doubled if they set up face-to-face meetings with purchasing before the RFP was issued.
- An optical reader manufacturer analyzed their CRM data and found that involving their technical people in the sale didn't make any difference when the customer was a bank, but increased the success rate to other financial services customers by 32%.

The list goes on, but what's important here is the method. This is Science with a capital 'S'. It's systematic hypothesis testing and knowledge building. And this kind of approach to model building from CRM data will play a bigger and bigger part in the future of selling.

Another transformation in the sales profession has been the development of better pipeline management models. Sales managers today would be lost without sales funnels that break down the selling cycle into manageable steps that let them predict and forecast how the sales opportunities they manage are progressing through a pipeline. Again, this has evolved greatly over the last 20 years. Writing in 1987, I complained that most pipeline models were based on how suppliers wanted to sell, not on how customers wanted to buy. In 20 years pipeline management has progressed from this simplistic view of the selling cycle. Today's pipeline models are customer responsive. A manager who understands metrics can use them to forecast, to diagnose performance problems, and to target coaching help.

I could catalog many other changes that have transformed the field of sales into a business science. For example, new channel strategy models have altered the role of salesforces and brought clarity to how face-to-face selling works with other channels to create customer value. New strategy models, especially in key account and global account selling, have turned planning into a truly strategic process and raised the bar for sales management. The integration of sales and marketing had brought important concepts into selling, such as segmentation and value propositions. All these changes mean that a sales manager today can no longer survive as a seat-of-the-pants generalist.

In saying this, I wish I could be confident that I was preaching to the converted. It should be self-evident that sales management is a sophisticated activity, light-years away from the old "cheatin', lyin' and stealin'" stereotype of selling. Unfortunately, the evidence is that old stereotypes persist, even in the most unlikely places. What has prompted me to write this Foreword – beyond giving support to Beth Rogers' excellent book – is a sense of outrage about how sales management is seen in high places. Let me be very specific: the way in which sales is viewed by many Boards of Directors is, at best, dangerously naïve and, at worst, a business disgrace. I'll give you an example. I advise the Board of a public company in the United States. Three years ago, at my first meeting with the Board, they were discussing how to fill the vacant position of Chief Marketing Officer. The issue was one of qualifications: would a general MBA be acceptable in an otherwise qualified candidate or did the sophistication of marketing demand a specialized MBA in marketing? It was a good and useful discussion. Last year the VP Sales job needed to be filled. The same individuals who had argued so convincingly that a specialist MBA was a prerequisite for the Marketing position seemed quite content to accept VP Sales candidates with no qualification beyond track record. When I pressed them they told me that while marketing was a science, sales was just a craft. Shame on them! How are we ever to develop a generation of sales managers who can prosper in today's sophisticated selling world if senior management think like that?

I'm being hard on the Boardroom here – perhaps too hard. My clients did have one very convincing defence. "And where do you suppose we would find a candidate with an MBA specializing in sales?" they asked me. It's a fair point. As far as I know, such an animal doesn't yet exist. Although there are dozens of Marketing MAs in the USA and Europe I don't know of an equivalent in Sales. In Europe, only the University of Portsmouth has a mature Sales Management programme at Masters' level.

It's a chicken and egg problem. Top management doesn't demand academically qualified candidates because there are none. Business Schools, on the other hand, have been reluctant to introduce MBAs in Sales until there's demand from companies. Each is waiting for the other. A pox on both their houses, I say. While we wait, the sales field becomes ever more complex and the need for advanced business education in sales is ever more urgent. Sooner or later the dam will break.

What can an ambitious sales manager do in the meantime? It's not as if help is easily available in terms of articles and books. Last year I carried out a survey of books published in the sales field. I started with a raw count. There have been more than 5,000 books written for salespeople but less than 50 for sales managers. Of these sales management books, most are simplistic and tactical. There's only a handful of strategic books to help sales managers to cope with the complexity of today's sales challenges. This is one of them.

When I pick up a book on sales management I have a simple test to help me to assess in 30 seconds whether it's worth reading. I flick the pages and look at the pictures. If I see no diagrams, no graphs and no models I can usually make an accurate prediction that the book is of the old school. It will be the usual mixture of war stories and seat-of-the-pants advice. That sort of book was good enough 20 years ago. It's not good enough today. Try it with this book. You'll find your eye skimming over facts and figures; you'll see charts and diagrams; you'll find strategic models. That's the kind of book we need. Thank you, Beth Rogers, for writing it.

Neil Rackham
Visiting Professor
Portsmouth Business School

Acknowledgments

For the most part, writing a book is a solitary and difficult endeavor, so it is particularly satisfying to be able to thank all the people who have helped to make it more sociable and achievable:

First and foremost, I am very grateful to my mentor Neil Rackham – Visiting Professor of Sales Management at Portsmouth Business School and author of many inspiring books – for his constant encouragement, advice and practical help. I would also like to thank everyone at John Wiley & Sons Ltd involved in the production of the book.

Further, I would like to thank the following: my colleagues and students at Portsmouth Business School, who have encouraged me to pursue my specialist knowledge of sales management (www.port.ac.uk/pbs); the alumni of MA Sales Management (Portsmouth); The Institute of Sales and Marketing Management – it is an honor to be a Fellow and the Research Director of the ISMM (www.ismm.co.uk); Brian Lambert, CEO, United Professional Sales Association (www.upsa-intl.org); Professor Malcolm McDonald and Dr Tony Millman, who, apart from providing references for this book, chose me to undertake Cranfield School of Management's first research project on the subject of key account management in 1994.

I am also grateful for the assistance of former colleagues from the Cranfield Marketing Planning Centre, especially Professor Lynette Ryals, Professor Hugh Wilson and Terry Kendrick, who have also made direct and indirect contributions; John Andrews, and all members of the Sales Training

Association; The Marketing and Sales Standards Setting Body, including Chief Executive, Chahid Fourali and all the members of the Sales Steering Group (www.msssb.org); Ian Corner, an expert on CRM/SFA implementation; Dr Kevin Wilson, for establishing the Sales Research Trust.

I must also express my gratitude to all the following people and organizations who have given specific permission for models and quotations: Professor Tim Ambler, London Business School; The American Productivity and Quality Center, Houston (www.apqc.org); The Association of the British Pharmaceutical Industry; Avaya (www.avaya.com); Bain and Company, New York (www.bain.com); Peter Bartlett, Value Care Partners Ltd (www.valuecarepartners.com); Renee Botham, Managing Director, Touchstone, London (www.touchstonegrowth.com); The Service Sector Statistics Division, Bureau of the Census; The Caux Round Table, Saint Paul, MN, Den Haag, Tokyo, Naucalpan (www.cauxroundtable.org); The Chartered Institute of Purchasing Supply (www.cips.org); Val Heritage, The Communication Challenge Ltd (www.communicationchallenge.co.uk); Hugh Davidson, Visiting Professor, Cranfield School of Management; Don Baker, Editor, *Dayton Business Journal* (http://dayton.bizjournals.com); Jim Dickie, Managing Partner, CSO Insights (www.csoinsights.com); EICC (Electronic Industry Code of Conduct: www.eicc.info); Gartner Group (www.gartner.com), especially Ed Thompson, CRM/SFA expert in Europe; Antonella Grana of AIDA* Marketing e Formazione, and AIDA clients PEMAGroup/Metalpres and Vagheggi Spa (www.aidamarketing.it); Professor Andres Hatum, Comportamiento Humano en la Organizacion, Buenos Aires, Argentina (www.iae.edu.ar); Terry Kendrick, University of East Anglia; Philip Lay, Managing Director, TGC Advisors LLC, San Mateo, CA (www.tgc-advisors.com), publisher of *Under the Buzz*; Emeritus Professor Malcolm McDonald, Cranfield School of Management; Olympus Medical, Center Valley, PA (www.olympusamerica.com); Dr Tony Millman; Tim Mutton, Managing Director, TPM Marketing and Consultancy Ltd (www.tpmmarketingandconsultancy.co.uk); Professor Nigel Piercy, Warwick Business School; Ronald Stagg, Director of Corporate Services, Purchasing Management Association of Canada, Toronto (www.pmac.ca); Professor

* AIDA is an ISMM accredited training center based near Venice, with a mission to develop the best training for Italian managers and entrepreneurs to enable them to compete in the home and international market.

Lynette Ryals, Cranfield School of Management; Professor Asta Salmi, University of Helsinki, Finland; Dr Christoph Senn, Columbia University; Professor Benson Shapiro, Harvard Business School; Mike Smith, Director, Tennyson, Chichester (www.tennyson.uk.com); David Evans, Managing Director, Research, The Supply Chain Executive Board* (www.sceb.executiveboard.com); TACK International, Chesham, Bucks, UK (www.tack.co.uk); Ken Teal, Wessex Innovation Service (http://www.shealtd.co.uk); David Todman, Sales and Marketing Director, APV; Professor John Ward, Information Systems Research Centre, Cranfield School of Management, and lead author of "Benefits management: delivering value from IS and IT investments"; John Wilkinson, University of South Australia (www.unisa.edu.au); Professor Hugh Wilson, Director, Cranfield Customer Management Forum (www.cranfield.ac.uk/som/ccmf); Stuart Morgan, Editor, *Winning Edge*; Robert L. Reid Jr, Director of Procurement and Risk Management, Winthrop University, Rock Hill, South Carolina; Diana Woodburn, Marketing Best Practice Limited (www.marketingbp.com).

I would also like to thank all the authors whose work I have referenced in the text and the bibliography; and also all the companies, organizations and business professionals who take part in research to enable the public knowledge of best practice to be developed.

* A division of the Corporate Executive Board. A provider of business research and executive education based in Washington DC.

About the author

Beth Rogers is regarded as a leading thinker on the topic of sales management, and is also sought out for her ability to provoke the thinking of others. She manages the primary postgraduate program for sales managers in Europe. Beth is also Research Director of the Institute of Sales and Marketing Management, and a Fellow of the Royal Society. She was elected Chair of the UK Government's National Sales Board in 2005, and was instrumental in the launch of National Occupation Standards for Sales in the UK.

Her extensive practical experience in both sales and marketing in the information technology sector has been supplemented by in-depth consultancy in a variety of organizations, together with research and teaching. She has worked with major corporations in Europe, the USA, SE Asia and Australia, and with small businesses in the South and South-east of England, both in manufacturing and services. Beth has also contributed to public and voluntary sector organizations.

Beth is a popular author and speaker on sales management. Her previous books include co-authorship of *Key Account Management – Learning from Supplier and Customer Perspective*. She has written many articles on sales and marketing-related topics over the past 18 years, and is a regular contributor to *Winning Edge*. She has also provided comment for the *Daily Telegraph* and *Sunday Times*.

Beth works with employers, her alumni, professional institutions and fellow experts to raise the profile of the sales profession.

Introduction

"Everyone lives by selling something"

Robert Louis Stevenson, Scottish essayist (1850–1894)

It is hard to imagine anything more fundamental to the economy than selling. It makes the world go round. Or, if you want a formal governmental definition:

> *The sales function "creates, builds and sustains mutually beneficial and profitable relationships through personal and organizational contact".*
>
> Quoted with kind permission from
> The Marketing and Sales Standards Setting Body, UK

If you have chosen this book you probably agree with me that it is about time that salespeople and sales managers had equal esteem with other professionals. Unfortunately, around the world, from the USA to Japan, and from New Zealand to Sweden, selling is regarded as an occupation not worthy of much respect – an occupation on a par with politics and tabloid journalism.

Unfortunately (and the research has been done to prove this), selling has been consistently negatively portrayed by scriptwriters for over 100 years. They have given us Willy Loman, Herb Tarlick and Delboy Trotter. The most we can hope for a stereotypical sales character is that he (and they are overwhelmingly male characters) may be lovable as well as being a rogue!

In the sales profession we have to be aware that when selling is bad, it is horrid. Companies have a significant challenge to rise above the negative stereotypes and occasional real-live scandals and develop sales professionals who are very, very good and command respect. There is considerable support for salespeople, from organizations such as the United Professional Sales Association, the Strategic Account Management Association, the Institute of Sales and Marketing Management and other professional and government-sponsored bodies. The UPSA's Compendium of Professional Selling and the UK government's vocational standards for sales are freely available to any sales manager or salesperson.

There are more salespeople than accountants, engineers, lawyers and marketers. Selling takes place in all industries and in some public sector organizations. Millions of people are full-time salespeople (15 million in the USA alone) and millions more recognize selling as part of their job. Despite many years of marketers trying to sideline the sales function as operational, tactical and in decline, the sales profession is in fact thriving in terms of quantity and quality. Nevertheless, sales has been the Cinderella of the management world for a long time. Yet what could be a more worthy topic of discussion than the way in which a company makes its revenue?

Many businesspeople say to me that the strategic management of supplier–customer relationships is "the next big thing" that companies needs to address. In studies going back many years, chief executives have recognized that the sales managers' responsibility for handling the customer interface can be the most important thing in generating company success. With inspired leadership and the right application of skills and systems, strategic relationship development can deliver competitive advantage. Companies are starting to realize that they cannot manage customers or even key accounts because the power of customers gives them the means to "manage" back. So where do they go?

They go back to the drawing board and take a good hard look at "the art of the possible". Supplier strategy cannot drive customers, but there are pathways for mutual gain. The greatest advocates for strategic sales management companies who are designing those pathways are their customers. Whether they long for low-touch, remote and transactional relationships with particular suppliers for particular goods and services, or whether they want a joint venture with others, customers appreciate the suppliers who understand their needs and develop the capabilities to meet them.

The main reason why selling should be respected, and the key to its success, is the rare skill of "boundary-spanning" – understanding the customer's point of view and reconciling it with the needs of the company for profitable growth. That is a complex activity to manage, and this book alone could not possibly provide all of the answers, although it does offer some possible solutions and provide signposts to others. It is here to facilitate the strategic thinking that sales managers have to apply in 21st-century businesses.

However, not all sales managers have been prepared for this role. Customers cry out for more highly skilled salespeople and sales managers, but investment in sales skills (worldwide) is only just starting to improve. Of course, many sales managers have succeeded by learning from experience. With experience in industry and self-employment besides teaching, I appreciate "the university of life" and its relevance. But sometimes life can be a lot easier if we take time out to think.

This book is a summary of "state-of-the-art" strategic sales management thinking, designed for practitioners who recognize that a bit of knowing can accelerate the success of a lot of doing. It is based on extensive consultation with sales management professionals, employers, sales management experts and professional institutions. It is short and succinct because sales managers are busy people with limited time to read. But as sales managers also travel a lot, they can consider this knowledge as a traveling companion to dip into when their plane is delayed or the freeway is gridlocked.

This book is divided into three parts.

Part I is about business strategy. If, as a sales manager, you are going to impress your chief executives, and if you are going to coach your account managers to impress their Board level contacts in customers, a solid grounding in business strategy is necessary. I've had the pleasure of seeing some of my students go from being account managers at graduation to Sales and Marketing Director within three years. That's because they had invested in developing their general understanding of business and sales strategy together with their analytical and creative thinking skills.

Chapter 1 introduces the strategic language of organizations and what sales managers need to know about it in order to take part in strategy formulation. If you are going to lead your sales team to greater achievement, a certain way of getting customers' attention is to understand their point of view. You need to know how a purchasing manager develops purchasing strategy. You and those you coach will start to recognize where value matters to the buyer and where it does not.

Chapter 2 demonstrates the purchasing professional's strategic tools. Research suggests that purchasing decision-makers think that suppliers do not understand their needs. This chapter gives a purchaser's view of suppliers – how they are categorized and how your performance as a supplier is measured. This is essential reading for superior "boundary spanners".

What about your own strategy? You need your own strategic tool to stimulate your thinking. Following a long development path since the first matrix was designed for B2B sales in 1982, this book offers a simplified approach to mapping customer relationships to classify their investment requirement. Chapter 3 discusses the relationship development box – a tool for strategic sales management, which identifies different categories of relationship and shows how different sales models are appropriate for each.

Part II is about those different categories of business relationships and sales models. Making mistakes with strategic relationships is possibly the most career-retarding thing a sales manager could do, so let's avoid them! The customers with whom we most want to deal tend to draw resources and management attention, but have you realized that the customer also regards the relationship as strategic? Are you able to lead company resources allocation in other departments in a way that meets the customer's needs? Chapter 4 looks at developing strategic relationships.

Customer retention is an important objective in a difficult economic climate, but as your company also needs growth you can never stop trying to find new customers. Even the best-managed strategic relationships can run out of steam, so where are the next relationships to come from? Chapter 5 looks at prospective relationships, and discusses what is known about the dynamics of buyers' switching behavior and what is needed to motivate change. It also explains how to avoid the pitfalls of wasting money on acquisition quests, and presents criteria for success. Different resourcing models are also explored.

Most companies have a large number of customers that may admire the brand, but they only need your product in small quantities or for occasional use. Good sales managers do not neglect them. For many valid reasons, these "tactical" customers do not need a strong relationship with you as a supplier.

Your strategy should be focused on the distributors, business partners or outsourcing partners who can serve these customers better than you can. Chapter 6 looks at successful ways to work with partners, and the use of desk-based selling (telesales and web-driven sales) as options for success in this category.

The most difficult strategic decision a sales manager has to make is to distinguish between strategic and "cooperative" relationships with customers. Even if a customer buys a lot from you, and even if the relationship is cordial, it may not be growing, so investment is not appropriate. The customer may need your product or service, but behave in an adversarial way about it, in which case it is unwise to invest where switching probability is high. How then do you restrain yourself, and allocate resources effectively in this most difficult of categories? Chapter 7 looks at "cooperative" relationships. How do you classify these customers that you want to keep, but who are not investment prospects? How can you achieve cooperation in situations where conflict seems inevitable?

Some business relationships will break down – for a variety of reasons, good and bad. Risks, after all, can be opportunities as well as threats. As a strategically minded sales manager, you need contingency plans for these situations. Chapter 8 examines exit strategy. Business relationships do not last forever and you need to know when to quit and how to respond to customer defection.

Part III looks at some of the new skills you as a sales manager require to respond to the 21st-century world of strategic selling. A lot has been written about training, forecasting and compensation schemes. This section of the book looks at some new challenges and how to address them.

Some people would argue that a company's most valuable and most intangible asset is its reputation. Salespeople are standard-bearers of the company's reputation. You are expected to ensure high standards of behavior, despite the contradictions presented by some of the targets that salespeople are given. Chapter 9 discusses reputation management, corporate governance, and how this affects you in managing the sales function.

"Of course, we salespeople do the best we can, but the marketing department gives us such lousy leads." If you want to be taken seriously by Board members, start talking to marketing and get these problems sorted out. Marketing can only support sales, and sales can only contribute to better marketing if there is dialogue and teamwork. As a strategically minded sales manager, you need to be leading that. Chapter 10 reviews sales and marketing integration, from mutual respect and strategic alignment to day-to-day operational co-working.

Do you know how important it is to the motivation of your salespeople that they respect you as a leader? The research evidence is overwhelming. Sales managers with concern for their people as well as the tasks they have to achieve are the most successful. Chapter 11 examines the sales manager/account manager as a team leader. The sales manager not only needs to think strategically and maintain a long-term view, but also has to guide a large team of salespeople who themselves are teaming with other parts of the company. This chapter discusses ideas about leadership and the skills required.

You might want to do something about leading, but no one wants to do anything about processes. You don't have to do any "processing" yourself; but you do need to know how to mentor a process expert to make sales processes work for you and your team, rather than frustrate you. Chapter 12 covers sales process management and the impact of technology. Streamlined processes must underpin each sales department, and by preventing the mismanagement of resources through quality processes, sales managers can reap the benefits of effectiveness and efficiency.

So, read on, dip in and, above all, enjoy!

PART I

Strategy

For decades sales has been stuck in an operational silo. "Go out and get the numbers!" How bizarre. What is the top line on a Profit and Loss Account? Yes – sales. What happens to the bottom line without a top line? It goes negative.

Looking after the top line is what sorts the winners from the rest. Therefore a lot of companies are starting to manage the delivery of the top line strategically.

That's good news for you as a sales manager. But if it is going to be good top-line strategy, you have to contribute to strategy formulation, not just implement it. That involves you in three issues:

1. You need to understand strategy in general.
2. You need to understand the strategic input of purchasing decision-makers in your customers.
3. You need to have your own strategic tool for analyzing business relationships.

1

The big picture

"When people talked about 'Sales Strategy' I used to laugh. As an oxymoron, even 'Military Intelligence' paled in comparison. In those days, 'Sales Strategy' was nothing more than simple tactics ruthlessly executed. But that was then. Today the wrong sales strategy sinks companies."

Neil Rackham in *Sales and Marketing Management*, Spring 2000
Reproduced with kind permission from Professor Neil Rackham

The place of sales in business strategy

The role of marketing has been hotly debated over the years, whether it is strategic, tactical, or not even necessary. The role of sales is rarely questioned. Ever since Stone Age tribes traded pots for shells, selling has been necessary. Of course, you cannot have a seller without a buyer, but more of that later.

The evolution of business in the 20th century favored those with professional qualifications such as accountants, who frequently made the switch from money management to general management at Board level. Marketers too, armed with MBAs and compelling concepts like branding and segmentation, became more strategic and also jostled for a place on the Board. Not so sales. Most Sales VPs got on with selling, consoling themselves that the monetary rewards of selling provided a more attractive prize than power. Nevertheless, company politics did not go away. As soon as a quarterly target was missed, the sales force became the reason for the failure of the business strategy.

Can sales continue to sit on the strategic sidelines? In this era of customer orientation, it is more important than ever that sales managers should be involved in strategy-making, despite assertions from some business gurus that marketing is strategic and sales is operational. Who else but salespeople are close enough to understand the relevant decision-makers in the customer organization? If a company truly wants to align its strategy with customers' strategies, it is no longer appropriate for salespeople to be the tactical, operational doers, whose feedback is filtered through layers of management and skepticism.

In this era of customer orientation, it is more important than ever that sales managers should be involved in strategy-making, despite assertions from some business gurus that marketing is strategic and sales is operational. Who else but salespeople are close enough to understand the relevant decision-makers in the customer organization?

Professor Nigel Piercy and Nikala Lane at Warwick Business School have identified ways in which the sales function contributes to strategy-making, and call it the five Is: – involvement, intelligence, integration, internal marketing and infrastructure development. We will discuss many of these functions in Part III, with a specific focus on infrastructure development in Chapter 12. At the moment, let's just look at the big picture.

Intelligence is the easiest to discuss. Professional salespeople should be closely scrutinizing the customer and their business environment and applying their skills to selective supplier–customer relationship development. Some companies may assume that marketing does all that research, and for some categories of relationship, an aggregation of information about customer needs may be all that is necessary. But in business-to-business, many customers are large and complex, and the account manager's understanding should be complete.

The account manager can identify opportunities for relationship development with certain customers, but operations have to deliver it. That's where internal marketing is essential, but it also leads on to involvement and integration. If sales is not involved in strategic decisions at the same level as operations, what does that say about the status of the organization's knowledge of the customer? Sales can only be integrated into the rest of the organization when it is represented at the highest decision-making level. Where else can sales explain what customers are doing, and how the organization can add value?

Selling has always been a "boundary-spanning" role – representing the company to the customer and representing the customer within the company. Companies cannot call themselves "customer-focused" unless they have that "voice of the customer" in the Boardroom. Is it just wishful thinking that sales should have a place at the Boardroom table? Not at all.

Selling has always been a "boundary-spanning" role – representing the company to the customer and representing the customer within the company.

We live in an era where a company's top five customers frequently generate more than half of an organization's revenue. These key customers have a significant impact on all parts of the business: they influence, or even decide, R&D priorities; and they affect every element of the business chain, from systems design to distribution. Increasingly, it makes no sense to have a Board on which the voice of these key customers is not represented. Marketing can represent the voice of the many anonymous customers who, in aggregation, are called "the marketplace", but only sales has the closeness and depth needed to speak for these key customers who have such a profound effect on a company's strategy and future.

Selling with strategic focus has implications for the way sales activity is organized. It also has implications for the knowledge that salespeople, account managers and sales managers need. In order to operate at Board level, you need a certain language, and a historical and cultural background of strategy-making. This chapter gives an overview of business strategy models that sales managers and account managers need to present their case internally and to work with senior customer personnel on relationship development.

So what are the strategic roles of the sales function?

Involvement – in strategy formulation
Intelligence – industry and customer knowledge and analysis
Integration – working across functions to develop value
Internal marketing – of the customer to colleagues
Infrastructure development

Source: Piercy and Lane (2005)

What is the "big picture" that drives strategic thinking?

No company operates in isolation. When business strategy is converted into sales targets without sufficient involvement of sales in the strategy formation, there's often a serious disconnect. It sometimes seems that Chief Executive Officers and their strategy formulation teams assume that the company can drive itself anywhere, regardless of economic cycles, the activity of competition or customer behaviour.

It sometimes seems that Chief Executive Officers and their strategy formulation teams assume that the company can drive itself anywhere, regardless of economic cycles, the activity of competition or customer behaviour.

Real strategy is not like that. Strategic plans cover not only "where are we now?" and "where do we want to be?" but also the methods of getting there. Plans must be modified by consideration of the global and local business environment (see Figure 1.1).

Quite early in a strategic plan, there is usually a "PEST" analysis, of the political, economic, social and technological trends that impact on the company. Just keeping up to date with new laws affecting the operations of the company is a demanding activity. Economic conditions affect all players in the global economy, but some industries are more sensitive than others to economic swings. Food retail is a good place to be in a recession as we all need to eat, but the size of a knowledge services firm, such as systems integration, can change significantly depending on economic prosperity or recession.

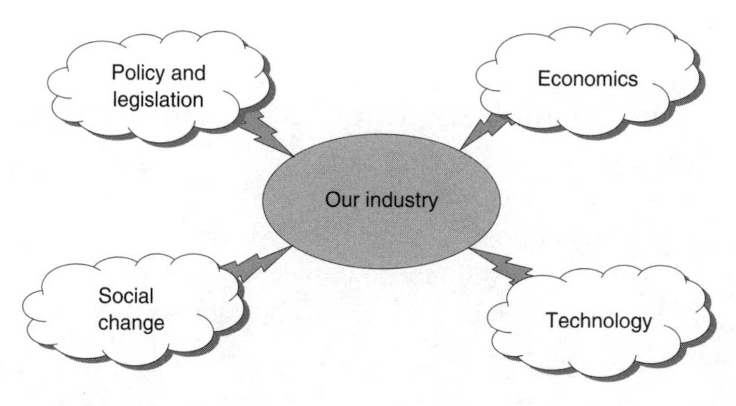

Figure 1.1 *The business environment.*

Social trends are very important, even for business-to-business companies. In retailing, it is vital to know the patterns of the catchment area of each store, by age, income, cultural origin and family size (demographics). This enables plans to be made to get the right stock to the right stores at the right time. All demand in a supply chain is derived from aggregated consumer needs and wants. If the rising generation of consumers is concerned about the environment and social responsibility, then raw materials extraction companies need to ensure that that is reflected in their activities.

Other external impacts, such as the weather, local sporting success or national tragedies, also have to be taken into account. This analysis is a means of identifying some genuine opportunities and threats for the business.

Political/legislative factors

- Corporate governance
- Health and safety at work
- Equal opportunities/diversity
- Employment law, governing individuals' rights at work
- Consumer protection
- Tax and duties on products/services
- Regulations governing use of land and property
- Environmental regulations
- Copyright law
- Privacy law, e.g. regulations covering spam e-mail and unsolicited telephone calls
- Prohibition/legalization of substances and activities.

Adapting to the external business environment

In 1989 in Argentina, inflation reached approximately 5,000%. The 1990s saw increased stability, but also deregulation, which opened up competition.

In a study of companies adapting to this dramatic economic change between 1989 and 1999, researchers found that flexible, adaptive companies had the following characteristics in the way they gathered information about their business environment:

- They had formal and informal ways of gathering information about the external business environment.
- They attempted to create an external orientation.
- They adopted new models for processing, analyzing and using external information.

> *"Every employee is aware of the importance of having an open mind and catching all they can from the sector, competitors and customers."*

Source: Hatum and Pettigrew (2006)

An important role of VP Sales is to contribute to an understanding of how PEST factors are affecting the company, and to take the lead on identifying how these factors are affecting certain customers in particular industries. Changes in external pressures can affect the way they want to buy, as we will see in Chapter 2.

You may ask how objective a PEST analysis can be. Some businesspeople can have their own fears or enthusiasms about any or all of the PEST factors, which is why other sources of opinion should be reviewed. Research institutes, industry watchers, government departments and consultants all produce analyses of trends and predictions. Since these analyses are based on reliable sources, businesspeople should take notice of them, at least for developing a Plan B in case Plan A, or "business-as-usual", does not give the expected results.

Early in my career in the IT industry, I worked on a strategic plan that was heavily influenced by a technology trend. IT analysts' reports were predicting that most companies would decentralize their IT installations from mainframe computers with dumb terminals to client/server networked technology. Client/server versions of mainframe software had to be developed in order to meet this trend. Subsequent reviews suggested that the mainframe software performance was still buoyant but the client/server software was not being accepted very rapidly. Global economic recession had arrested the customers' desire for change.

The analysts' predictions were not necessarily wrong. The rise of the Internet in the 1990s ensured that networked servers with their personal computer clients became the norm, so it was a good idea to have prepared new products for the new world. Mainframes did not disappear, they merely changed into super-servers, so the plan could be seen in hindsight as pessimistic compared to the reality that emerged. Nevertheless, it would have been desperately wrong to ignore the analysts' predictions altogether and assume that a steady sales performance for a mainframe software product with over 20 years' heritage was going to continue forever.

Competitive pressure in our industry

Too many companies, not enough differentiation

> **Merging to survive**
>
> Sometimes, there are just too many companies competing to deliver similar value. In 2006, two Taiwanese companies merged to create a large-size display panel supplier that could rival the Korean market leaders. Demand for large-size TFT–LCD (Thin Film Transistor–Liquid Crystal Display) screens was weak and prices were declining, putting pressure on revenue and profitability in the industry. Scale and capacity were the keys to survival.

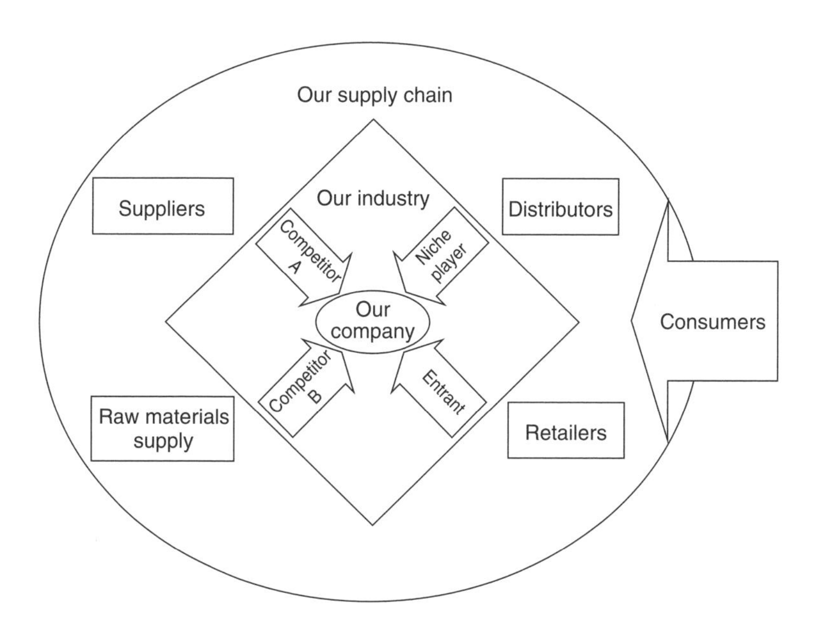

Figure 1.2 *Industrial supply chain.*

Decisions to deal with competitive pressure through merger are usually done collectively and at a high level. VP Sales should be able to contribute to them based on feedback from salespeople about particular competitors. Salespeople must know what their direct competitors are doing. Unfortunately, research report after research report suggests that salespeople have such faith in their own products and services that they do not pay enough attention to learning about competitors and why they might be more successful in developing relationships with customers. A recent survey of 426 salespeople found that respondents were not confident that they had a good understanding of the competitive environment or industry benchmarks (The Communication Challenge Ltd, 2006). When salespeople understand "the big picture", they are able to impress the customer with their knowledge, and demonstrate a clear framework of differentiating value to address their needs.

Salespeople must know what their direct competitors are doing. Unfortunately, research report after research report suggests that salespeople have such faith in their own products and services that they do not pay enough attention to learning about competitors and why they might be more successful in developing relationships with customers.

Besides understanding current competitors, salespeople also have to be constantly alert to the possibility of new entrants coming into the industry. Sometimes, the effect of an entrant can be dramatic. A distinctive European brand entered the US vacuum cleaner market in 2002, and gained more than 20% of market share within four years. Meanwhile, the parent company of the former market leader decided to sell it.

Working closely with other supply chain players in strategic relationships may help a company to cannibalize its own products or services before someone else does. As the long-term nature of a relationship reduces risk, innovation becomes more of an opportunity. A balanced portfolio of customer relationships can help to reduce risk if a particular strategic relationship is lost to a market entrant.

Meanwhile, the biggest competitor that any company should fear is "do nothing". In the IT industry, a high proportion of proposals are lost to the customer's inertia and unwillingness to act, which can often be linked to uncertainty and risk in the business environment.

Supply chain influences: upstream suppliers

> **Recession prompts OEM competition with channel**
>
> With business hard to find in the dot.com bust after the dot-com boom, the direct sales teams of some of the major players in the IT industry appeared to be reaching deeper into the small and medium-sized business customers that were usually served by channel partners. Where it occurred, this conflict risked reducing margins for both the supplier and the reseller. It is worth noting that it was the front-line salespeople in the resellers who were the first to realize the situation.

If our immediate suppliers hold significant power in the supply chain, or if the companies extracting raw materials create bottlenecks as their ability to supply – and their prices – vary, our opportunity for profit is lower. Of course, the prices we pay for goods may be affected by the suppliers' bargaining power, but we may be able to partner with suppliers to ensure some long-term stability in prices. There might be different types of suppliers that a company could work with to ensure a better balance of mutuality. The worst we might fear from our suppliers is that they have enough power and brand value in the industry to by-pass whatever value we create and build relationships directly with our customers. We will look later at how value has to be justified in all aspects of the supply chain. There are also legal constraints on supplier power. When a company has more than 25% of the market share, they attract the interest of anti-trust legislators. This reduces to some degree their enthusiasm for wielding their power.

Derived demand: how consumers drive supply chains

If your company is extracting tin, it is because millions of people want to buy food in tins as that extends the food's shelf life. So, if all demand is "derived demand" from the consumer, why do we think that we can push our value down the supply chain? Many strategists now talk about the "demand chain". In fact, the idea of a demand chain was identified in the 18th century by the Scottish economist/philosopher, Adam Smith:

> *"Consumption is the sole end of all production; and the interest of the producer ought to be attended to, only so far as it may be necessary for promoting that of the consumer."*
>
> Adam Smith, *The Wealth of Nations*, Book IV, Chapter VIII (1776)

Consumer power generally expresses itself as an insatiable hunger for more choice at lower prices. This contributes to the fearsome reputation of retailers in the supply chain. I once interviewed a purchasing manager in a medium-sized retailer who admitted pushing an account manager too hard on discount. The account manager walked away from the negotiations, and supply ceased. The next week the buyer had the hassle of explaining to his manager why an important brand was missing from the shelves in stores, and backed down. In a large retailer, this would have been high risk indeed.

Many retailers have progressive supplier development programs that can help small companies to grow and be profitable and successful. Power brings with it public expectations of responsibility. For example, retailers can be called upon to address power imbalances throughout the supply chain.

Customer power reaches up the supply chain

For four years, a group of agricultural workers in the USA conducted a campaign to gain public support for their demands for better wages and working conditions. Student groups, religious organizations and celebrities joined a boycott of fast food chains that were dealing with the workers' employers. To end the boycott of their brand, one chain implemented a "pass-through" to ensure that the workers got an increase in their piece rate.

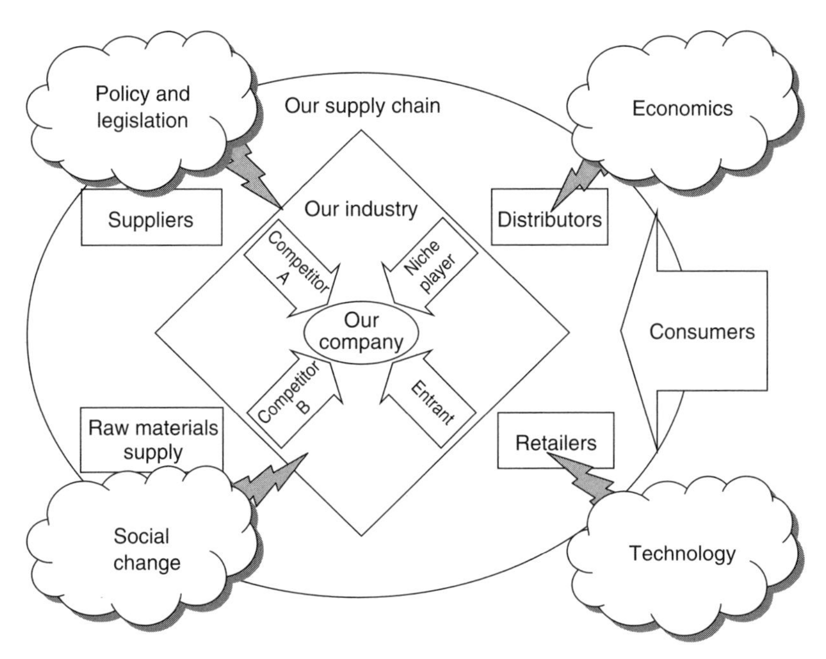

Figure 1.3 *The big picture.*

You may not be in an industry that deals with retailers, or even distributors. Perhaps your business involves working directly with industry customers. This has been my experience in the IT industry. This can be equally challenging as large companies who represent a significant proportion of their suppliers' revenues are bound to be tempted to use that power when necessary. If industry conditions allow it, reinvigorating your customer base to ensure a broad portfolio of relationships is essential to minimize the risks associated with large and powerful customers. We will discuss this more fully in Chapter 3.

The components of the whole business environment are shown in Figure 1.3.

Opportunities and threats

All the external factors in the business environment are sources of opportunities and threats, so when we talk about a SWOT analysis, the "O" and "T" sections should be derived from PEST and the demand chain. That is the big picture that company strategists have to address; and VP Sales has to contribute to an understanding of what this picture is. The way that strategists use this information to change the company's position in a turbulent business environment is by changing investment in the company's relative strengths and weaknesses to enable it to perform more effectively.

Strengths and weaknesses

In 1985, strategy guru Michael Porter introduced a concept called the "Internal Value Chain" to track exactly where companies add value to immediate customers. From the different functions identified in the internal value chain, we could make a judgment on what we do well, and what we don't do well. This was an extremely helpful tool at the time.

Looking back from 2006, this "chain" model seems to have been rooted in the concept of a company having different functions that pass things on to another department (Figure 1.4). In modern organizations that concept can be seen as a weakness, as it is at the handover stage that things tend to go wrong. The lack of internal integration can result in inefficiencies and dissatisfied customers, and functions within the company should at least be interlocking cogs in a finely tuned machine. We can all think of many ways that companies differentiate their value, even in B2B organizations, that must be inherent in all functions. Perhaps a company could be a "green" leader, known for an excellent record on everything from controlling its factory emissions to recycling paper and print cartridges. "Green" value leadership can now be important in winning government business in some parts of Europe.

Two things are certain about a company's strengths. One is that it does not matter a hoot what we who work for the company think are our

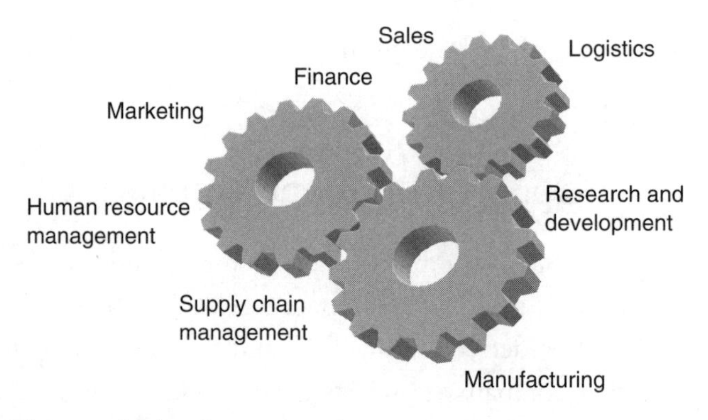

Figure 1.4 *The internal value chain.*

A strength is only a strength if it is seen as a strength by customers, and if they think that it makes us different from our competitors.

strengths, or even what the Chief Executive Officer tells industry analysts. A strength is only a strength if it is seen as a strength by customers, and if they think that it makes us different from our competitors. Let's look at a value differentiator that almost every purchasing decision-maker will tell you is important: "Being easy to do business with." What does that mean? Customers who want it talk about simple processes – reliability, friendly service, speedy problem resolution, and much more. It is a powerful company-wide competence where it exists, and if customers tell you that you are easier to do business with than competitors in a particular way, then that is worth putting in a SWOT analysis.

On the basis of building on strengths, addressing weaknesses, exploiting opportunities and minimizing threats, companies can make strategies for themselves. But we have all seen many SWOT analyses that have simply been long lists of vague ideas or wishful thinking. As such, they can hardly inform strategy. A variation that is much more rigorous is a grid designed by key account strategist Diana Woodburn.

Her principles include the minimizing of the SWOT lists to a few key factors that are specific and relevant. These few things then need to be forced together to generate some truly strategic thinking. Do we have a strength that is neatly aligned with an opportunity? For example, what if a bureaucratic company has just taken over a nimble and flexible competitor, and one of our strengths is "ease of doing business with us"? We should be

	Strengths 1 2 3	Weaknesses 1 2 3
Opportunities 1 2 3	S/Os Strategic wins!	W/Os Investment?
Threats 1 2 3	S/Ts Risk management	T/Ws Danger area Contingency plan

Figure 1.5 *A SWOT matrix. (Reproduced with kind permission from Diana Woodburn of Marketing Best Practice, www.marketingbp.com.)*

able to leverage that all the more if our nearest rival gets restructured into its new owner's straitjacket or submerged in post-acquisition navel-gazing. If we are in a highly competitive industry such as printing, but are recognized for our expertise in using recycled paper and biodegradable inks, we should be swinging into action whenever new "green" legislation is passed.

The alignment of weaknesses with threats is also possible, and will require investment to avoid difficulty. Counteracting threats with strengths and addressing weaknesses that might cause opportunities to be lost is also important. Looking at SWOT this way tells us more about the strategy that is needed.

What's all this analysis for?

"Everybody's got a plan, until he gets hit", according to a heavyweight boxing world champion. But as Louis Pasteur (1822–1895), French microbiologist and inventor of pasteurization of milk pointed out, "chance favours only the prepared mind."

Analysis can lead to paralysis, decision-making that takes too long, and strategic plans that are inflexible and get ignored. An inside-out approach to analysis and planning can make a company internally focused with the possibility of being wrong in its view of the world. There are many variables that affect the future of any business, and contingency planning for all of them would be wasteful. Risks associated with any sort of investment seem to get constantly higher and more complex.

Portfolios reduce risk

The analogy of supply convoys in World War Two was used in a *McKinsey Quarterly* article to explain how companies need to operate in a complex and rapidly changing world. The weather was one problem – that could be difficult to manage despite meteorological forecasts and navigational equipment. Even more of a problem was enemy activity; attack by submarine, air or other ships was a constant risk, despite the best efforts of the intelligence services. Convoys were deployed, with supply ships mixed with troop ships and destroyers, which improved the chances of each ship and the supplies crossing the ocean safely.

These convoys were the military equivalent of "portfolios" in business. In order to get your enterprise through the dangers of the business environment, you have to work with a variety of initiatives, in a collection, some of which will make it and some which will not. The key to success is a disciplined search for the right collection and a flexible approach to future change.

Source: Bryan (2002)

Readers might also reflect that many companies may make strategic plans, but manage themselves to quarterly objectives. This is ironic because expectations of future performance, not last quarter's results, should theoretically drive share prices. But try telling that to a CEO who has just missed a sales forecast for the second consecutive quarter.

It is difficult to manage for the long term – anyone knows that from their own personal development – but consultants like McKinsey suggest that it is possible for companies to have a long-term value orientation yet deliver short-term performance. For example: some companies are known for having a long-term focus on innovation and managing progress in the short-term by measuring the proportion of sales coming from new products (Davis, 2005).

Some companies are known for having a long-term focus on innovation and managing progress in the short-term by measuring the proportion of sales coming from new products

Portfolio analysis

A portfolio is a collection of, for example, artwork, investment, property, products, skills or customers. Having a collection of things in a business sense is sometimes referred to as a combination or spread for the purpose of reducing risk and maximizing opportunity. Definitions of portfolio management describe a business process by which a company formulates strategy to

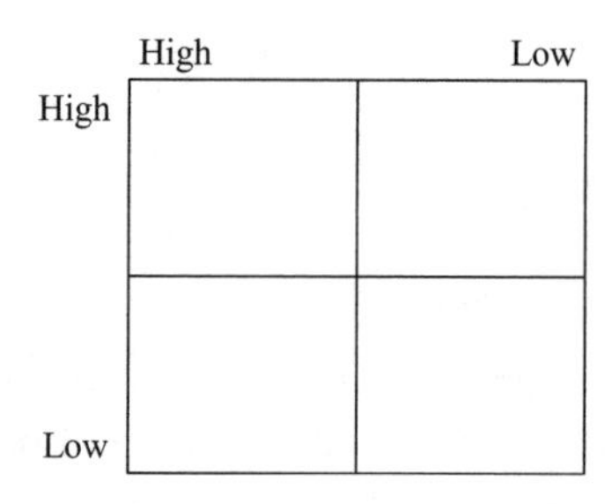

Figure 1.6 *A 2 by 2 matrix.*

achieve its overall objectives: how it decides on the mix within the collection in order to prioritize resource allocation, accepting a risk/reward trade-off.

To visualize the mix, strategists use a diagram and call it a matrix. The meanings of matrix include "the formative parts of an animal organ" and "mass of rock enclosing gems", but in its most general sense, according to the *Oxford English Dictionary*, it means "the place in which things are developed". Strategists and marketers have been working with matrices to categorize items within portfolios for decades.

These portfolios usually involve a 2 × 2 box, with axes marked high and low (Figure 1.6). The horizontal axis works from left to right. Once you get used to these universally useful boxes, the world of strategy is yours for the taking!

Product portfolio management

The Boston Consulting Group's Growth-Share Matrix, designed in the product-led 1960s, is still probably the most well-used approach to analyzing a company's product portfolio, and the earliest example of a strategic tool for professional marketers. The vertical axis measured the market growth rate and the product's position on the horizontal axis shows the relative competitive position through market share. The Profit Impact of Marketing Strategy (PIMS) program, which has been managed by the Strategic Planning Institute since 1975, found that high return on investment was closely related to high market share. PIMS is still collecting and analyzing data from hundreds of companies (see www.pimsonline.com).

Some researchers have pointed out that the cost of acquiring market share varies considerably from market to market, and that correlation does not prove causation, so we must treat generalizations carefully. Nevertheless, the BCG matrix has stood the test of time and gained popular appeal with its stereotypical product types of "Wildcats", "stars", "cash cows" and "dogs".

Correlation does not prove causation

In my first statistics seminar as an undergraduate, the tutor handed out two lists of numbers by calendar month. One was the number of births in the country; the other was the number of storks in the country. More storks are present in the summer, when the birth rate is higher. On the basis of his lists, we could conclude that there was a statistical correlation between the number of storks in the country and the birth rate. His point was, of course, that the correlation does not prove that the storks brought the babies.

Business unit portfolio management

To accommodate more variables and shift the focus of matrix management to markets, McKinsey, working with General Electric, developed a nine-cell Attractiveness–Capabilities matrix. From General Electric's point of view, something was needed to address the problem of its business unit managers planning too conservatively, which resulted in a weak plan at corporate level when the unit plans were aggregated (Lorange, 1975).

The vertical axis "industry attractiveness" addressed the industry sector in which the unit operated. A score for the business unit was derived from factors such as market size, market growth and profitability, weighted and scored to create a compound overall score. To score "business strengths" on the horizontal axis, the unit was judged on market share, growth, product quality, technology skills, economies of scales and experience, marketing capability and profitability relative to competitors. The importance of the business strength score was that it was deemed to be something that the unit could change with the right allocation of resources over time.

With a score on each axis, each GE business unit would land in one of the cells in the matrix. Each of the nine cells in the matrix was allocated a label indicating strategic direction. For example, high industry attractiveness and strong business strengths would result in investment for growth;

medium industry attractiveness and weak business strength would result in a strategy of "manage for cash". Given the continuing success of GE, who can argue against the power of the tool to focus resources where growth could be maximized? So, the company got a balanced plan rather than a conservative plan, ambitious where success was achievable, tactical where market conditions were unfavourable.

So, the company got a balanced plan rather than a conservative plan, ambitious where success was achievable, tactical where market conditions were unfavourable.

This model is indeed sophisticated, but includes variables that are difficult to measure objectively. There may be independent benchmarks for market share and product quality, but how can we determine the relative strength of a company's marketing capability?

The model attracted interest from other large corporations, but some wanted to adapt it. Shell wanted to incorporate more qualitative variables and called their amendment of the BAA the Directional Policy Matrix (DPM), a name that seems to be more widely used in strategy textbooks than the original (Figure 1.7).

All these matrices (Growth-share, BAA, DPM) used circles to indicate a product or business unit's position, with the area of the circle being proportional to sales volume. Most companies who adopted strategic portfolio matrices found that they improved the skills of the managers involved in working with them and the quality of information used in strategy-making.

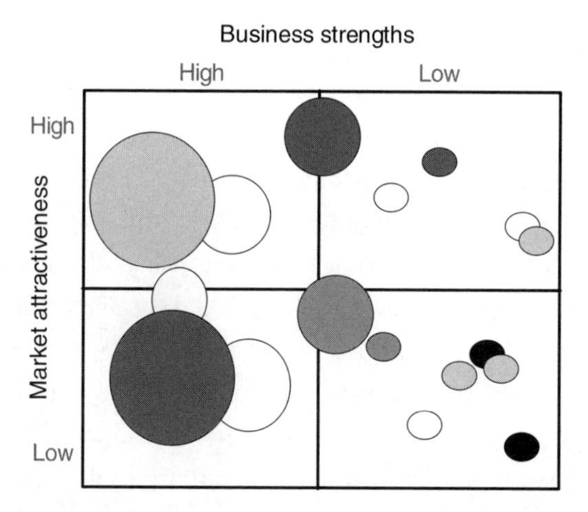

Figure 1.7 *A variation on the directional policy matrix. (Adapted from Professor Malcolm McDonald with kind permission.)*

They perceive the analysis as far more objective, and the process as far more efficient, than other approaches. At least all assumptions and sources of information are logged so that participants in the process can trace why decisions have been made. Of course, the matrix is only a "snapshot" of the portfolio at a point in time. The positioning of the circles should provoke questions, rather than being a definitive answer.

Of course, the matrix is only a "snapshot" of the portfolio at a point in time. The positioning of the circles should provoke questions, rather than being a definitive answer.

By the 1980s, the DPM was taught in business schools around the world. It was designed for a global conglomerate, and it worked very well at that level. It still needed more adaptation in order to work for smaller companies, or units within large corporations. This is where the customer portfolio became significant.

The development of customer portfolio analysis

Large customers are not necessarily profitable

The Supply Chain Executive Board, a division of the Corporate Executive Board, has analyzed 1.26 million order records from six companies in three industries in an ongoing study of supply chain "costs to serve".

The least profitable 20% of customers represent only 11% of volume of orders. But these are **large** orders – over 20 times the revenue of the average order – and they generate **large** losses. For every dollar of revenue earned, they reduce profit by 87 cents. A large order from a customer seems attractive, but large orders still cost a lot to fulfill. The implication is that customers who order in large quantities are not necessarily strategic to their supplier.

This research, which is discussed more fully in Chapter 3, is referenced with kind permission of David Evans, Managing Director, Research, The Supply Chain Executive Board.
A division of the Corporate Executive Board.
A provider of business research and executive education based in Washington DC.
(www.sceb.executiveboard.com)

Customer portfolio management was designed to address this sort of problem – challenging the assumption that volume drove profitability. Volume might have been king in the 1950s, but by the 1980s the world economy was a different place, and achieving success was more complex.

In 1982, Renato Fiocca examined the use of portfolio matrices in what were then called "industrial markets", but we know today as B2B (also incorporating B2G, business-to-government). He suggested that the core for strategic analysis should be the customer. He pointed out that in most industrial markets there are a limited number of important buyers. Buying processes are complex; supply chains have their own power structures and close relationships or partnerships between buyers and sellers are possible.

Fiocca intended that his matrix would help decision-makers in B2B markets to improve profitability because they could allocate resources to the most promising business relationships and withdraw them from others.

In B2B, we are familiar with large customers being referred to as "accounts". Fiocca called his model the "account portfolio matrix". The attractiveness of the customer's business was scored on the vertical axis. The score on the horizontal axis was based on the strength of the relationship between the supplier and the customer.

Customer "attractiveness factors" were about the market in which they operated. Fiocca included market size, the customer's market share and the customer's strength compared to their competitors, covering financial strength and their technical skills and intellectual property. The "relative buyer–seller relationship" encapsulated the strength of "our" relationship as supplier to the customer versus the customer's relationship with competitors. Fiocca included personal friendships and complementary culture as strengths as well as the "share of purse" versus competition, and the number of years that the supplier–customer relationship has been in place.

Since Fiocca created the model presented in Figure 1.8, there have been other modifications and simplifications. In the mid-1990s, I was a researcher in a team led by Professor Malcolm McDonald at Cranfield School of Management working on key account management. We identified Fiocca's account portfolio analysis as an important tool for distinguishing key accounts from other accounts, but rather than use a nine-cell model we decided to use a four-cell model into which we hybridized some elements of the directional policy matrix.

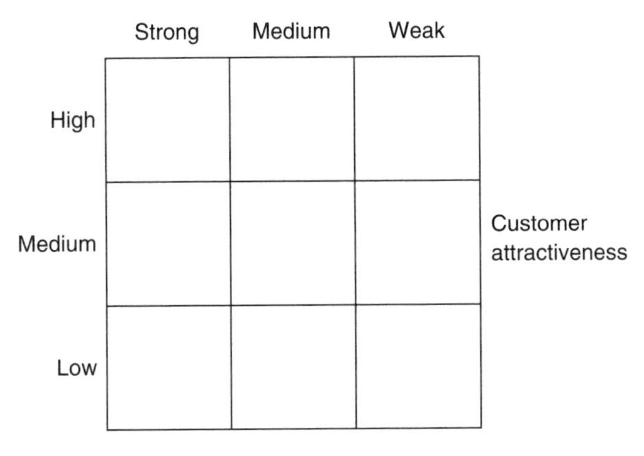

Figure 1.8 *Account portfolio analysis. (Adapted from Fiocca, 1982.)*

In practice, our model moved further on from Fiocca's in trying to focus on the relationship between the buyer and the supplier. In my work with small companies and with companies from developing economies in recent years, I have tried to improve its usability even further (Figure 1.9).

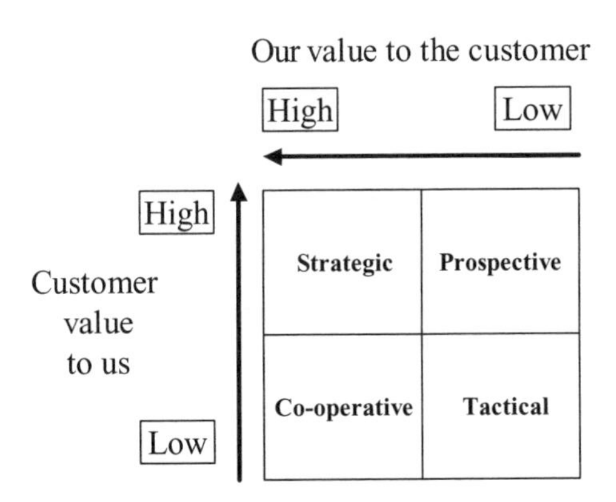

Figure 1.9 *The B2B relationship development box.*

My research into buyer–seller relationships has usually involved key personnel from the supplier and members of the customer's buying decision-making unit. There are innumerable examples of senior managers in a supplier thinking that they are doing very well with a customer when in fact the customer has a less rosy view of their achievements and the quality of the relationship. It is a phenomenon that was identified by Professor Malcolm McDonald as "supplier delusion". So it is important that the horizontal axis should represent the customer's point of view.

There are innumerable examples of senior managers in a supplier thinking that they are doing very well with a customer when in fact the customer has a less rosy view of their achievements and the quality of the relationship.

When account managers have asked purchasing managers about how they compare to competitors, it is clear that because all suppliers are expected to be able to meet core expectations of product quality and delivery accuracy for a reasonable price, it is "soft" factors such as accessibility of key staff and problem-solving that distinguish them. True perception of business strengths comes from a customer viewpoint.

Although the research and calculation involved in identifying appropriate factors, weighting and scoring systems can be difficult and time-consuming, there are two main strengths in portfolio approaches.

First, the steps involved in compiling the customer attractiveness scores are more likely to deliver a greater degree of objectivity than models with axes based on single, qualitative or judgmental factors. The requirement to consult the customer about their rating of "our business strengths" (versus competitors) can also be a contribution to objectivity, which should lead to better decisions about resource allocation.

After all, while suppliers are looking out to their customers from the inside, those same customer organizations have purchasing professionals looking out to their suppliers from the inside, analyzing them and making judgments about them. Chapter 2 examines their strategic perspective.

The labels for the quadrants of the relationship development box are designed to describe business relationships simply:

- *Strategic*: To describe a relationship as strategic is instantly understandable; it is one where both parties to it anticipate long-term gain.
- *Tactical*: A tactical relationship is instantly recognizable as one where both parties are not investing, but doing mutually advantageous business on a transaction-by-transaction basis, looking for mutual short-term gain.

Where there is a difference in either party's perceptions, more care is required.

- *Cooperative*: If a customer recognizes a supplier's business strengths but potential for business development is limited, the relationship can still be long-lived, but it will not attract significant investment from either side. The relationship is cooperative in that there is some mutual dependence, but it may not necessarily be comfortable or even friendly.
- *Prospective*: If a supplier is targeting a customer or potential customer, but the customer is not yet convinced of the supplier's strengths, the relationship can be described as prospective.

In describing the axes of this model in workshops and classes, I find myself repeating again and again that the vertical axis represents the strategic value of the customer to the supplier, and the horizontal axis represents the strategic value of the supplier to the customer. This way, we can marry the purchasing analysis with customer analysis and form a tool that both buyer and seller can use to describe their relationship at a point in time. It is supposed to be a relationship portfolio analysis rather than an inside-looking-out customer analysis.

In terms of strategy-making, investment focus is in the high/high box. But a healthy supplier needs to spread risk, and generate development activity in the other quadrants at low cost. We will return to the relationship box in Chapter 3, and examine each of the quadrants in Chapters 4 to 7. In the meantime, let's take a look at strategic purchasing: how customers analyze their suppliers.

2

The purchaser's view

"80% of companies believe that they deliver a superior customer experience, but only 8% of their customers agree."

Quoted with kind permission from Bain and Company

What are buying decision-makers in your customers trying to achieve?

Purchasing definition

"Purchasing is the process of procuring the proper requirement, at the time needed, for the lowest possible costs from a reliable source".

Quoted with kind permission from
Director of Procurement and Risk Management
Winthrop University, Rock Hill, South Carolina

Research by Swinder and Seshadri (2001) has identified four purchasing strategies that are connected with better company performance:

- Win–win style negotiation with suppliers
- High-quality communications with suppliers

- Reducing the supplier base
- Developing long-term relationships with strategic, high-performing suppliers.

Most organizations recognize that more can be achieved with suppliers if a company can act like a good customer, offering some long-term commitment and process integration. From a supplier's point of view it is critical to note the research findings that the main factors that lead to a purchasers' favorable attitude are the quality of a relationship, the length of a relationship and a supplier's reputation rather than dependency on a supplier. You should also note that value delivery has to be proven before relationship quality can be developed.

In many situations, purchasing professionals are eager to work with suppliers to develop mutually advantageous business relationships based on value. In a recent survey by TACK International, 24% of buying decision-makers said that price was not their top criterion. Yet we have all heard anecdotes by the water cooler from salespeople who are dealing with purchasing managers who knock them to the floor, stand on their throat and demand an outrageous discount. Inevitably, these stories have created an exaggerated stereotype of the merciless purchasing manager who would cheerfully buy the wrong product if it were cheaper. If we are getting mixed messages from the purchasing profession, perhaps it is because we, as sales management professionals, do not know enough about how they analyze us as suppliers.

The impact of purchasing professionalism on brand

"Professionalism in purchasing, with its ongoing external trading relationships, is key to supporting and/or enhancing the brand; sometimes this can be the only differentiating factor between companies."

Quoted with kind permission from
The Chartered Institute of Purchasing and Supply (www.cips.org)

In 1984 Peter Kraljic wrote in the *McKinsey Quarterly* about the challenges facing the purchasing profession. They included:

- The proportion of costs associated with purchased goods increasing
- The need for more flexible and responsive materials planning, worldwide
- The need to secure supply of strategic products for the long-term, requiring long-term contracts, process integration, or even joint ventures or acquisitions
- Broadening sources of supply, but concentrating on the best suppliers

Purchasing managers were, and still are, faced with strategic questions such as:

- To what degree should purchasing should be centralized or localized?
- How much risk is acceptable in key sources of supply?
- Should we make-or-buy in product sourcing?
- Should we have in-house or outsourced services?

It is the role of professional salespeople to help them to address those challenges.

Who makes buying decisions?

The nature of business-to-business buying decision-making is complex. A purchasing manager may be in charge of the process, but other decision-makers in the company are consulted or may have greater influence, depending on the category of purchase, which we will discuss later. The number of people involved in commercial buying decisions mainly depends on the size of the company. In a small company, there may be as few as three people who debate supplier value. The Chief Executive Officer of medium-sized firms may delegate much of the purchasing process to other managers, but have final approval. Some firms use external experts to help with major buying decisions.

I have interviewed many purchasing decision-makers over the years, and even small companies like the principle of a "decision-making unit". Having a number of managers involved helps to minimize risk and ensure commitment to the purchase agreed. Managers actually debate "value" in the proposals offered by potential suppliers. The fit of the solution to their specification and their confidence in the supplier's abilities to fulfill promises made in the proposal are examples of the value elements they take into account. Individual buying decision-makers are particularly concerned about the risks they take when choosing a supplier.

In a small company, a bad decision about a machine tool for the factory or an IT system can mean that the company does not survive. In a larger company, although more financial risk can be absorbed, no individual wants to make a decision that ruins their career. That's why commercial organizations ensure that they have robust purchasing processes. Government and voluntary organizations are even more cautious about audit trails for purchasing decisions, since taxpayers and donors perceive the money spent as "theirs".

In a small company, a bad decision about a machine tool for the factory or an IT system can mean that the company does not survive. In a larger company, although more financial risk can be absorbed, no individual wants to make a decision that ruins their career.

A company's purchasing of goods and services that are consumed in production can account for over 50% of total costs. Unlike other areas of the business, 100% of savings on consumed goods and services go to the bottom line. Compare this with, say, the savings created by the introduction of more efficient systems or new equipment. Typically, an initial investment is required that can take three or more years to deliver a return.

In order to ensure best value is achieved, the purchasing function has been growing in importance in most industries over the past 20 years and the purchasing profession has been improving its skills levels. Purchasing professionals have a combination of skills encompassing strategy formulation, process management, team-building, decision-making, behavioural skills, negotiation skills and financial knowledge. Their command of strategy is focused on their professional niche – the ability to analyze the company's supply base, structure categories of supplier relationships and plan activities with suppliers.

In order to ensure best value is achieved, the purchasing function has been growing in importance in most industries over the past 20 years and the purchasing profession has been improving its skills levels.

Portfolio analysis in purchasing

Subjects for regular debate among buying decision-makers are: which suppliers are strategic enough to be partners in a business relationship, and how should we deal with non-strategic suppliers?

A partnership approach is not always efficient

A case study of a Finnish company in the electronics industry reveals how, even when overall purchasing strategy favors interdependence with suppliers – or, at least, cooperation – relationships with minor suppliers will be handled tactically. The value of procurement in the company in the year of the study (2001) was 30 million euros, of which 70% was for components; 50% of purchases were considered strategic and 20% "bottleneck"; 10% of suppliers account for 90% of purchases.

The degree of mutual dependency between strategic suppliers and the company has prompted the electronics company to ensure continuity of supply by taking share ownership in some of their key suppliers. The Finnish company fosters a positive attitude to conflict with suppliers. They believe that discussion, analysis and resolution of conflict can accelerate development of solutions. The researchers in this case noted that the company's bias toward partnership-style relationships was not necessarily efficient in terms of resource allocation. They applied portfolio analysis and advocated streamlining the purchase of volume commodities via e-procurement.

Source: Ahonen and Salmi (2003)

The purchaser's portfolio matrix

By rating a purchased product or service in terms of its importance (i.e. the amount of value and profit that it adds) on the vertical matrix, and the complexity and risk inherent in its conditions of supply on the horizontal axis, Rackham and de Vincentis in *Rethinking the Salesforce* (1998) explained that purchasers work with four strategies:

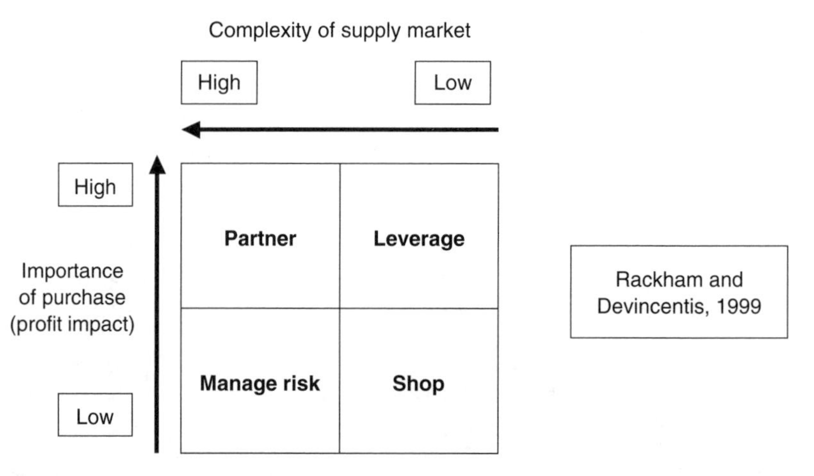

Figure 2.1 *The purchaser's portfolio matrix. (Reproduced with kind permission from Professor Neil Rackham.)*

- *Partner*: High profit impact, high supply risk
- *Manage risk*: Low profit impact, high supply risk
- *Leverage*: High profit impact, low supply risk
- *Shop*: Low profit impact, low supply risk.

Partner

The evidence for focus on a supplier's capabilities

A recent survey involving 3,300 participants indicated:

> "A focus on the capability of a supplier – such as quality or delivery – more positively influences the financial performance of a firm's procurement operation."

62% of companies procure most of their business needs from their top 10 suppliers. These organizations "report a 52% lower median cost of the procurement cycle per purchase order."

However, diminishing returns set in if organizations try to arrange strategic relationships with more than 5% of their supplier base.

Source: Performance Benchmarks: Procurement (2006)
American Productivity and Quality Center

For more than 30 years, APQC has worked with organizations from around the globe to identify best practices. Research quoted with kind permission of the APQC

The possibility of a close business relationship between supplier and customer is high where the product supplied has a high profit impact and the supply market is complex. Supplier and customer can share goals and co-develop solutions for end-customers. Business for both requires a long-term approach, rather than transaction-by-transaction bidding. Generally, this is where suppliers want to be with their customers, but it is not a position without risk. Partnerships can break down and can leave suppliers exposed. The costs of partnerships are high for both parties, and experts recommend caution before seeking a partnering relationship.

Test for new values

The test of a partnership is its capacity to create new value that cannot be achieved from a conventional buy–sell relationship. Andre Boisvert, who set up many hi tech partnerships, advises: "If all you are doing is swapping four quarters for a dollar, stay a vendor."

Source: Rackham, Friedman and Ruff, *Getting Partnering Right*, McGraw-Hill (1996)
Quoted with kind permission from Professor Neil Rackham

Also, the hype from the customer may be greater than the commitment. For example, a McKinsey survey in 2005 found that 70% of IT managers expressed a preference for closer relationships with IT suppliers, but only 30% were trying to implement them (Dail and West, 2005).

Purchasing professionals need to focus on the best suppliers of strategic goods and services. They work hard to understand supplier capabilities, and most companies have reduced their supplier base since the 1980s. Poor or average suppliers are dropped, and purchasing professionals expect high standards from the few suppliers who are listed. They are also prepared to help the best suppliers to do more for them as customers.

But remember the risk management responsibility of purchasing managers. They may believe that they need to avoid dependence on a single "best" supplier to protect themselves from quality or service problems, and they may also fear price changes, policy changes in the supplier due to a merger or change of chief officer, or even natural disasters. For example, it was widely reported that when a fire broke out at one of their key suppliers in

Kariya, Japan, Toyota had to shut down a significant number of assembly lines (Bartholomew, 2006).

Purchasing managers need to feel that they have some sort of control in the relationship. A purchasing manager told me many years ago that although one of his two suppliers for a key raw material was clearly superior to the other, he gave some occasional business to the second supplier to encourage competition in the supply market and to keep the main supplier "on their toes".

Purchasing best practice

The key findings of an in-depth study by the American Productivity and Quality Center into sourcing from world-class suppliers revealed that:

- Best practice companies actively seek best sources. Excellence includes technical performance as well as quality and cost.
- They certify suppliers' operations.
- Their environmental standards are high.
- They enter into legally enforceable contracts.
- They have local employees in the supplier's country.
- Their measurement criteria are consistent across geographical boundaries.
- They achieve credit terms directly with suppliers.

Source: Lock and Meimoun (1999) Published by The American Productivity and Quality Center

For more than 30 years, APQC has worked with organizations from around the globe to identify best practices. Research referenced with kind permission from APQC

Nevertheless, closeness to one supplier can reduce risk in other ways. A strategic supplier will prioritize supply to a key customer, ensuring stability of supply for them. One raw materials company I worked with had allocated goods to customers on a pro rata basis when supply was constrained. When they categorized

Nevertheless, closeness to one supplier can reduce risk in other ways. A strategic supplier will prioritize supply to a key customer, ensuring stability of supply for them.

their customer relationships using a portfolio box, they focused on forecasting the needs of strategic customers and could proritize supply to them. Also, within a close supplier–customer relationship, process integration can be achieved, which simplifies complex tasks, and reduces costs. Partnering can also improve service to the end customer.

You can be a critical asset to your customer if, as a supplier, you consistently perform well, continually improve, are financially stable and have a positive approach to relationship development. Your customers will invest in your cost competitiveness if you are a critical supplier, e.g. by giving you the opportunity to rate them as a customer and changing the way they do things to eliminate waste for your benefit.

Of course, you have to perform well on key performance indicators set by the purchasing manager in the customer before trust can develop between your two organizations. Trust is developed before commitment. Once both have committed to long-term contractual arrangements, it can be said that a strategic relationship exists between your organizations, and that process integration and joint investment in new product development may follow.

Another factor in successful strategic relationships is flexibility. A long-term contract cannot be set in concrete. It is what happens in contractual "gray areas" that determines the quality of a business relationship. One IT company with which I worked had a policy that if the customer had a problem with their remote managed services, they would fix it first and refer to the contract later, if at all. Knowing that they could rely on their supplier in that way, customers were not only happy with long-term agreements, but many acted as references for the supplier when they were bidding to prospects. Building up a network of intangible "give and take" around a core contract for goods and services can actually reduce a lot of hidden costs and risks for both parties to the relationship.

It is what happens in contractual "gray areas" that determines the quality of a business relationship.

Some customers find partnering easier than others. There are indications that companies that have extended purchasing processes for important items, requiring multi-functional and multi-level decision-making, develop a preference for partnering. It probably saves them a lot not to repeat purchasing decision-making too often!

Manage risk

If the complexity of the supply market is high and it is difficult to obtain alternatives, the supplier has a certain amount of power. However, if the profit impact of their product or service is low, the purchasing manager has little incentive to partner. Investing in a relationship for non-strategic products and services is not necessarily money well spent.

Nevertheless, in order to reduce hassle in sourcing non-strategic products and services, purchasing managers will probably prefer a cooperative relationship with suppliers. Because it is difficult to obtain alternatives, they may take a long time to choose the right supplier and be prepared to enter into a long-term arrangement with them, but they will expect a competitive price in return for long-term contracts. Typical products in this category include merchandising and other marketing services, and facilities management services such as security, catering and maintenance.

Customers in this situation may be retained, but loyalty should not be assumed. In fact, where switching costs or the hassle involved in switching are high, buying decision-makers may be dissatisfied, but still stay with a supplier.

The role of switching costs and switching risks

A study in Australia found that despite failure of the core product or service, inflexibility, poor technical support, poor communication and failure to take responsibility for problems, customers did not necessarily switch supplier. Even in cases of sustained dissatisfaction and unresolved complaints, there was an expectation that alternative suppliers were just as bad.

Switching costs and switching risks are a considerable deterrent to switching suppliers. Although purchasing decision-makers are very objective, a good relationship with the supplier's key account manager made up for a lot of organizational failure.

Source: Yanamandram and White (2006)

Suppliers should not be complacent if they have the luxury of being an incumbent where switching is difficult.

Suppliers should not be complacent if they have the luxury of being an incumbent where switching is difficult. A relationship of convenience may last a long time, but if it is a difficult one, it can become very adversarial. Fixing problems in a low trust environment creates hidden costs for both sides. Those who make the purchasing decisions will spread negative comments about the supplier throughout their networks, which becomes a barrier to acquiring more customers. They may also demand considerable compensation for contractual failings or start behaving badly themselves, for example, by withholding payment well beyond normal payment terms. In the meantime, of course, the buyer is forever searching for new suppliers in the market, substitute products or services, and improvements in the performance of competitors.

Leverage

A letter to suppliers from the director of trading at a specialist UK retailer was recently featured in a trade magazine. The letter demanded longer payment terms, price reductions and a greater contribution to joint marketing. As will be noted from industry codes in the later discussion in this book on reputation management, it is not considered best practice to delay payments to suppliers. Nevertheless, not all companies who publicly aspire to best practice actually implement it, and salespeople have to work with that reality.

In industries where commoditization prevails, "leverage" is likely to be dominant. It is also common in public sector buying strategy. Important products may have a significant impact on the customer's business but, if a supplier can be easily changed, then raw competition is likely to produce a better deal for the buying organization. Price matters. Buyers may offer volume, but they are not looking for value creation through partnership.

Suppliers frequently mistake high-volume customers for "key" accounts, and waste money investing in additional services or offering expertise. In fact, the supplier needs to take costs out of this type of relationship.

A purchasing manager knows the negotiating power of being a large customer, and if supply risks are low, they have every temptation to use that power. It is likely in "leverage" supply situations that the product is a commodity being bought in volume. For maximum leverage, the customer must have their own internal technical expertise so that they are not dependent on the supplier for advice on using the purchase or for other types of support.

If your purchasing contact is putting significant focus on renegotiating your existing contract to achieve gains such as improved payment terms and shifting inventory to you, these tactics are indicative that they perceive you as a supplier to be "leveraged".

Standardization

If a purchasing manager's primary interest in a supplier is for large volumes of standard product, they need to make sure that they are getting a standardized product. This is a situation in which some aspects of quality and service can be traded for lower prices. Suppliers do not like giving up the opportunity to serve large customers with their expertise, but market conditions force the issue.

There are places in the world where large quantities of commodities can be purchased cheaply. The purchaser knows that that may introduce some risks. Will delivery be reliable? Will the "standard" quality be too low and result in wastage? The last thing that a purchasing manager wants is that sort of hassle. Colleagues protesting over an inadequate product delivered late is a nightmare. Purchasing managers have no wish to be involved in such a situation. The winner is the supplier with an established reputation who can offer something standard and reduce process costs.

Adoption of e-procurement

E-commerce has been associated in the minds of salespeople with a purchasing professional's drive for leverage. The primary motivation for applying information technology to processes is usually to save money. In industrial organizations, the buying process is complex and time-consuming. For non-strategic purchases, that seems to be wasteful. More efficiency and transparency should reduce costs. Research on e-procurement has

In industrial organizations, the buying process is complex and time-consuming. For non-strategic purchases, that seems to be wasteful.

recorded more improved efficiency than improved effectiveness. Nevertheless, the purchasing manager is pleased if the purchasing process can become quicker and cheaper! E-procurement can result in information being managed better, and a reduction in "maverick" decisions.

Suppliers must keep in mind the extent to which purchasing professionals are driven by awareness of the cost of time. The supplier has no choice but to understand the customer's need and to respond with information targeted at particular decision-makers within the company, in easily accessible electronic communications. Since the supplier will also be utilizing third-party sources of information on the Internet, keeping such market influencers as industry analysts informed is also sensible.

The demands of e-procurement create a challenge for the IT function of a supplier. Not only must sales and marketing processes be able to link to the customer's e-procurement process, but in order to continue taking time and cost out of any transactions, fulfillment will have to be efficient and information will have to be exchanged quickly. As suppliers' and customers' inventory control systems are now often linked, this can create data security challenges and the weight of the law tends to put the onus on the supplier to keep the customer's confidential information secure. Some customers, for some categories of purchase, value speed of delivery and efficiency of processes more than product differentiation.

Process improvement

A case study of a chemicals company and their largest customer sheds some light on what can be achieved by process improvement utilizing information systems. The relationship was described as fairly adversarial, but obviously the amount of business undertaken between the two required some degree of cooperation. Inventory rationalization was the key by which the supplier demonstrated cost reduction to the customer. Collaboration on inventory data sharing enabled the customer to reduce stock levels and save money.

The same supplier, working with another large customer with a cost reduction challenge, helped the customer move from the use of a special formula product to a standardized product.

Source: Corbett and Blackburn (1999)

Shop

It is likely that e-procurement will eventually dominate in this category, and it is even more likely that purchasing managers will be willing to take more risks. They can take time to look around without spending too much time identifying minor savings. A bid-by-bid approach is suitable, unless a supplier can provide an alternative with even lower hassle. Relationship-building is completely inappropriate. It is the ideal situation for e-tendering and reverse auctions.

E-marketplaces

In 2000, GM, Ford and DMX set up an e-marketplace called Covisint for the automotive industry. These three companies alone control 46% of transaction volume in the industry. Covisint was intended to be a secure platform linking suppliers and customers in e-procurement, supply chain management and new product development processes. Suppliers can offer online catalogues for buyers to browse. There is an online bidding system where buyers post requirements and process proposals from potential suppliers against their buying criteria. Sometimes, reverse auctions are launched where suppliers can see other bids and are challenged to lower their prices. Within a year of launch, 2,600 companies were using Covisint (Jelassi and Enders, 2005).

At the time of writing, Covisint is used by 30,000 companies in 96 countries and has expanded into the healthcare sector. (*Source*: www.covisint.com.)

Reverse auctions

In reverse auctions, the supplier competes for the opportunity to supply the customer. As bids come in, they are transparent to all the competing suppliers. Suppliers have to put in lower prices to beat their competitor's last bid. Having these auctions online as well means that the buying company has a very cheap process for collecting bids and dealing with a wide variety of potential suppliers.

Buyers claim that reverse auctions generate huge savings. In 2001, General Electric planned for $600 m in savings generated by online reverse auctions (Kwak, 2002).

Transparency may appear to contribute to savings, but sealed bids can generate as much in savings as open bids. Transparency affects the perception of the suppliers, who feel that they are watching their margin being eroded. Some wonder if the buyer is manipulating the process. Purchasing managers need to set policies for their reverse-auction process to ensure that suppliers perceive that it is fair.

There is considerable risk for buying decision-makers who get too dependent on reverse auctions as their main means of achieving cost savings. They may identify a low-cost supplier who proves to be unreliable. Then the costs of rectifying the mess they leave can be punitive. The purchasing manager of a city council told me that he had once engaged a new low-price supplier to do some highway maintenance. The supplier got as far as digging up the road, but then went bankrupt, which left the manager with an enormous problem to solve.

Some companies have tried to overcome these concerns by ensuring that a total cost of ownership analysis is applied in their reverse auctions, which takes into account supplier quality, technical support and other non-price-related factors.

Many suppliers recognize the role of information technology in reducing purchase costs for all parties in the supply chain, and have used it to improve their competitiveness.

The value of innovation

The French office supplies company, Brun Passot, recognized that customers considered its product range to be a non-critical purchase. As early as 1989, the company set out to help customers to automate purchasing stationery through the provision of computer terminals and purchasing software that linked to the Brun Passot server. This application could send product information, quotes, delivery information and process payments. It was a considerable investment for the supplier, but paid off for them in terms of improved volume of orders, cheaper processing of orders and faster stock turn.

For customers, such as COGEMA, who had 700 employees responsible for ordering stationery spread across 72 locations, the benefits were also worthwhile. They saved 30–40% of costs compared to their manual procedure. Once having established themselves as innovators in process improvement, Brun Passot kept up the pace by offering customers access to a wider range of products and to their EDI expertise.

Source: Jelassi and Enders (2005)

Supplier performance measurement

Whatever the relationship that exists between suppliers and customers, both will only be able to monitor its success or failure if something is measured. However, each party will have their own internally focused measures of return on investment. Just as sales managers want to demonstrate returns such as increase in sales revenue and improved sales productivity, purchasing managers must also impress their Chief Executive Officer. The Chief Executive Officer is also under pressure, and the forced turnover of CEOs because of performance deficiencies has risen significantly since 2001.

Just as sales managers want to demonstrate returns such as increase in sales revenue and improved sales productivity, purchasing managers must also impress their Chief Executive Officer.

Purchasing decision-makers must therefore prove value of production and value of delivery, and that can be very complex. Take, for example, the implementation of an IT system, where they are relying on IT managers and operational managers for measurement and feedback.

Many IT managers complain that performance measurement only tells you when you are already in trouble. Costs are not easy to measure in complex change projects, and in any case the most important factor in any business change involving IT is time. System implementations spread over years usually grossly exceed the original budget. To avoid project drift, functionality often has to be sacrificed, and users then become dissatisfied with the system. Employee dissatisfaction can lead to poor use of the system, and poor internal process quality can lead to

Many IT managers complain that performance measurement only tells you when you are already in trouble.

customer dissatisfaction. Where does all that leave the purchasing manager? Usually, negotiating compensation from the supplier.

One purpose of performance measurement is to prevent this kind of nightmare scenario. Even if the measurement is imperfect and less than totally objective, it helps in several ways. For example, it can improve the qualification of suppliers by eliminating the risky ones. It can provide early warning of project drift or cost overruns.

So, for any purchasing decision, proactive monitoring and measurement is necessary to minimize risk.

In a research report published in 2002, 70% of survey respondents said that they regarded supplier performance measurement as "very important" or "critical", but implementation was not as widespread. The report found that measurement improved supplier performance by 26.6% on factors such as quality, price, on-time delivery, lower lead times, contract compliance and responsiveness (Minahan and Vigoroso, 2002).

However, one-off cost reductions are not always what a purchasing decision-maker wants. Continuous improvement might be more important, but it still needs to be tracked. Of course, there is actually a cost in measuring things; for example, the application of metrics to an IT project can add up to 8% to costs. The purchasing manager and the IT manager have to consider how much will be saved – especially hidden costs – or risk avoided.

What gets measured?

In a 2006 article with Professor Ryals of Cranfield School of Management, we identified from published research on purchasing three levels of supplier performance measurement.

Measures per transaction

At the core of any supplier performance measurement system are three key elements of "value for money":

- Price
- Quality conformance
- Delivery reliability

These can be measured per transaction.

The key elements may vary in importance, depending on the type of company, and there are trade-offs within these three criteria. Obviously, a company focused on quality will accept higher prices, and companies frequently pay higher prices for faster and reliable delivery. There are also interdependencies. In one case study penalties were charged by the customer for late delivery or parts rejected, but the supplier still assumed that if the accepted parts were on time, then they had at least partly met the criteria. From the customer's point of view, the order was a complete failure (Carbone, 2004).

Purchasing decision-makers would argue that some suppliers never even make the grade on their basic requirements, and that it is remarkable how they stay in business. Expectations of value have been raised in the past 30 years. Japanese manufacturers became global giants by focusing on quality, and other emerging economies have offered basic production efficiency at low cost. There is a constant "raising of the bar". Without satisfaction at the transactional level, the purchaser's perception of product value is minimal and the potential for a long-term relationship with the supplier is zero.

Without satisfaction at the transactional level, the purchaser's perception of product value is minimal and the potential for a long-term relationship with the supplier is zero.

Support factors

Closely behind doing what is required at a transactional level, research indicates that the next most urgent buyer demand is that suppliers should be "responsive". Some companies rate response flexibility higher than price. Responsiveness, which is a simple way for suppliers to enhance satisfaction, is often the first subjective measure to appear in purchasing criteria. Although companies could have some objective measures, such as how quickly a company answers the telephone, it is probably perceptions of responsiveness that really matter.

The quantity and quality of communications is a contributing factor. Communications need to be constructive at all points of contact to maintain the impression of responsiveness. Even the quality of communications items such as the layout of invoices may be measured, or at least create perceptions.

However, judgments about the interpersonal skills of a supplier's personnel are likely to be dominant in creating perceptions of responsiveness. Can they envisage how the customer sees the issues (empathy)? Can they have an open discussion? Can they demonstrate quality reasoning in their negotiations?

The issue of maintenance and technical support is also surprisingly subjective. Suppliers sometimes assume that their technical support is valuable, but it depends on the type of product they offer, the skills level in the customer, and the geographical spread of their operations. Technical support can be valued, but customers also expect that suppliers will make some guarantees about technical problem resolution. It is therefore expectations of technical support and perceptions of technical support delivery that will determine how a supplier is rated.

As previously mentioned, beyond response and support, customers are interested in suppliers who can offer process innovation, such as participation in e-procurement and supply chain automation.

"Intangible" factors

Purchasers will be more favorable toward suppliers where the company has a good reputation and where its personnel are capable of developing business relationships. Branding is a much-neglected subject in business-to-business markets, yet some of the biggest brands in the world are B2B companies, such as Microsoft and IBM, or they have significant B2B divisions, e.g. Mercedes, which has a truck division. The longevity, financial stability and technological capability of suppliers do matter to purchasing decision-makers. It may not be possible for any supplier to suggest that nobody was fired for choosing them, but the personal risk involved in making a purchasing decision is mitigated when the supplier's reputation is widely admired.

The longevity, financial stability and technological capability of suppliers do matter to purchasing decision-makers.

Corporate social responsibility

One intangible factor valued by many organizations for legal or moral reasons is consistency in corporate responsibility across the globe.

HP, Dell and IBM together with Celestica, Flextronics, Jabil, Sanmina SCI and Solectron launched the Electronics Industry Code of Conduct for global supply chains in 2004. The Code promotes standards for socially responsible business practices throughout the supply chain. As companies become more dependent on suppliers in developing economies, they have found it to be more effective to jointly monitor labor and environmental practices and plan improvements. The coalition has now grown to over 20 members.

Additional information can be found on the website at www.eicc.info.

Reference provided with kind permission of EICC.

It has been mentioned above that demonstration of value, i.e. satisfactory performance on core functionality, is a prerequisite for developing a relationship with a customer, but does not itself necessarily lead to loyalty. Both parties need to assess and exchange information regularly to be sure that core value has been delivered. Suppliers can demonstrate further commitment to a customer by understanding their goals and anticipate future needs and sharing ideas.

A customer needs to be confident that the supplier will not act opportunistically, and building the right level of confidence can take time. When a supplier is trusted as a partner, the relationship with the customer usually moves toward joint investments, e.g. jointly managing assets used in the relationship (stock, machinery, vehicles, etc.). At this stage, measurement becomes a joint issue, rather than something that the buyer does to the supplier.

Latest best practice

Supplier performance management is still evolving. One purchasing institute is encouraging its members to adopt a 360-degree appraisal process, inviting the supplier to rate the buying organization as a customer.

At any level of performance measurement, perception is truth. Buyers perceive that they meet top supplier managers more often than they do, and that they give them more information than they do! Buyers think they do more relationship building than suppliers think they do; and suppliers think they fulfill their contractual obligations better than they do (Blancero and Ellram, 1997). A misunderstanding or an instance of complacency may upset the perception of "justice" in business relationships. With such widely different perceptions, a transparent procedure is needed to resolve disputes.

Categories of supplier performance measures are shown in Figure 2.2.

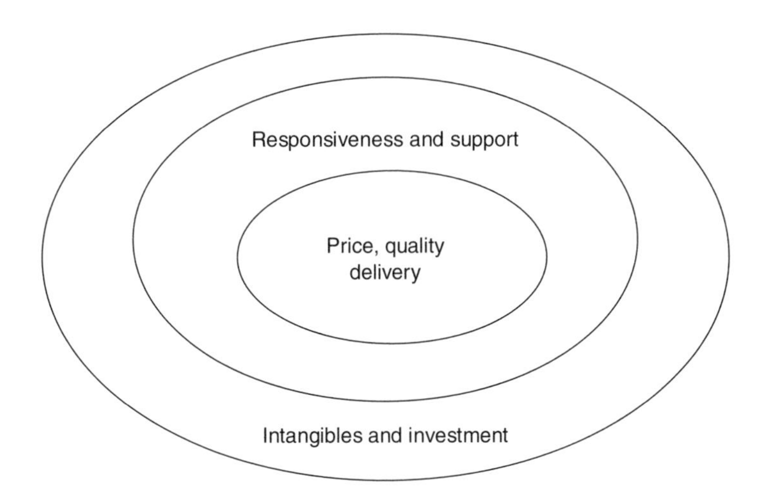

Figure 2.2 *Supplier performance measures.*

Human factors

In order to sell effectively, salespeople must make an accurate assessment of how their customers are judging them. In this chapter, we've covered some of the criteria that customers use to make decisions, such as price, reliability and risk. On the surface, assessing which of these criteria is really important to a particular customer would seem fairly straightforward, but in real life it can prove to be difficult. For example, when a customer says, "You cost too much", it would be easy to assume that price is the central issue, although this is often not the problem.

Early in the sales cycle, "You cost too much" is likely to mean: "We're not yet convinced of the benefits of changing." In the middle of the cycle, cost objections often mean: "We've found a competitor who is cheaper." As the selling cycle moves into its final stages, "You cost too much" may have a completely different meaning. It could, of course, be a genuine reflection that cost is the primary decision criterion. Or it could be a negotiating tactic. Or (see Xerox study) it could be a polite and acceptable way to cover up customer concerns about the risks of moving ahead.

Hidden perceived risks

A study carried out in Xerox by Neil Rackham interviewed buyers in lost sales where Xerox had been turned down by the buyer in writing on the grounds of cost. It turned out that in 64% of cases, price was not the most important factor. The real reason was a perceived risk that the buyer was unwilling to share with Xerox. Interview responses included:

"I didn't trust the salesperson."

"My boss preferred IBM."

"The Xerox presentation was smooth – too smooth."

"It's a new model and we felt it needed more of a track record before we committed to it."

Source: Neil Rackham, *Major Account Sales Strategy*, Chapter 6, McGraw-Hill (1989)

Quoted with kind permission from Professor Neil Rackham

It is a human thing to be economical with the truth. An excuse not to place an order is not necessarily a deliberate attempt to mislead. It can be a way of saying that you did a good job, but there were irrational reasons for placing the business elsewhere. Most of the content of this chapter has focused on professional purchasers making rational choices between suppliers. There are many other interested parties in buying decision-making units – line managers, financial managers and end users of the product being considered. There are also people who would like to sideline or even sabotage an individual purchase or a supplier relationship.

There are also people who would like to sideline or even sabotage an individual purchase or a supplier relationship.

Although purchasing systems are designed to filter out personal biases and focus on organizational objectives, subtle influences on people in the buying decision-making team may affect the most considered of sales proposals. Sales managers need to be aware that a tender does not necessarily mean an outcome for one of the potential suppliers. In many cases, a supplier's biggest competitor is "do nothing".

Business purchases are made by human beings, with all their frailties. In addition to the rational reasons for doing or not doing something, we all have to cope with irrational influences on our business and ourselves. These influences may come from the business environment; for example, in a recession many purchases that would normally be made are delayed. Influences may come from the organizational culture; for example, a long-established company may have policies that prevent purchasers from choosing innovative solutions.

Last, but not least, any purchasing decision-maker will be influenced by their individual circumstances. To take risks in a risk-averse organization could have unpleasant career consequences. To integrate suppliers more closely into the company might mean a loss of control over information or resources, and create insecurity. To choose the best supplier in an open tender might mean losing trusted contacts in the incumbent supplier who have become personal friends.

Salespeople tend to be aware that perceptions of rational choices are themselves subject to the buyer's own individual outlook on life. Anyone only ever notices a small proportion of what they see and hear, screening out boring bits and unhelpful messages. And our own biases lead us to distort messages. Classically, what is half full to an optimist is half empty to a pessimist. We are subject to conditioning and may have conscious and unconscious beliefs and attitudes about products and services, messages and the way that they are delivered, companies, brands and images. We may be unaware of our true long-term interests, or have incomplete information about our options.

Nevertheless, it is also human to repeat actions that have been followed by positive consequences, and avoid those that have been followed by negative consequences. Suppliers that focus on delivering positive consequences to customers should succeed.

Conclusion

Purchasing professionals use analysis models and measurement systems to ensure that supplier relationships are managed appropriately and fairly. Although the influence of individuals may be a moderating factor, for most of the time and in most circumstances, sales professionals are dealing with predictable outcomes based on parameters set by the customer. Understanding purchasing strategy will help the thoughtful salesperson to succeed, but as a sales manager you will also need to coach them to develop their intuition about buyers' perceptions. Realistic appreciation of the nature of the business relationships between your company and the customer will also be important. We are moving on to analyze that in Chapter 3.

3

The B2B relationship development box

There is only one thing that we all have in common – that we are all different!

Popular proverb

Total delivered cost

The Supply Chain Executive Board (SCEB), a division of the Corporate Executive Board, has analyzed 1.26 million order records from six companies in three industries. These orders covered the business of 5,825 customers, and represented $3.65 bn in revenue.

By studying "total delivered cost" per order (cost of goods sold plus costs to service the order), SCEB discovered that just over 5% of the revenue generated was unprofitable.

The least profitable 20% of customers represented only 11% of volume of orders. But these were large orders – over 20 times the revenue of the average order, and they generated large losses. For every dollar of revenue earned, they reduced profit by 87 cents. A large order from a customer seems attractive, but large orders still cost a lot to fulfill. The implication is that customers who order in large quantities are not necessarily strategic to their supplier.

Even within the 80% most profitable customers, large but unprofitable orders are still observed. These unprofitable orders can reduce profit by 6%, and are highly likely to be driven by costs to serve such as customization and logistics.

Source: David Evans, Managing Director, Research, SCEB (www.sceb.executiveboard.com)

In Chapter 1 we looked at business strategy and the role of sales within it, and in Chapter 2 we looked at how purchasing professionals classify and deal with suppliers. In each of these chapters we discussed value and identified the need for a tool to capture the supplier's and customer's perceptions of value.

So what form would such a tool take? A good example of a value assessment tool is the business-to-business (B2B) relationship development box, which enables you to identify those relationships with customers that justify the investment of strategic resources, and those where low cost approaches are required.

Let us first remember where B2B customer analysis originated. Customer segmentation in business-to-business markets has historically been a rather simplistic matter.

Traditional ways of segmenting a B2B customer base

The following ways to segment business customers have been very common:

Segmentation by company size

Many companies divide their customer base into "corporate", "small/medium enterprises" (SMEs) and "small office/home office" (SOHO).

Segmentation by company location

Global companies start by dividing the company into international trading blocs – Americas, Europe, Middle East and Africa (EMEA) and Asia Pacific

(AP) – and then into countries within those blocs and major cities or regions within the countries.

Segmentation by Standard Industrial Classification

Companies organize themselves into divisions focused on industry sectors according to what customers make or do – for example, automotive, shipbuilding, pharmaceuticals, clothing manufacturing, IT services, etc. Industrial classification codes cover a great degree of detail in classifying company activities, as shown below.

Extract from the North American Industry Classification System (NAICS)

2002 NAICS Code	2002 NAICS Title
22	Utilities
221	Utilities
2211	Electric Power Generation, Transmission and Distribution
22111	Electric Power Generation
221111	Hydroelectric Power Generation
221112	Fossil Fuel Electric Power Generation
221113	Nuclear Electric Power Generation
221119	Other Electric Power Generation
22112	Electric Power Transmission, Control, and Distribution
221121	Electric Bulk Power Transmission and Control
221122	Electric Power Distribution
2212	Natural Gas Distribution
22121	Natural Gas Distribution
221210	Natural Gas Distribution
2213	Water, Sewage and Other Systems
22131	Water Supply and Irrigation Systems
221310	Water Supply and Irrigation Systems
22132	Sewage Treatment Facilities
221320	Sewage Treatment Facilities
22133	Steam and Air-Conditioning Supply
221330	Steam and Air-Conditioning Supply

Source: www.census.gov/naics
Reproduced with kind permission of The Service Sector Statistics Division, Bureau of the Census

Problems with traditional methods

In recent years, each of these traditional ways to segment customers has come under attack from both academics and practitioners. Segmentation by customer size was introduced more than 50 years ago. For a long time customer size was the most widely adopted form of business-to-business customer segmentation. It was based on the plausible assumption that larger customers would be more profitable. So the top tier of large customers – the major accounts or key accounts – justified more sales resources, special treatment and preferential terms. As a consequence, these accounts had a higher cost of sales. But, because these accounts were more profitable, the higher cost was justified. There is some evidence (see Rackham and de Vincentis, 1999) that until the 1990s larger accounts were indeed more profitable, so this segmentation worked.

For a long time customer size was the most widely adopted form of business-to-business customer segmentation. It was based on the plausible assumption that larger customers would be more profitable.

During the 1990s there was a progressive uncoupling of account size and profitability. Sales managers began to discover that middle market accounts were often more profitable than the big Fortune 500 customers on whom they had been lavishing their sales resources.

Segmentation by company location has also proved increasingly difficult as national boundaries evaporate, customers source globally and purchasing decision-making becomes more centralized. A customer in Spain may therefore be purchasing in China for a project in Dubai. A sales organization that is rigidly geographically-centered will find it difficult to compete for this kind of business.

Segmentation by industry has proved very effective for some companies, as it expedites learning. A salesperson dedicated to one industry will find it easier to learn each customer's business and the special needs of the industry. In competitive sales, salespeople with better industry knowledge are more likely to win the business, but many companies have a product range that doesn't easily fit into any industry classification and a sales force structured around such an industry model may be more costly and less flexible.

Organizing the supply-side business according to traditional segments is not wrong, as companies must organize themselves by some method. Traditional forms of segmentation are better than segmentation according to "who shouts loudest". Assumptions can be made about the type of products and services that customers want based on an understanding of the size and scope of their organization, or what it makes for its customers, and focusing expertise on those needs is important.

There is, however, another dimension to categorizing customers that has become increasingly important since the "right-sizing" revolution of the 1990s. As we saw from the discussion about the purchasing professionals' point of view, customers have different ways of categorizing suppliers and, in most case, the best sales skills in the world are not going to change the customers' minds about how strategic you are to them.

Customer-aligned segmentation by relationship development categories

In order to adapt to the world of customer power, your resources have to be allocated to customers according to the type of relationship that you can sustain with them. We need a tool to accommodate our strategic view of a customer, combine it with their strategic view of us, and reach a conclusion about the characteristics of the relationship in its own right. Although things change over time, and of course sales managers want to make change happen where it is possible and appropriate, we need to start with a "warts and all" snapshot of the state of play between our customers and us today.

In my experience, Fiocca's account portfolio matrix (explored in Chapter 1), was a revelation both to large corporates and smaller businesses. Although salespeople have long been encouraged to allocate their time efficiently between their customers, efforts to manage company resources effectively across the whole customer base have often been fragmented. The coming of powerful Customer Relationship Management systems has enabled the capture of more data on which to make resource allocation decisions, but even so, customer portfolio management has remained an inside-looking-out activity.

Customers, particularly sophisticated purchasing professionals, do not appreciate being "managed" by suppliers, and equally "supplier management" by customers is inappropriate terminology. Researchers in the Industrial Marketing and Purchasing (IMP) Group, who have been studying the nature of supplier–customer interaction in business-to-business markets for over 20 years, argue that any particular relationship between a supplier and customer is something that works in its own right. Both parties contribute to it, but neither can claim to manage it exclusively.

Customers, particularly sophisticated purchasing professionals, do not appreciate being "managed" by suppliers, and equally "supplier management" by customers is inappropriate terminology.

The IMP Group say that companies are not independent actors; they cannot make decisions based entirely on their own objectives. Interaction between suppliers and customers means that they are part of a relationship. The success or failure of a relationship is not confined to a single company, although each sees success in its own terms. A company's direction interacts with the direction taken by the customer and other participants in the chain of supply. That is an important concept to grasp. Therefore, if a company is to be successful in managing sales, it has to be a successful participant in a variety of business relationships. This is why the B2B relationship development box tries to capture the customer's attitude to the supplier, as well as the supplier's attitude toward the customer, identifying types of possible relationships and transitional stages.

As with all strategic analysis, senior managers must be convinced that there is a compelling business case for it. Company reports often state that customers are the most critical assets in the business, but chief executives continue to allow product strategy or operational demands to drive the business. If you believe that relationships with customers are the real hub of strategy and want to act upon it, the B2B relationship development box can be a key illustrative tool and decision-support model.

Why do we use the B2B relationship development box?

The steps involved in compiling the customer value scores are more likely to deliver a greater degree of objectivity than models with axes based on single, qualitative or judgmental factors. Also, the requirement to consult the customers about their rating of our value as a supplier (versus competitors) is also a contribution to objectivity, which should lead to better decisions about resource allocation.

Using the B2B relationship development box

Any use of tools carries the danger of focusing you on the strategy formulation process rather than the content of strategies. It is important to ensure that the variables used in the model are enduring factors that truly influence the long-term success of the business. Even the critics of portfolio analysis say that boxes facilitate visualization and can aid decision-making when used with caution. So, let's proceed to considering how it can be used – with caution!

It is important to ensure that the variables used in the model are enduring factors that truly influence the long-term success of the business.

There are challenges in using tools like this matrix (Figure 3.1). Who decides the value factors, and how they should be weighted and scored? How can estimates of future value be made, especially when considering relationships that are in the very early stages of development? An ambitious small company is going to see things quite differently from a mature company that needs to consolidate financial strength. Within a large company, different functional experts will have different views about the company's priorities.

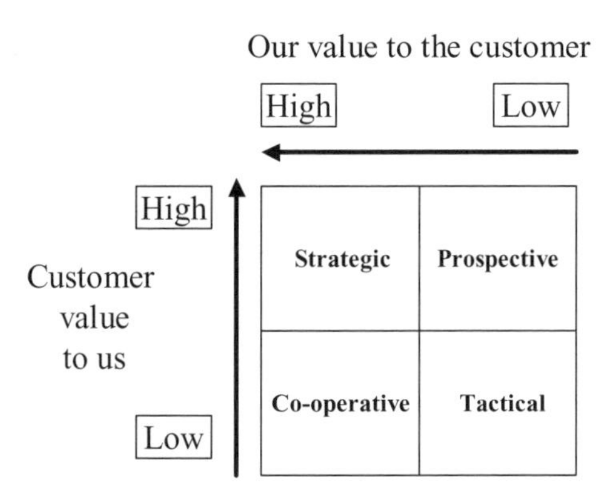

Figure 3.1 *The B2B relationship development box.*

In my experience, there needs to be a discussion between you and other key decision-makers, including finance, operations and marketing. Tools like this analysis box have persisted because they enable strategy-making teams to encapsulate their knowledge and to discuss strategic choices. Of course outcomes are important, but the value of any strategic tool is its ability to provoke thought and constructive debate. Managers, particularly sales managers, are frequently accused of too much "doing" when they are paid to think. Tools that help your thinking process are worth exploring.

To use the B2B relationship development box, your assembled team should start with the vertical axis – the customer's value to us as a supplier.

Vertical axis – what is customer value?

Step 1: Decide on value factors

Quantitative factors

What factors of value should we use? What makes some of our customers more valuable than others? Companies initially focus on quantifiable value factors because they are perceived to be most objective. Of course, even quantifiable factors must be handled with care (see box).

Working with numbers

- Know what you know, what you don't know and what you are assuming. Test them all.
- Seek hard data, but make sure that it is presented in a way that is meaningful. For example, an average can be very misleading if the range of numbers around it is very wide.
- Find out how the data was collected. For example, data drawn from small sample sizes can give misleading impressions.
- But even if data is "statistically significant", it may not be useful.
- Check that numbers come from a well-respected source.
- Check that a consistent process has been used to measure the statistics over time – trends matter more than the metrics themselves. Movements over time, movements in relative positions or against an

independent benchmark tell the whole story. Care must be taken to keep measurement stable over time so that results are comparable.

- Don't get too worried about the exactness of data. "A fuzzy sense of what matters is far more important than precise calculation of the irrelevant". (Professor Tim Ambler, London Business School.)
- When comparing trends, remember that correlation does not prove a causal link.
- Remember that numbers can be wrong, either because someone compiling them or programming the computer made a mistake, or because they are being presented in a misleading way.

The importance of different quantifiable value factors is not universal to all suppliers, so you need a weighting system. To many suppliers, the most valuable customers are those who appreciate their technical value-added enough to pay premium prices for it. They are perceived to be the customers who generate profit, which is what the shareholders want. For others, customers who order large volumes are very attractive, because large orders keep the factory running at optimum capacity. Other companies may prefer customers who generate growth opportunities through their own growth rate, buying into new product lines or acting as a regular reference site.

Typically, you need to choose a few quantifiable factors, such as sales volume with us as a supplier, the growth rate of their business (for example, their turnover grew by 5% last year) and the profitability of the customer's business with us at the operating profit level. The profitability factor is universally popular, but many companies have difficulty measuring profitability per customer beyond a typical gross margin less customer-specific discount. So what is customer profitability?

Getting a handle on customer profitability

Since customer relationship management (CRM) systems are available, the lifetime value of a customer appears to be something that we can know and should know. But our understanding of the value of the

Since customer relationship management (CRM) systems are available, the lifetime value of a customer appears to be something that we can know and should know.

customer needs to start simply and build up. You know that discount is costly. There cannot be a sales manager alive who does not have a war story about a sales representative returning to the office and triumphantly announcing the procurement of a big, big deal, only to discover that the discount offered made the deal unprofitable even at a gross margin level. Everyone in business needs to know some basic financial facts. Let's start with the accountant's motto:

> *"Revenue is vanity. Profit is sanity. Cash flow is reality."*

Sales volume sounds great, but you need to make a profitable sale. Having made a profitable sale, you then need to collect the money.

A profitable sale is not just one that covers the cost of making the products; it must also cover a lot of attributable overhead.

- How much technical support will this particular customer consume for this particular project?
- How much does it cost to provide a salesperson for this customer?
- What general property and administration costs should be allocated to this customer?
- Does this customer have any special delivery requirements?
- How long does this customer take to pay?

Each day over the allowed credit terms means that the customer is borrowing from you instead of their own bank, which means that you are borrowing from your bank to cover the customer's debt, perhaps at premium interest rates. That alone can be the significant difference between a deal being profitable and incurring expensive losses. It may seem harsh that accountants call customers "debtors", but they have a point.

Real profit

	Sales
minus	discount
minus	cost of production
equals	Gross margin.

	Gross margin
minus	delivery costs
minus	technical support costs
minus	sales commission and other salesperson-related costs
minus	property and administration overhead
minus	cost of servicing debt
equals	**Real profit.**

If your company's costing system is activity based, it helps to ensure accuracy in determining profit per customer. Unfortunately, most companies' costing systems are focused on product/service profitability, but some financial software is still flexible enough to provide granular information about costs associated with individual customers.

Lifetime value is a calculation based on the profit generated by a customer over time, taking into account the time cost of money. Has dealing with this customer over 10 years produced a better return than if the company had left its investment in this relationship in the bank?

To decide on value factors is one thing, being in a position to measure them objectively is more difficult to achieve. Nevertheless, the pursuit of objectivity usually delivers worthwhile knowledge and knowledge sharing between departments and functions in the company.

Qualitative factors

Every company with which I have worked has wanted to include some kind of qualitative factors alongside the quantifiable ones. But when we are in business, there is normally some driving force behind what we regard as an intangible benefit brought by a customer, and it is worth the effort to try to assign some measurable payback. The following presents some examples of intangible attractiveness factors.

The value of customer endorsement

Many service companies rely heavily on the goodwill of satisfied customers to reassure prospective customers about their value add. Even where a product can be tried out by a prospect, to have a reference from an established customer about a potential supplier's approach is very helpful. It is a badge of honor for salespeople to secure a customer's consent to be a case study on the website, or even to take part in advertising campaigns.

> *"Customer X is a great reference account, but we couldn't take a prospect to see customer Y."*

We appear to be saying that customer X can reduce our cost of customer acquisition, but can they really do that? Is it proven that the selling cycle on a deal with customer Z was genuinely shorter thanks to a visit to customer X than it would otherwise have been without that visit? Challenge your assumptions. If the sales cycle is shortened, that is a measurable benefit to us as a supplier. If we do not believe that a visit to customer X shortens the sales cycle, what else might we consider to be of great value?

We intuitively know that reference visits reassure prospects, and by reducing the prospect's perception of risk in doing business with us, the reference customer has contributed to our success. Perhaps it is too difficult to pursue measurement; in which case, let's look at the situation from a different angle.

Customer X is giving us something back. They are spending some time with a prospect and that has a value in itself. It may be a small thing to try to quantify, but it is a way of comparing the relative value of customer X versus customer Y, who may even refuse to allow you to quote their name as a customer.

The customer's partnership approach

> *"Customer X is willing to consider long-term arrangements, but customer Y wants to reverse auction every bid on their website."*

So customer X is offering to reduce our forecasting risk and eliminate the costs of constantly rebidding. That has a value.

The customer's personal approach

> *"The Purchasing manager at customer X smiles and offers the sales representative a cup of coffee and a cookie. The purchasing manager at customer Y wrestles the rep to the floor and puts his foot on his throat."*

This is a slight exaggeration, of course! Some personalities are easier to deal with than others. Stress is an unpleasant thing and it can cost the supplier money if the customer's purchasing manager is so aggressive that your representative has to spend time off work. But fortunately such a situation is very rare. The whole reason for doing the relationship development box is to be objective. Decision-makers do discuss personalities and their effect, but usually do not allocate any weight to this as a value factor (although it might be a consideration in allocating personalities to the account team!).

Step 2: A scoring system

Even with quantifiable factors, a scoring system has to represent a logical indication of relative value. If a customer regularly does a lot of business with us, surely that is a good thing, and the higher the amount of business, the higher the score? It is not necessarily good if it means that a particular customer dominates share of business, because that increases risk. For example, the stock value of a global software and services company that had won Outsourcing Excellence Awards went up 5% when the company announced that its reliance on a particular customer had been reduced from representing one-fifth of its turnover to one-twentieth within two years.

So care needs to be taken to identify what constitutes a high score on an attractiveness factor and what constitutes a low score. Relativity is an important consideration. If margins in your industry sector are small and being squeezed even further, a customer that is just 0.5% more profitable than another might score very highly.

Step 3: Weighting attractiveness factors

The relationship development matrix requires attractiveness factors to be allocated a score out of 100. That sounds easy, but when you spread those

100 points across five or six attractiveness factors, even more debate ensues! If profitability is very important and gets a weighting of 40, that only leaves 60 points to accommodate growth, volume and qualitative factors (see Table 3.1). Any factor that only gets 5 points at the end of the discussion is usually dropped.

Step 4: Final scores

All that remains to be done on the vertical axis is to allocate scores out of 10 per customer, apply the weighting factor and wait for the surprises. Previously loved big accounts gain less than 500 out of 1,000, while unnoticed middling accounts often indicate great potential.

Of course, we could stop here and just allocate resources according to customer value. That would be logical if we believe that we really can manage our customers, rather than our customers managing themselves. This is where I have to depart from the "custom and practice" in some companies – where forecasts are made and quotas are set as if the growth the supplier needs to achieve could dictate what the customers want. As a veteran of the product push days of the IT industry, I know that it can come to a grinding halt when the customers decide they have had enough hype and stop buying.

You could waste a lot of time and money trying to develop business with customers who are not interested in developing with you, or any supplier. Remember the IMP Group observation that a buyer–seller

You could waste a lot of time and money trying to develop business with customers who are not interested in developing with you, or any supplier.

Table 3.1 *Final scores.*

Value factor	Weight	Cust. X score	Weighted score	Cust. Y score	Weighted score	Cust. Z score	Weighted score
Profitability	40	7	280	3	120	5	200
Sales volume	20	3	60	9	180	7	140
Growth rate	25	4	100	2	50	8	200
Reference value	15	9	105	3	45	6	90
Totals	**100**		**545**		**395**		**635**

relationship is an entity in its own right? We can identify what it is by finding out, and mapping how the customer rates us.

Horizontal axis – how does the customer measure our value as a supplier?

Professional purchasing managers will have a formula for the balance they require between the key criteria of cost, quality and delivery (timing and convenience). Given that many competitors can usually meet those core requirements, most will take other factors into account when choosing a supplier, as discussed in Chapter 2. You may be compared to competitors on technical capability, the professionalism of service employees and/or relative financial strength. "Softer" factors such as accessibility and problem-solving may also be critical differentiators.

"Softer" factors such as accessibility and problem-solving may also be critical differentiators.

Usually, purchasing professionals share their supplier performance criteria and ratings. Even where no comparable competitor is active in the account, purchasing benchmarks from other categories of supplier may be applied. Allegedly, a pharmacy chain told a shampoo supplier to benchmark itself against a condom supplier whose processes were regarded as best practice.

Of course, some buying decision-makers may not share their ratings, or it could be that your engagement with the customer is at such an early stage that they have no activity on which to judge you. Assumptions have to be based on informal feedback. This is not ideal, but is a viable step when learning the mechanics of the tool.

At this point, people usually wonder why, if each customer is using totally different criteria, it helps the supplier with resource allocation. The B2B relationship box is a means of judging the worth of investment in a relationship in a general sense. The box alone cannot determine whether investment in particular capabilities such as quality, delivery or technical support are needed, although it is likely that, by consulting with customers, you will discover the weaknesses you need to address.

Interpreting results – the quadrants of the B2B relationship development box

High customer value, high supplier value

Let's call these relationships geese – the geese that lay the golden eggs. It was also guard geese that once saved ancient Rome from invaders. They are loyal and productive pets.

Logic dictates that customers who are valuable to you and who value your business strengths offer development opportunities. They may well be willing to try your new products and buy other categories of product and service from you. To most companies, the most compelling question is whether customers in this quadrant are willing to pay more to justify the investment.

Research in this field suggests that perceived value is the key to pricing, and you can apply price differentials if you can provide tailored offerings that customers really value. Purchasing decision-makers are often prepared to pay more to suppliers whose products/services generate very high levels of satisfaction. Also, willingness to pay is stronger when the customer has a long-term cumulative experience of satisfaction.

Willingness to pay is stronger when the customer has a long-term cumulative experience of satisfaction.

In a McKinsey survey of 200 Fortune 1000 companies in 2005, most were able to raise revenues and profits by more than 20% on average through collaborative initiatives with customers. This study also came with a hazard warning: suppliers who were not able to collaborate effectively actually lost money trying (Hancock, John and Wojcik, 2005).

Collaboration requires tailored service and flexibility in processes. Investment in collaborative activity with customers is a source of success for many. Risks must still be managed; and over-focusing on strategic relationships can weaken your flexibility (see Piercy and Lane, 2006). Strategic customers sometimes leave strategic suppliers, perhaps because of a merger, or because of a change of policy or chief officers. Or perhaps, if they believe they have gained influence in a supplier, the temptation to renegotiate on price appears. Chapter 4 will look at strategic relationships in more detail.

Low customer value, low supplier value

Let's call these relationships bees, because if you have a lot of them and they are very well-organized, you can make honey.

Suppliers, large and small, are not always comfortable with how to manage tactical accounts when their ideas on customer alignment have been affected by years of hype about "delighting all customers". In fact, customer orientation and tactical management of deals for cash flow advantage are not necessarily concepts in conflict.

A silicones manufacturer with a global reputation for innovation faced price competition in the 1990s. Although silicones are very diverse materials, in the late 1990s smaller producers were able to sell some silicones in a commoditized way – low price, no service. It was clear to the branded manufacturer that there was a category of customer focused on cost who would take risks to achieve a low price. So the branded manufacturer set up a sub-branded e-commerce channel to deal with price-driven customers. It concerned industry analysts at the time, but delivered good overall results even in the short term.

Suppliers need to provide a non-contact or low-contact channel for customers who just want a cheaper standard product. Telesales teams (sometimes outsourced) have replaced field forces in whole or in part in a number of organizations. Other companies have used the Internet successfully. This is a case in point of the seller–buyer relationship existing in its own right. Suppliers who will not or cannot be a party to transactional relationships (the purchasing category "shop") are creating risks for themselves. A significant minority of purchasing professionals just do not want any supplier wasting their time with relationship-building, and most others do not want it for specific purchase categories.

Suppliers who will not or cannot be a party to transactional relationships (the purchasing category "shop") are creating risks for themselves.

We will look at tactical relationships in more detail in Chapter 6.

High customer value, low supplier value

Let's call these relationships fish, because you need a lot of patience to catch them.

The challenge of converting prospects and new or occasional customers into regular customers is the most difficult one that you face, particularly if you are in a smaller company that needs to grow. If your target customer is happy with their incumbent supplier, waiting for the opportunity to demonstrate differential strengths is frustrating. Should time and sales resource be invested? Suppliers are often tempted to use price offers to accelerate the opportunity for change. Alas, the lifetime value of customers acquired by discount can be half the lifetime value of those who chose you for other reasons. Nevertheless, you must reduce the risk of change for prospects, so some element of trial purchase or enabling the prospective customer to pilot your service may be necessary.

If your target customer is happy with their incumbent supplier, waiting for the opportunity to demonstrate differential strengths is frustrating.

There is less advice in the world about acquiring business-to-business customers, compared to the many wise words that have been written about customer retention and its contribution to profitability. We have all experienced the longer sales cycles that come with mature and risk-averse markets, and the difficulties of making a first contact with prospects when legislation restricts e-mail and telephone access. Companies agonize about the cost of acquiring new customers, and know that they must indeed be selective and "gain to retain" in order to achieve customer lifetime value.

But how do most companies get the purchasing manager's door open so that they can discuss specific needs? Outsourcing customer acquisition to specialist agencies is an area of growth. They can focus on the challenge for you, and more ideas are given in Chapter 5.

When things are going well with a core group of key and major accounts, there is a temptation to avoid investing resources in customer acquisition. Relying on growth through current key accounts can be risky. The existence of the prospective quadrant should be a regular reminder of the need for new customers, regardless of other pressures on sales resources. Prospective relationships are discussed in more detail in Chapter 5.

Low customer value, high supplier value

Let's call these relationships goats. Goats are admirable creatures and very productive but, due to their intelligence, can be rather difficult.

Perhaps the most controversial question for you when it comes to allocating the scarce resource of skilled salespeople, is how to service customers who are important to keep but whose business is static. The relationship between your two companies is usually long-standing, and needs to be protected. So how would a "non-strategic" customer feel about infrequent contact from a good salesperson and more contact by telephone? Would visits by a sales agency be accepted?

Growing companies have as many challenges as any other organization in injecting objectivity into decision-making about allocating resources to relationships. Relationships with large customers who are not getting any larger but have a lot of voice, can absorb a lot of resources. This can affect profitability, although it is still desperately important to the supplier to maintain volume.

Salespeople developing this type of relationship are often concerned that they have lower status, but in fact these relationships offer a critical stability to you because of their regularity of business. Their appreciation of your value is worth retaining, but these are cases where the purchaser is probably classifying you as a supplier as "manage risk" or "leverage".

"Cooperative" does mean working together, but it does not necessarily mean comfort and friendliness. You need to look for opportunities to reduce relationship costs through the standardization of activities, which will require careful negotiation with the customer. This is actually a very skilled job and the account manager who can do it deserves high symbolic rewards.

"Cooperative" does mean working together, but it does not necessarily mean comfort and friendliness.

"Cooperative" relationships are usually immediately recognized by small companies, who feel the resource pressure acutely. The problem is that many of them have not developed a standard business model – the business has developed account by account and all offerings are tailored. That is operational management's challenge. Meanwhile, motivating the account manager of stable, cooperative relationships is challenging, especially as they still need to act as the customer advocate to ensure that the customer does not become dissatisfied.

Cooperative accounts will be discussed in more detail in Chapter 7.

Cautionary note

Remember that the matrix is a snapshot at a point in time. Business relationships change over time. We positively want prospective relationships to become strategic in the future, as today's strategic relationships may lose momentum and become co-operative. Circumstances may catapult co-operative relationships into the strategic box, or off the matrix altogether. Tactical relationships can also change over time. Whatever resource allocation seems logical to you today, make sure that your salespeople are constantly alert to change in customers. You also need to be prepared for the total collapse of business relationships (for more on this, see Chapter 8). Calling this sales management tool the relationship ***development*** box should help you focus on the potential for change.

Whatever resource allocation seems logical to you today, make sure that your salespeople are constantly alert to change in customers.

Conclusion

In every size of organization a balanced customer portfolio is valuable. Under competition law, all customers are equal. It is nevertheless the nature of business that different relationships with customers require different approaches and different resource allocation. The B2B relationship development box is a useful tool for capturing the complexity of the real business world.

Having completed an analysis like this, sales managers sometimes feel like shouting "eureka!", but it is only the beginning. Customizing sales strategy involves much more planning, which we will examine in Chapters 4 to 8.

PART II

Using the Relationship Development Box

We have a tool to identify different categories of business relationships with customers, which have to be developed in different ways. What are the strategic options for these very different relationships? Some categories have been neglected in the past. It is not very sexy to write about difficult long-term relationships or exiting relationships, but you need to develop strategies for all categories.

The following chapters examine each quadrant in turn, and the situation in which the relationship drops off the quadrant altogether:

- Strategic
- Prospective
- Tactical
- Cooperative
- Exit

4

Strategic relationships

"You only know a man when you have walked a mile in his moccasins."

Native American saying

"Strategic" relationships are possible where you believe, on the basis of rational customer attractiveness analysis, that the customer has strategic value to your company, and where the customer's buying decision-makers believe, on the basis of rational supplier performance evaluation, that you can add value to their company and its customers.

These relationships need to be of a high quality. Data from an admirably huge qualitative (51) and quantitative (400) study of purchasers' views suggest that relationship quality is crucial in determining their sustainability over time (Ulaga and Eggert, 2006).

What is a "high-quality" relationship? These researchers found that relationship value has first to be established, i.e. the purchasing company's satisfaction with a product/service. After that, the quality of the relationship becomes important. This is in contrast to traditional models of relationship building that have recommended that relationships should be built first and then value created. Many salespeople work fruitlessly to build relationships in a vacuum, hoping this will lead to business and not understanding that in today's world customers only want relationships with companies who have demonstrated a track record of value creation.

The mantra now is "create value and the relationship will follow" – not the other way around. Value in itself is quite complex, given that it is a subjective consideration of a pay-off between benefits and sacrifices relative to a competitive offering. There will usually be several perceptions of value among different company decision-makers, and salespeople must understand and balance these differences. Relationship quality is also difficult to define. Most definitions include trust, commitment and satisfaction, but these are also subjective perceptions.

Value in itself is quite complex, given that it is a subjective consideration of a pay-off between benefits and sacrifices relative to a competitive offering.

Nevertheless, collating the subjective views of a large sample of purchasing managers, Ulaga and Eggert give us some strong indications of how industrial customers determine their intention to stay in a relationship with a supplier. Relationship value – the perception that benefits exceed sacrifices – has a strong impact on satisfaction. Satisfaction raises the level of intention to expand business with an incumbent supplier, and decreases the likelihood of defection. Satisfaction leads to trust and that, in turn, leads to commitment. Relationship quality develops over time as the supplier creates value and the customer feels able to trust the supplier to deliver satisfaction.

Relationship quality develops over time as the supplier creates value and the customer feels able to trust the supplier to deliver satisfaction.

Ulaga and Eggert's extensive study has given us canned common sense – do what you promise to do in the early days of engagement with a customer and you will be trusted. Once a customer has learned to trust you, then long-term commitment to a business relationship is possible, and the risk reduction associated with it is achievable. The strategy that a supplier uses to develop a relationship of this strength has been called *key account management*.

What is key account management?

Of course, everyone in sales management has heard of key accounts – also called strategic accounts. They are customers identified by suppliers as important to the achievement of their strategy. So what do sales managers need to do with them?

Definition of key account management

Key account management is "an approach adopted by selling companies aimed at building a portfolio of loyal key accounts by offering them, on a continuing basis, a product/service package tailored to their individual needs. To coordinate day-to-day interaction under the umbrella of a long-term relationship, selling companies typically form dedicated teams headed up by a key account manager. This special treatment has significant implications for organization structure, communications and managing expectations."

Quoted with kind permission from Dr Tony Millman

Companies have to be sure that strategic relationships are indeed strategic before investing in a key account management approach, which can be expensive and complex. As discussed elsewhere in this book, large accounts are not necessarily key, satisfied customers are not necessarily loyal, and things change over time. It is also worth noting that the expectation of organic growth from "key" accounts needs to be tested. A new book by Hess and Kazanjian (2006) on organic growth in companies includes research suggesting that it is quite rare, and an average growth of 6% per annum would be impressive.

How key is "key"?

If we could think of companies having needs in the same way that individuals have needs, is the business relationship fulfilling needs for both organizations at the highest level? Psychologists believe that individuals evolve from fulfilling their basic needs for food and shelter, through pursuing needs for security and social enjoyment to seeking goods and services that enhance their self-esteem. Ultimately, we also have needs for "self-actualization" (Maslow, 1993). A classical example of a service that addresses "self-actualization" needs is education, where the vocations of teachers and students come together. Professor Malcolm McDonald and Diana Woodburn have suggested that this model (Maslow's hierarchy of needs) can be applied to the development of business relationships, with the truly strategic relationships providing "self-actualization" for both supplier and customer.

Seamless integration

PEMA Group, a mechanical engineering company, and METALPRES, a manufacturer of aluminum die castings, are customer and supplier, but also work as an integrated team to win automotive sector customers.

They work together to provide high levels of service and to integrate knowledge and solutions. The relationship is based on mutual trust rather than contract.

The automotive sector is very price competitive. PEMA and METALPRES can improve their status and reduce process, administrative and marketing overheads by co-developing and co-branding an offering.

Example provided by AIDA Marketing e Formazione, Italy. Quoted with kind permission.

The nature of KAM

Key account management is a strategy in itself, and has various characteristics in its implementation. These are:

- The business management skills of the account manager.
- Long-term planning.
- Special organizational focus, including key account teams.
- The development of value, such as joint new product development and/or process integration between the supplier and customer.

Historical context

Identifying "special" customers who justify a little more development has probably been going on since trade began. Although Peter Drucker highlighted the importance of the customer in the 1950s, supplier–customer relationships were not explored in business schools for some time later. Much of the early (1970s) research on business-to-business markets concentrated on the sales process and the role of decision-making units in the customer organization. In the 1980s, the IMP Group was the first research body to focus on analysis of buyer–seller relationships and their role in improving effectiveness and efficiency, information sharing and risk reduction.

In 1995, Kalwani and Nayarandas of Harvard Business School reported on the difference in performance between firms with long-term relationships and those with a short-term approach. They identified that suppliers with long-term relationships with suppliers enjoyed better profitability over time and sustained profitability in a recession. Since then, many companies have implemented key account management programs, with varying degrees of success.

More recently, Piercy and Lane (2006) of Warwick Business School have drawn attention to the risks inherent in focusing too much on a small number of strategic customers. Like any strategy, key account management needs to be applied with care.

How can suppliers make strategic relationships work?

The business management skills of the account manager

When I was doing the first stage of my research on key account management in the 1990s, I remember joking with a sales director who was commenting on what was expected of key account managers that it would help if they could walk on water and leap tall buildings at a single bound. Of course, you can get by on less, but let's be aware that expectations of account managers in strategic business relationships are escalating. You cannot just call a salesperson an account manager and hope it improves a relationship with a customer.

Being a standard bearer

Account managers can spend about 75% of their working day in different types of communication. Customer decision-makers expect them to communicate well, but also to be a "brand ambassador" for their company.

Account managers do more than sell; they are "representatives" in the true sense of the word. Although he or she is an individual (customers say that they do not want "clones"), an account manager has to convey the values of the supplier in how they look, what they say, what they do and how they do it. This is not just a matter of being "on message". Many people can present well. Fewer can listen sufficiently well to absorb the customer's needs quickly and adapt to provide the information and solution that the customer needs, without over-committing their employer.

Some buying decision-makers have mentioned to me that an element of "standard-bearing" is the "likability" of the account manager. This sounds very personal. We all have various ideas about what constitutes our reasons for liking someone. Some common factors of likability in business relationship include enthusiasm, showing appreciation, being polite and being interesting. Confidence must not stray into arrogance, and care for the customer must seem genuine, not contrived.

In my early research, I found that buying decision-makers always rated integrity as a crucially important quality in an account manager. In feeding this back to key account managers, they expressed surprise that their integrity was not taken for granted. We all have a constant capacity to doubt when there is a lot at stake. Customer personnel who have placed trust in an account manager and a supplier need to see demonstrations of integrity for reassurance. When things are going to plan and when they are not, an account manager and his team have to deliver on promises.

When things are going to plan and when they are not, an account manager and his team have to deliver on promises.

Can integrity sit well with managing politics in a customer's organization, or with colleagues? A standard bearer has to find a way. The company's "business practices guidelines" should help all employees to deal not only with big ethical challenges but also with day-to-day dilemmas.

Likability matters, and integrity must be encouraged and supported. The overriding feature of "standard-bearing" is professionalism, which requires an employer to invest in ongoing development of key account managers and the teams that support strategic relationships.

Being a "boundary spanner"

In short, boundary-spanning means that someone can see things from alternative points of view and find some common ground between them. An account manager is expected to represent the supplier to the customer and to champion the customer to colleagues. Constantly switching from one viewpoint to another causes stress, and you need to check that account managers are able to maintain balance and objectivity.

A successful boundary spanner makes a significant difference. In a study of 249 German companies, Walter and Gemünden (2000) reported that supplier–customer relationships managed by expert "boundary spanners" had significantly higher sales growth and significantly better "share of purse".

Supplier–customer relationships managed by expert "boundary spanners" had significantly higher sales growth and significantly better "share of purse".

How did they define "boundary-spanning"? They observed that accomplished boundary spanners were good at searching for information and knowing how to use it for the benefit of those in their network. They had influencing skills, and could build support. They could find people to help the customer and create cross-boundary contacts between people in different functions. They could coordinate activity and get results. They could establish cooperation and mutual understanding, and create a climate for communications. Their social skills include being perceptive and flexible, and developing empathy.

Are boundary spanners born or made? Walter and Gemünden certainly thought that employers could encourage boundary-spanning by giving account managers a budget for acquiring information, sufficient time to develop specific relationships, and administrative support. They also identified travel privileges as a desirable benefit. Of course, anyone who travels regularly in the course of their job is grateful for employer-financed comforts.

There is another reason to provide travel privileges to networkers. An entrepreneur once told me that he always traveled first class because then he could meet business decision-makers who were also traveling first class and extend his network. Boundary spanners are not just well connected within their own company and within the customer's organization. They need to have good contacts with influential third parties, and practice makes perfect.

Another thing that you can do to support boundary-spanning is to give account managers access to top decision-makers, and consult them about business strategy. In this way, their contacts perceive them as having influence.

> **Executive involvement at Siemens**
>
> In a division of Siemens studied by Christoph Senn between 2000 and 2004, strategic accounts were streamlined by 25% and program costs were halved. Also during that time, senior executives became involved in some strategic accounts. A total of 450 executive calls changed Siemens' image in a very positive way. During this period, in which there was 55% growth overall in the remaining strategic accounts, revenue from the strategic accounts with senior executive involvement doubled.
>
> Quoted with kind permission from Dr Christoph Senn
> University of Columbia, New York

Being a value creator

The simplest starting point for creating value is an honest understanding of what is important to the customer, and their rating of you as a supplier. As discussed in Chapter 2, customers may measure the performance of suppliers on many factors. In a strategic relationship, responsiveness, support, investment and innovation are likely to be among the criteria as well as basic performance on price, quality and delivery. If such things are not being measured, it seems difficult to imagine that the relationship is strategic or that you would be able to access the customer's "self-actualization" level of need.

Although customers are only convinced by company-wide capability to deliver whatever they perceive as value, your key account managers are in the front line observing and absorbing the unique needs of customers' business so that they can think creatively about new possibilities for value delivery. In my early research, 36% of buyers said that creativity was a desirable attribute in an account manager. Those who were not so concerned about creativity were still concerned that the account manager should be flexible, able to question existing situations and to reconfigure them.

Without the ideas of the key account manager, you may miss opportunities to help the customer to be special to their customers. To demonstrate what business authors Anderson and Narus (1998) have called "resonating focus" – i.e. making the offer to the customer superior on a few things that matter most to them – accounts managers are going to have to coordinate unique process and product development resources.

Partnering to deliver value

Olympus Medical maintains and repairs high-technology medical equipment, and concentrates on partnering with customers to deliver customized solutions. The company needs to deliver repaired instruments directly to doctors, not to the hospital loading bay. In some cities, local knowledge is critical to avoid delivery delays, and a local carrier is used. Their carrier in New York and Boston, Eastern Connection, makes very early deliveries directly to doctors' offices, avoiding the rush hour traffic as well as any delays within the hospital's internal distribution system. Drivers and service staff working on the account are given special training.

Quoted with kind permission from Olympus America Inc. (www.olympus.com)

You should focus company capabilities on things that matter most to customers. To be good at unimportant things is a waste of resources, to be bad at important things is a recipe for disaster (see Figure 4.1).

Can your key account managers marshal company resources to give customers a better return on their assets than they can manage themselves? Can they identify a way to make inventory turnover faster, improve productivity, enhance customer service or at least ensure better information flows in the supply chain? Of course, helping a customer to reduce costs is useful, but that may be a short-lived success. Key account managers need to identify solutions that will continue to deliver benefits. Therefore, key account managers must also be able to scrutinize the internal processes and the cost structures of customers.

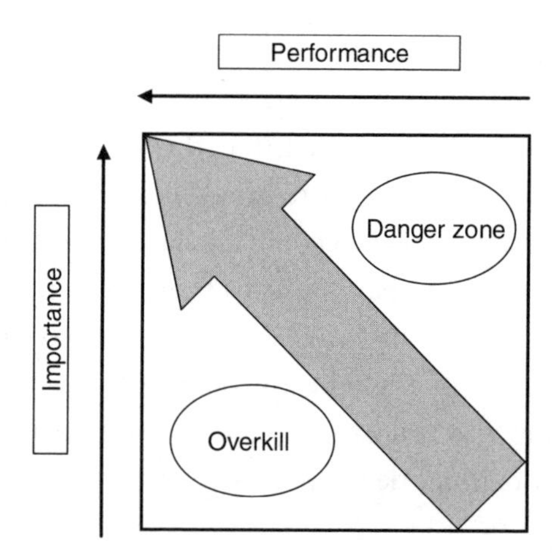

Figure 4.1 *The performance–importance matrix. (Adapted from Martilla and James, 1977.)*

Getting things done

I have gradually begun to appreciate that many account managers perceive that it is easier to deal with the customer, compared to the difficulties of negotiating with their own managers and colleagues to get things done on the customer's behalf. Many would argue that internal negotiation is the real crux of the job.

Negotiation is a process of preparation, debate, proposing, bargaining and looping back to debate if necessary before agreement. It ought to be rationally viewed as a normal part of life, but negotiation is often distrusted as a process in which side *A* loses and side *B* gains at side *A*'s expense. The distinction between "streetwise" negotiation and "principled" negotiation must be made.

Fisher, Ury and Patton originally defined principled negotiation, which requires participants to:

- separate personalities from the issue and focus on the objective;
- concentrate on the interests of parties, not on their position;
- search for options for mutual gain;
- insist on objective criteria.

These principles are particularly important in negotiating with colleagues, where the temptations to react to provocation, to escalate or to manipulate are great.

More recently, Lax and Sebenius (2006), who talk about "3D negotiation", have addressed the modern dilemma of negotiation without formal authority. At the time of writing, formal authority is much less likely to secure cooperation and commitment than it was in the past. It is essential to ensure that the right people are involved in the right sequence in order to get something done. Those leading the negotiation must not only architect and plan the negotiation in advance, but also design an agreement that creates different but complementary value to satisfy the interests of people involved as well as using thoughtful tactics at the table. It is important to ensure a genuine "no deal" option. This means that a key account manager must have the authority to call upon alternative resources, such as contract staff, if negotiation fails.

In summary . . .

Sales managers worry about recruiting key account managers because the skills required for the role are so diverse. Providing the right development to help them to achieve is expensive. Some companies organize intensive "academies" involving external training providers to teach and co-coach with sales managers. Being a key account manager is an excellent career development choice for sales achievers who want to explore their general management potential. However, natural extroverts may find the degree of analysis, administration and people management difficult. If you have this recruitment challenge, why not widen the net? I have met key account managers with backgrounds in engineering, marketing and accountancy as well as sales.

If you have this recruitment challenge, why not widen the net? I have met key account managers with backgrounds in engineering, marketing and accountancy as well as sales.

Long-term joint planning

If a relationship is strategic, then there ought to be a joint supplier–customer plan, or even a plan encompassing more relationships in the supply chain. Waiting for the customer to raise strategic issues is not enough. If no long-term plan is currently in place, the key account manager has to initiate one.

There are many benefits in doing so (Ryals and Rogers, 2007). To begin with, the customer may give the key account manager a better understanding of strategy than they previously had. The plan may create opportunities to make new contacts, identify problems to solve and demonstrate consistency and commitment to the customer. Internally, the plan offers a point of debate and a point of commitment.

It can be a long process which itself must be understood in detail by the key account manager and other contributors to the plan, including customer decision-makers. The key account manager will need considerable training in information-gathering, analysis and strategy formulation, and be equipped to manage the resulting action plan to fruition.

Many categories of company plans are done from the inside out, but this is not best practice in key account planning. Key account plans start from examining the customer's markets and the opportunities and threats within them. What should the customer be planning for the next three years? At this stage, the key account manager can discuss certain assumptions with the customer, and together they can confirm or adjust them.

However, as the customer may not see something in their business environment that an external observer can see, accepting the customer's analysis of their own situation is not always the best thing for a supplier to do. If the customer is blinkered, the supplier's position may also be at risk. One of the best ways for a key account manager to create customer value is to bring new marketplace and industry insights.

One of the best ways for a key account manager to create customer value is to bring new marketplace and industry insights.

Usually, there is mutual appreciation of the opportunities and threats facing the customer, and the strengths and weaknesses they have to deal with them. Then comes the great creative art of strategic account management – identifying how your capabilities as a supplier can be aligned to help the customer to overcome weaknesses or build on strengths.

Let's take an example of a capital goods supplier working with a manufacturing customer. Figure 4.2 shows the customer's SWOT, in the format we saw in Chapter 1.

Listing the SWOT in the manner suggested in Figure 4.2, and leaving four boxes blank to identify potential strategies that the customer might be

	OPPORTUNITIES • New tax breaks for investment • Derived demand for innovation • New channels to new markets	THREATS • Lack of science graduates locally • Recession stalling orders
STRENGTHS • Financial reserves • Engineering skills (R&D) • Brand reputation		
WEAKNESSES • Age of capital equipment • Poor administrative processes • Geographical scope		

Figure 4.2 *Customer's SWOT analysis with blank boxes. (Reproduced with kind permission from Diana Woodburn of Marketing Best Practice, www.marketingbp.com.)*

	OPPORTUNITIES • New tax breaks for investment • Derived demand for innovation • New channels to new markets	THREATS • Lack of science graduates locally • Recession stalling orders
STRENGTHS • Financial reserves • Engineering skills (R&D) • Brand reputation	New product development	Offer better payment terms to customers work with suppliers on NPD
WEAKNESSES • Age of capital equipment • Poor administrative processes • Geographical scope	Invest in new equipment Enter new markets with new supply chain partners	Process redesign, or outsource?

Figure 4.3 *Customer's SWOT analysis with completed boxes.*

(or should be) planning themselves and/or with you as a supplier, helps to concentrate the mind on specific, relevant solutions (Figure 4.3).

- If there is demand for innovation and a strength is R&D skills, new products development is a strategic imperative. If it is difficult to recruit new talent to do that, your customer may want to combine resources with you.
- If the recession is stalling orders and a strength is financial reserves, your customer could offer better payment terms to their customers, but might expect you to reciprocate.
- If the age of capital equipment is a problem, but new tax breaks are effectirely reducing the cost of new equipment, buying new equipment is desirable (to support new product development).
- If the customer's geographical scope is a restriction, but new channels to new markets are developing, the customer should leverage new supply chain options (and may need your support to do so).

- Poor administrative processes are not a good fit with new payment terms being offered to customers, so perhaps the time is right to outsource administration.

Of course, in this scenario the supplier wants to sell more equipment as much as ever, but both supplier and customer need to see the big picture of meeting market demand with new products and new channels, so that the sales/purchases have logic and meaning. With customer buy-in to the proposals suggested, moving on to setting joint objectives, strategies and action plans with budgets will be logical.

If either the customer or you, as the account manager's boss, observe that the plan is just wishful thinking, then it will be rejected. Neither the customer nor your senior managers need to hear that everything is rosy. Every company's business environment is tough. There are threats and no business can be perfect in dealing with them. Positivity alone does not change that, but positivity combined with workable solutions can impress.

I met a Chief Executive some years ago who always asked key account managers presenting their plans: "Where's the spark?" He hoped and expected that each plan would logically identify "a spark" which would lead to more and better business with the customer. If it didn't, it was not approved. Planning is an iterative process. First-timers soon learned that several drafts might be necessary!

Lots of account plans are blighted by sloppiness between objectives and strategies. I have seen many that appear to claim that a high growth rate will be achieved simply by having more meetings with the customer! Of course, life's not like that.

Objectives are what you want to achieve with the customer, expressed quantifiably and not as a wish. An effective plan must be measurable. The key account manager must also suggest a "how" statement to prove that by doing *x* we can achieve *y*, e.g. by providing 24 × 7 on-site engineering support we can increase annuity service income in the account by 10%. As the sales manager, you have to believe that statement to be 100% feasible, or you must send the key account manager back to the drawing board.

As the sales manager, you have to believe that statement to be 100% feasible, or you must send the key account manager back to the drawing board.

The best of strategies is useless unless driven by robust implementation. So many account plans peter out toward the end, proffering action plans without much in the way of action, let alone coherence about who is going to do what and when. Encourage your key account managers to work with a project manager to help them to juggle prerequisites, co-requisites, critical paths and milestones, not to mention risks and contingencies. It will be worthwhile.

When you are the recipient of a robust plan, bear in mind the natural caution that the writer has probably applied and see if you can apply some pressure to bring forward achievements or increase their effect. When you are happy that the plan is ready, make sure the key account manager writes a lucid executive summary that you can present to other managers and the Board. Board endorsement will help the key account manager with leverage for implementation.

Review the plan with the key account manager at least monthly, and be sure to distinguish between mistakes in planning and mistakes in execution. There are bound to be both.

Organizing for strategic relationships

If you and your key account managers are hoping to convince strategic customers that you can "do" key account management, your company must have a supportive organizational structure. A McKinsey survey found that organizations that could not collaborate across business units, geographies and functions were unlikely to realize returns on developing strategic relationships; in fact about 25% could actually lose money (Hancock, John and Wojcik, 2005).

For small companies, the challenge is primarily one of building key account teams with representatives from the different functions of the company and presenting the customer with an account manager who can "conduct the orchestra" and ensure that their business runs smoothly. Figure 4.4, frequently called the "diamond" diagram, suggests a harmonious alignment between supplier and customer, where accounts receivable sorts things out with accounts payable, good inwards sorts things out with goods outwards, engineers talk to engineers and senior managers do lunch with senior managers. The account manager and purchasing professional are working

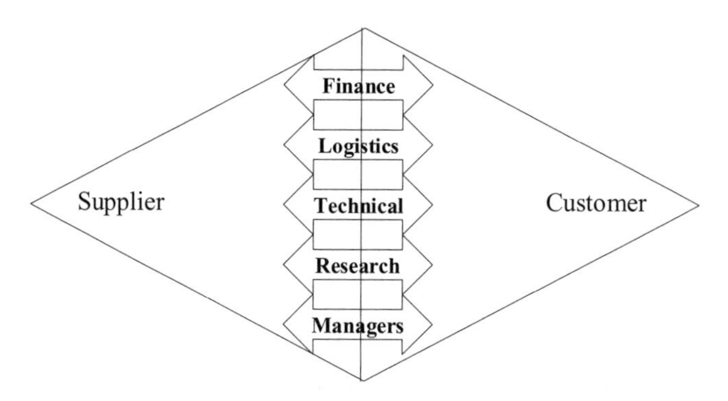

Figure 4.4 *The "diamond" diagram. (Adapted from Christopher and Jüttner, 2001.)*

away in the background to facilitate a company-to-company relationship. This in itself is easier said than done.

Nevertheless, cross-functional key account teams are an important step for all suppliers who aspire to be able to develop strategic business relationships. We have seen in the chapter on purchasing that customers frequently use "decision-making units" involving a variety of internal stakeholders, including technical, operational and financial experts as well as purchasing professionals, to make decisions about suppliers. It is not surprising that they expect decision-making units within your organization to match theirs.

Cross-functional key account teams form one dimension. When a company has several product divisions, a second dimension to the key account team is introduced, and then different geographical subunits create a third dimension. What happens when a multinational company with a traditional organizational structure (see Figure 4.5) migrates to something customers would perceive to be more responsive and focused on them?

In a traditional organizational structure, product sales live in product divisions, which have some power, and country sales report to regional managers. There are likely to be key accounts in each country or region, but when a company first examines its overall customer portfolio and identifies company-wide strategic relationships that have cross-divisional and cross-border relevance, the likelihood is that responsibility for the relationship at a corporate level will sit in a functional department in Head Office. Gaining commitment from product divisions and countries to work within an overall strategy may be challenging.

Head office/local office conflict is always possible when a few customers are identified as "key". Effectively, there is a reorientation of power from

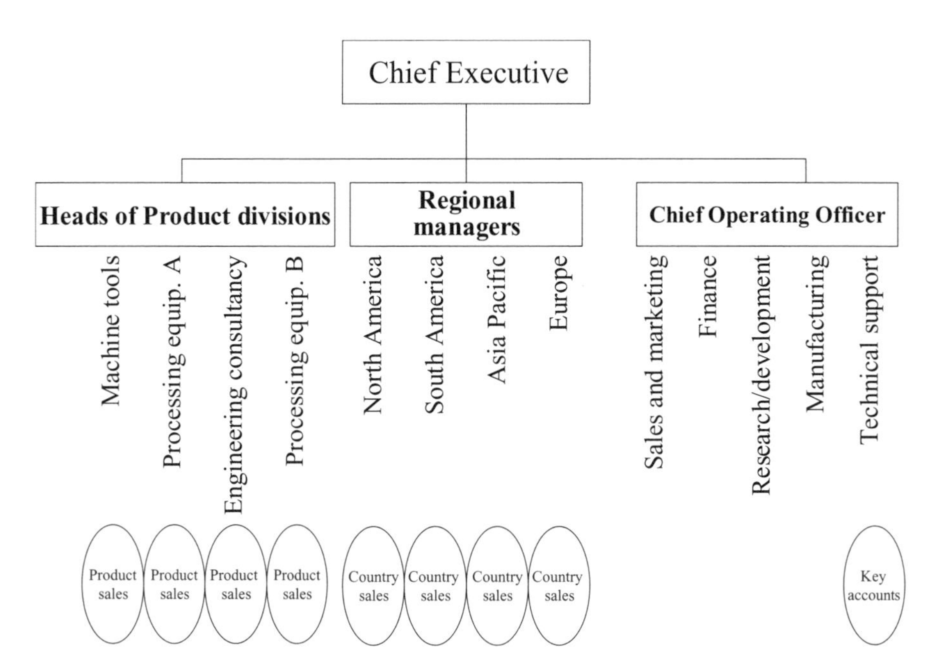

Figure 4.5 *Traditional organizational structure.*

divisions and countries to the center, which needs considerable commitment from senior managers. It involves a change in power structures and culture. Some organizations cannot cope; others find a way to make it happen.

Global key account implementation at an international hotel chain

When one international hotel chain implemented its global key account strategy, it had an even greater challenge than many companies – its hotels are run by independent franchisees. Local hotel managers were likely to be unsettled by losing power and control to global account managers at head office. But major corporate customers were demanding more than just rooms, and the hotel had a plan to respond.

The internal communication of change was the first big challenge, the company had 13,000 associates worldwide. New measurement standards were put into place so that credits could be allocated locally as well as globally when global accounts placed business.

There were also challenges in correctly identifying the geographically diverse customers that wanted more than just a single point of contact and a universal pricing agreement. When the hotel pointed out to a particular global key account that 10% of what they paid them was for cancelled rooms and offered a solution to minimize that waste, the customer was very interested. The hotel chain set up an electronic bulletin board so that other units of the customer could use the cancelled rooms. For the local hotels, this meant that catering business from occupancy of the rooms was not lost.

Small successes led to wider acceptance. Local managers realized that global accounts offered opportunities for incremental business, protection from economic bad times and better access to key decision-makers in the local offices of global accounts. The trade-off with power was worth it.

Source: Richard and Wilson (2000)

A number of companies now have key account divisions sitting alongside product divisions and country organizations. A key account division is certainly very convincing by way of an expensive commitment to ensure that strategic relationships are fully supported and developed. Three-dimensional key account teamwork raises the challenge of matrix management across four dimensions (Figure 4.6): customer, product, country and function.

Where is the country focus (Figure 4.7) for global key account activity? Many companies will site global account managers wherever the head office of the customer happens to be, and they have a "dotted" line report to the local country manager.

The link with product divisions (Figure 4.8) is not going to be so straightforward, when the customer may have a need for a variety of product categories from the supplier. The product divisions may need a dotted line relationship to the key account manager. A significant amount of their revenue may depend on close liaison with particular customers.

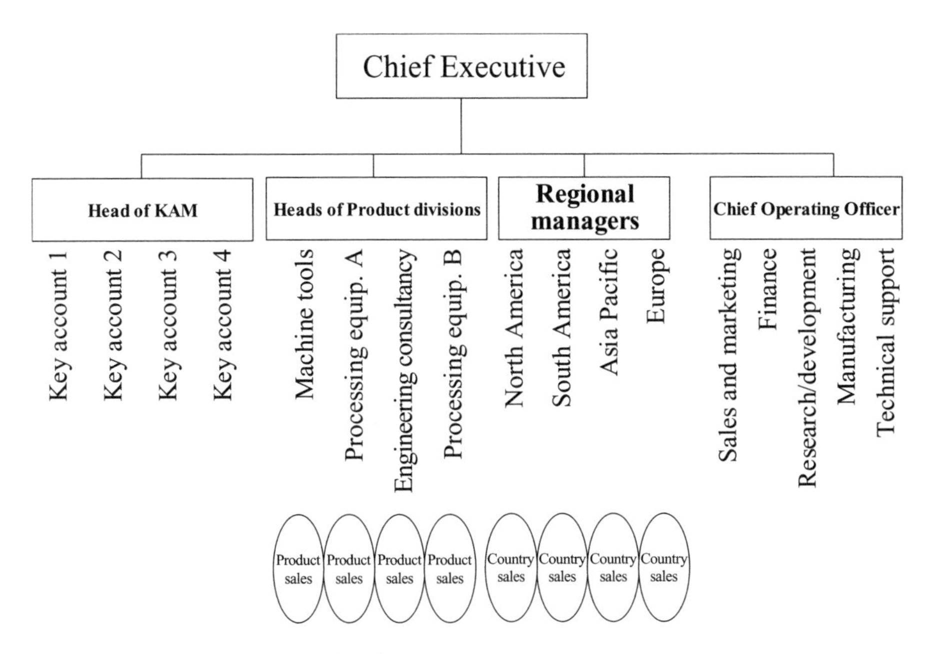

Figure 4.6 *Management across four dimensions.*

	KAM1	KAM2	KAM3	KAM4	KAM5	KAM6
Cust. HO Japan		✓				
Cust. HO Brazil	✓					
Cust. HO Canada			✓			
Cust. HO China					✓	
Cust. HO Germany						✓
Cust. HO USA				✓		

Figure 4.7 *Global key account activity.*

And in relation to functional teams, the internal "selling center" team may no longer be enough. In order to achieve the value creation and process integration that makes strategic business relationships thrive, cross-boundary teams (Figure 4.9) merging the buying center and the selling center can achieve the best possible progress.

	KAM1	KAM2	KAM3	KAM4	KAM5	KAM6
PROD1		✓			✓	✓
PROD2	✓	✓				✓
PROD3			✓		✓	
PROD4			✓		✓	
PROD5				✓		✓
PROD6		✓			✓	

Figure 4.8 *Divisional key account activity.*

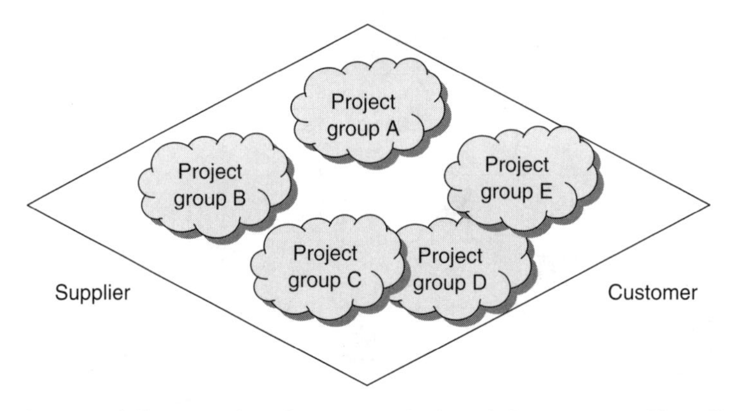

Figure 4.9 *Buying/selling cross-boundary teams.* (Adapted from: *McDonald, Millman and Rogers, 1996.)*

Cross-boundary teams at steel processor

"Improving customers' competitiveness was, in a strategic sense, as important as improving its own competitiveness."

Paladino, Bates and da Silveira (2002)

The state-owned steel company of Argentina was privatized in 1992, at a time of collapsing world prices. The company had a serious problem with quality, and needed to work with key customers on value chain integration to ensure mutual survival in the global market.

The company embarked upon an internal program of quality improvement, including knowledge management, leading to certification. Alongside this effort, it worked with its customers, who were also suffering from the changes in the business environment. In 1994, the company set up product and process improvement teams with 17 strategic customers – to coordinate and integrate their value chains. The teams were tasked with improving current products, developing new products, improving relationship and lowering transaction costs. Each cross-boundary team defined its own goals, milestones, and monitored progress.

Between 1994 and 1997, the company's sales increased 45% and profits nearly trebled from US$ 32m to US$ 91m. Its exports increased by 384%, productivity improved and the company's safety record improved. Between 1997 and 2000, results stabilized and were consolidated.

Source: Paladino, Bates and da Silveira (2002)

Indeed, many companies who regard themselves as having a leadership role in their supply chains have explored the idea of supply chain competition. If players throughout the supply chain of a product work as a team, then value creation for the end-customer could become very efficient.

Value creation including product development and process integration

Companies can turn even the most basic of generic products into a value-creating solution. Examples I have come across include a supplier of specialist ceramic pipes solving a customer's problem with breakages by offering to manage the use of its product in the customer's factory. Although the service cost more, total cost of ownership to the customer was reduced because breakages were virtually eliminated. One supplier, whose business with key accounts involved thousands upon thousands of small transactions, allowed the customer

Companies can turn even the most basic of generic products into a value-creating solution.

to self-invoice, as it saved so much time for both parties in reconciling their records. Obviously the customer was only ever going to pay for what they thought they had received, so why not have a process to reflect that?

Sometimes it is the purchasing team who make the suggestion for process improvement. Retailers have been the driving force behind collaborative planning, forecasting and replenishment (CPFR) with their fast-moving consumer goods suppliers. Both the retailers and the customers report better communications, more effective sharing of information about costs, better service levels, better end-customer satisfaction, reduced inventory overhead and better all-round flexibility in operations (Daugherty *et al.*, 2006).

In business-to-business, industrial customers are driven by derived demand from consumers, and expectations of more for less are escalating. It makes sense in many circumstances for suppliers and customers in B2B markets to work together to improve overall competitiveness.

It is beyond the scope of this book to discuss process mapping and new product development, and once opportunities have been identified by a key account manager, and recognized by you, your colleagues in operations and engineering would be likely partners in developing the idea. However, reviewing the techniques discussed in Chapter 12 to resolve sales process problems can also be applied in cross-boundary discussions to see where there is potential for either or both.

A concluding thought

Professor Nigel Piercy and Nikala Lane (2006, 2007) have challenged the assumption that a "key account management" approach to key customers is universally good for shareholder value. If you are dependent on a small number of customers for business development, it can increase your vulnerability as a company. They provide some evidence that even "key" customers will exercise their power to achieve lower prices and commoditization of products and services. This threatens your profitability.

Consider also that even "key" customers defect. Whether it is through merging with another company or the result of a new Chief Executive with a new policy, it happens. The effect can be very public and affect the share price of the dumped supplier. You need to maintain objectivity when reviewing the business relationships that are genuinely strategic.

With this in mind, let's consider in the next few chapters how other types of relationship can be managed to balance your risk.

5

Prospective relationships

"When you find a senior contact in your customer's organization who is going to be your advocate – that's the key to success. That's when a prospective relationship warrants serious investment."

Quoted with kind permission from David Todman, Marketing and Sales Director, APV.

David spent fifteen years in the manufacturing sector developing strategic relationships from nothing.

As we discussed in Chapter 3, the challenge of converting prospects and new or occasional customers into regular or even strategic customers is difficult and can be expensive. For many companies organic growth is too difficult an option. At face value, buying a smaller competitor would seem an easier growth strategy.

We have been hearing from researchers for years that existing customers are more profitable than new ones. Some companies now devote the majority of their sales and marketing budgets to customer retention. It is, after all, easier to sell more to a current customer than to gain a new one. However, no retention strategy can keep 100% of customers. Even with an outstanding sales effort and impeccable customer service, current

Even with an outstanding sales effort and impeccable customer service, current customers get acquired and sometimes they change their purchasing strategy. Or, their business may decline for reasons beyond your control.

customers get acquired and sometimes they change their purchasing strategy. Or, their business may decline for reasons beyond your control.

Suppliers who fail to acquire new customers will stagnate. The secret of portfolio management is to ensure that quadrants in the portfolio are balanced, which means that investment has to go into developing prospective relationships. Some prospective relationships may drop into the tactical quadrant (Figure 5.1), but there must be some expectation that a few will become strategic relationships in the long term.

How much investment you should make in developing prospective relationships could be subject to endless calculation of "optimal" spend. Although it is better to underspend on acquisition than on retention (Reinartz, Thomas and Kumar, 2005), in terms of return on investment some overspend on customer acquisition is better than underspend. Some might also say that if you are good at retention, you can risk a little more on acquisition.

In this chapter we shall look at some options for investment in developing prospective relationships from targeting to higher levels of involvement (Figure 5.2).

The simplest way to look at new customer acquisition is to consider the issues facing start-up companies. However, many of the same issues are just as relevant to existing companies that are selling new products in new geographical territories, or are just trying to penetrate new accounts where they have no reputation with buyers.

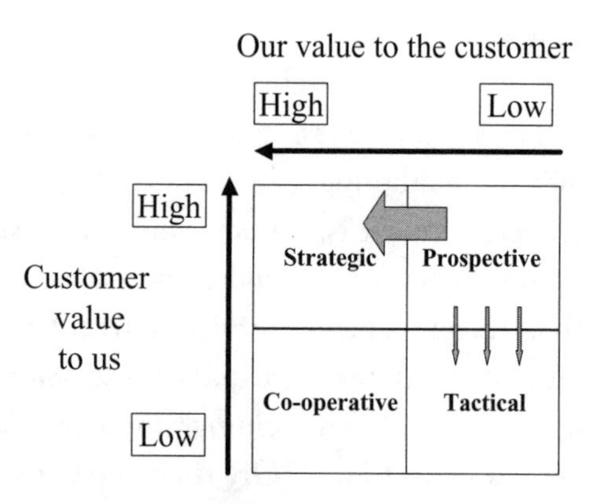

Figure 5.1 *Developing prospective relationships.*

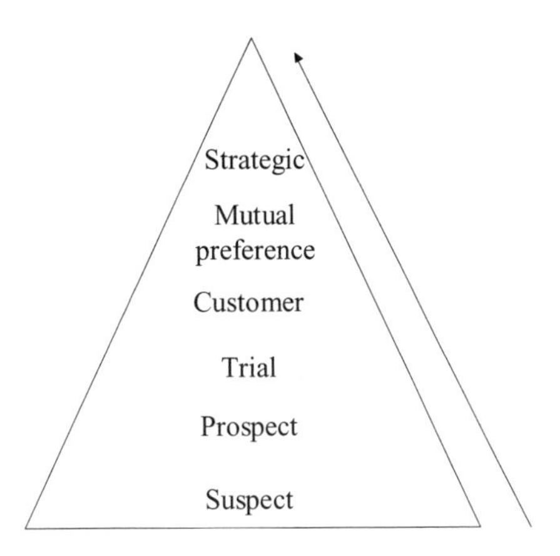

Figure 5.2 *The development stages of prospective relationships. (Adapted from Millman and Wilson, 1994, and MacDonald and Woodburn, 2001.)*

Encouraging references – some lessons from start-ups

Start-up companies in B2B often have just one customer. Sometimes, it is the former employer of the entrepreneur, or a business contact of the entrepreneur from a previous job, perhaps in a large company. Challenges arise when the start-up seeks the second customer. Many successful entrepreneurs report that getting their second customer was many times more difficult than getting their first one. The easiest way to overcome the barrier of acquiring second and subsequent customers is to get your first customer to act as a reference.

That is easier said than done. In a study based on software start-ups in Thailand, but with similarities with my observations of high-technology start-ups in Europe, Ruokolainen and Igel (2004) found that some relationships with the first customer fail. Those failures were associated with disputes about intellectual property rights rather than the functionality of the software.

If you are in a start-up company, you have to evaluate the commitment that a first customer has to your survival as a supplier. If that commitment is there, and you as a supplier work hard to improve the first customer's business performance by applying your product or knowledge with unique skill, then there is potential for the first customer to act as a reference account for the second and subsequent customers.

It is not ISO 9002 registration that makes you a "quality" supplier, especially if prospective customer number 2 has never heard of you.

It is not ISO 9002 registration that makes you a "quality" supplier, especially if prospective customer number 2 has never heard of you. You are a quality supplier only if your first customer will confirm to others that you are producing high-quality products, and that the causes are traceable. For example, is it clear that your quality results from hiring experienced engineering workers in effective teams operating up-to-date machine tools? Your reference account also has to believe that you can apply those capabilities to another company's needs.

You have then to consider an additional factor. What is the first customer's status as a reference? Do they have a good brand or technical reputation that will influence prospective customer number 2?

These observations are also helpful for larger companies who need customer endorsements in order to reduce the perceptions of risk that prospects might have about dealing with them. Some websites have large quantities of comforting case studies from satisfied customers. At some stage, however, a prospect may want to contact a customer directly, so you have to consider carefully the contact that would be of most assistance to each prospect.

Larger companies may also ensure that they proactively encourage "positive word-of-mouth" from customers to prospects. Customers are probably very well placed to recognize a similar need. Asking for contacts in other companies is a big hurdle for salespeople. Some buying decision-makers may pass on contacts; others could be defensive. Only your salespeople can judge whether the relationship is strong enough for such an approach, but they may need coaching to become comfortable in asking the question.

Fortunately, it is more common these days to find marketing departments thinking creatively about making opportunities for "word of mouth" to happen, although business-to-business (B2B) cannot leverage publicity events in quite the same way as business-to-consumer (B2C). Rules governing acceptance of hospitality are also becoming stricter in many companies. However, the organization of interesting learning opportunities, where customers are encouraged to bring their industry contacts, can be helpful.

For example, in some research I supervised for a property company, it was discovered that property decisions were not necessarily made in the best of situations with the best knowledge of alternatives, or with sufficient post-decision monitoring. So the property company organized seminars about realizing returns on property investment for local professionals who might be involved in decisions about leases and facilities, e.g. management accountants.

In my experience, achieving reasonable attendance at seminars requires at least two of the following:

- A relevant and interesting subject.
- A well-known and entertaining speaker.
- Interesting venue, such as a tourist attraction or sports stadium.
- Endorsement, e.g. from a professional association.

Only one of the above will not be enough when there are so many competing pressures on people's time.

The tasks involved in developing prospective relationships

Segmentation, targeting and positioning

One thing is clear from the few research studies on the topic of customer acquisition. Quality is more important than quantity. Targeted relationship development can improve return on investment by two or four times as much as an "open offer" approach to attracting new customers (Sargeant and West, 2001). If your targeting of prospective relationships is well honed, your approach to them will be differentiated, and you should enjoy better response rates and better levels of business over time.

Targeted relationship development can improve return on investment by two or four times as much as an "open offer" approach to attracting new customers.

"Open offers" involve high acquisition costs – you have to pay to get an open message broadcast widely. The customers acquired are usually not retained for long and their coming and going could erode overall profitability (Banasiewicz, 2004).

In a perfect world it would be nice to generate both quality and quantity in new business relationships. But a desirable quantity depends on your company's scope and capabilities. So, it is necessary to start any review of prospective relationships with some sensible objectives:

- What percentage growth is achievable?
- What return on investment is required?

The first step in profiling prospective relationships is identifying the companies that you don't deal with today but who might have a need for your solution. That is where the attractiveness factors on the relationship development box come in. You can identify the type of company that would make a great customer for your business, and start the process of identifying whether they would see you as a great supplier.

If you start from a sector approach to segmentation, it is a relatively simple desk-based job to draw up a list of prospective customers from Standard Industrial Classification codes or business directories (see Chapter 3). You can even buy lists, and you can also buy lists based on company size, location, or any other sort of "firmographic" characteristic. Could there be a needs-based approach?

Needs identification

Design agencies estimate that every three months major FMCG companies have some new packaging requirement; in other sectors it may take 6–12 months before there is an opportunity for the prospective customer to receive a proposal from a prospective new supplier. Some market intelligence about the timing of prospects' decision-making can give general guidelines. Of course, each prospect will be different and some prospect-specific homework using their website and press announcements is necessary.

If you can make some intelligent assumptions about a prospect's needs and demonstrate your understanding in your first contact with them, your letter may avoid the fast track to the garbage can.

As a consultant, I once worked with some in-house business development staff who were trawling company announcements in the financial press looking for signs of change in the organization that would indicate the need for new communications equipment. For example, the team targeted a company that was featured for successfully diversifying out of a declining sector. It was found that the company's information technology structure was indeed in need of significant upgrading and updating.

Doing homework on a target company should include checking out information on their website and how they are mentioned in the media. Researchers can learn the language of the prospect's industry through trade journals, e.g. learning the acronyms. Identifying potential key issues is essential preparation prior to making contact.

This desk-based activity is not exclusively the job of your salespeople. Close relationships with the marketing department should enable you to focus some of their activity on the homework and planning needed not just to identify leads, but also to qualify them in a meaningful way.

Initial contact development

Not all companies make it easy to identify their decision-makers from their website, but company reports, either posted on the company website or derived from other public records, will give a researcher a starting point. Once again, lists can be bought. Lists from reputable sources should have been screened so that you do not run the risk of contacting an individual who has registered under "do not contact" laws which, in some countries, protect businesses as well as consumers. It is advisable to send a letter to named individuals in the first instance.

Privacy legislation

In Europe, the Privacy and Electronic Communications Regulations 2004 created a requirement for potential suppliers to seek permission from prospective customers for e-mail and telephone contact. Although the law is primarily concerned with the privacy of private individuals, in the UK protection for businesses was also considered necessary. Companies can register with the Corporate Telephone Preference Service. Any company making an unsolicited marketing or sales call to a company on the register could face a heavy fine. Business associations lobbied for permission legislation to counter lots of unwanted contacts enabled by new technology.

Understanding needs in detail

Since the 1970s, the sales profession has had the benefit of Neil Rackham's SPIN model to guide salespeople at this stage of creating prospective relationships. If the marketing department or business development agency have done their work, the salesperson will have a meeting with a buying decision-maker. Rackham's team examined 35,000 sales calls and concluded that the most successful ones followed a rational pattern of questioning. Rackham then designed a model, used in sales training around the world, to help salespeople to use questioning to establish a prospect's explicit needs. The model, as you probably already know, is called SPIN.

For example, a salesperson from a high tech company receives a brief from the business development team that prospect X is interested in a technology upgrade. He or she will ask situation questions about the size, age and complexity of the current installation, then move carefully into asking questions designed to persuade the customer to explain their problems, such as "Does performance slow down at busy times of day?"; "Do you experience unplanned network outages?" When the customer has explained a little bit about the shortcomings of the current system, whether they relate to network availability, application performance, data security, or a policy decision to move to a new operating protocol, the salesperson will have gathered a list of implied needs.

The next step is to ask about the implications of the problems expressed – for example, does system downtime result in lost customers, or poor productivity? If so, the salesperson must move to a need-payoff question: How much would it be worth to the customer if they could solve that availability problem? Once need-payoff questions have been answered, the customer's explicit needs are on the table, together with some indication of their urgency.

We can now move on to creating value for the prospect and demonstrating our credibility as a supplier (Figure 5.3).

Proposal submission

In a focus group with purchasing decision-makers in small businesses, it was clear to me as a researcher how the participants were acutely aware of the risks they run in choosing a new supplier. The wrong choice could destroy

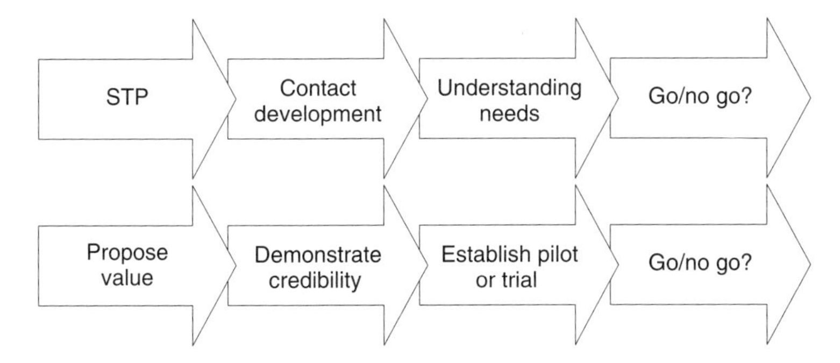

Figure 5.3 *Steps in creating prospective relationships.*

their entire business. Consequently, the development of trust was crucial, and closely linked with perception of competencies. If the proposal tendered was good enough to get through to a shortlist, it was normally an indication of the professionalism of the proposal and the strength of the customer references. Perceptions of the professionalism of proposals included everything from correct spelling to whether or not the content showed an appreciation of the buying company's needs as well as a value-creating solution.

Perceptions of the professionalism of proposals included everything from correct spelling to whether or not the content showed an appreciation of the buying company's needs as well as a value-creating solution.

Sales proposals need to cover a variety of information and it is often helpful to have a template- or software-facilitated process. Just like a sales call, a written proposal should concentrate on the customer's needs. It also needs to express your value as a supplier for a variety of different stakeholders – the technical decision-maker, the financial decision-maker, the purchasing professional, etc. Submitting proposals electronically enables you to build pathways through the information submitted to meet the needs of different reviewers. The required elements in a proposal are:

- Covering letter
- Executive summary
- Understanding of the prospect's needs and challenges
- Demonstration of unique value creation in the solution proposed

- Financial information – total cost of ownership over time, rather than unit costs
- Establishing your company as a credible supplier, such as customer references
- "Hygiene" factors, e.g. information about conformance to legal or industry standards
- Explanation of risk management approach – what you will do if something goes wrong
- How the business relationship will be managed
- Responses to specific questions that may be posed by the customer.

The work involved in producing proposals can be massive, and should be a team effort. An administrator can review the customer's Request for Proposal and sort the desired "hygiene" factors such as accreditations and legal compliance from the content. Meeting "hygiene" factors should be "business as usual" for most companies, especially if you have public sector customers. Legal compliance should already be answered in the proposal template.

In collaboration with technical colleagues, the salesperson should be able to decide from the content of the Request for Proposal (RFP) if there are any areas of confusion or concern. There should be a formal bid/no bid review, including at least the following factors:

- Customer relationship with current supplier
- Match of the RFP with our capabilities – skills and scope
- Potential profit
- Growth potential
- Financial risk
- Business risk
- Timescale
- Impact on people (e.g. extensive travel involved)
- Future reference value.

If you and your fellow reviewers are confident that the business can be won, you then need to apply a lot of creativity to the proposal. Brainstorm everything that needs to be done and every possibility for adding value to your solution. Then get a strict project manager to draw up a plan and make sure that all the contributors adhere to it. Have someone check that the proposal is written in plain and persuasive language using correct spelling. It is surprising how many proposals are not shortlisted because the reviewers at the customer's business observe that they have not been prepared with the care that they expected.

One buyer told a colleague that he turned down an otherwise good proposal for an $8 million piece of business because the name of another company had been left in the boilerplate in place of theirs. "It just stuck in my craw," he said. "If they couldn't get our name right, could we trust them?"

Allow plenty of time for managerial review and do not leave submission to the last minute – your courier may get stuck in traffic! And if you are looking for a detailed guide to writing persuasive business proposals, check out Sant (2004) in the bibliography.

Not all demonstrations of value are written. Sometimes the salesperson has to demonstrate it in the sales call. Take, for example, a new medical treatment for asthma sufferers, which instead of dealing with the symptoms of asthma attacks, acted to prevent them. It may sound like a great step forward for medicine, but sales were low even six months after launch. However, two salespeople were selling 20 times as much as everyone else.

Demonstrating value

The salespeople emphasized the lifestyle benefits of the drug for the children who needed it. These children would be able to own pets and participate in sports. The salespeople also recognized that allergists were not used to administering medication by intravenous drip, so they guided the doctors in using the drug and showed the administrative staff how to fill out the paperwork.

Source: Anon., *Harvard Business Review* (2005a)

A similar approach is taken by Vagheggi Spa, a cosmetics firm based in Italy. The salespeople help their customers in health and beauty spas to understand and apply the products to achieve best results for their customers. (Example provided by AIDA Marketing and Formazione.)

Follow-up

As with anything in marketing and sales, it is often the follow-up that determines success. In my early career at IBM, win/lose reviews were taken very seriously, so that we could learn from success and failure. If you are going to be skillful at developing prospective relationships, you need to know what the prospective customers think of your strengths and weaknesses.

If you win, there is still more monitoring and measurement to do. For example, what were the costs of acquiring the customer? What was the initial revenue, and what is the forecast for the customer's lifetime value?

The strategic options for growth

Buy a smaller rival

Growth by acquisition of a rival company sounds like a great quick fix. Some companies have been successful in growing by acquiring. Others have found that acquisition focuses both acquirer and acquired on internal matters, and no increase in overall company value is achieved.

Many of the anticipated benefits of "synergy" turn out to be illusions. A CEO who built his group of companies by acquisition told a new colleague to ignore all talk of synergy and savings from consolidation. He told him to assume that synergy and savings would be non-existent, and focus the acquisition trail on business fundamentals.

In fact, innumerable cases of mergers and acquisitions suggest that shareholder value may be diminished in the medium term.

Strategy consultants frequently see companies buying in economic growth periods when prices are high, and being forced to sell acquired units in recessions when prices are low. For the company that wants to grow, and is prepared to take on the managerial risk of assimilating different company cultures into its own, acquisition might be cheaper and smoother when the local economy or even the global economy is quiet.

Integrated marketing communications

Financial Directors are always seeking to pin down return on investment from marketing and improve it. Marketers are tasked with integrating

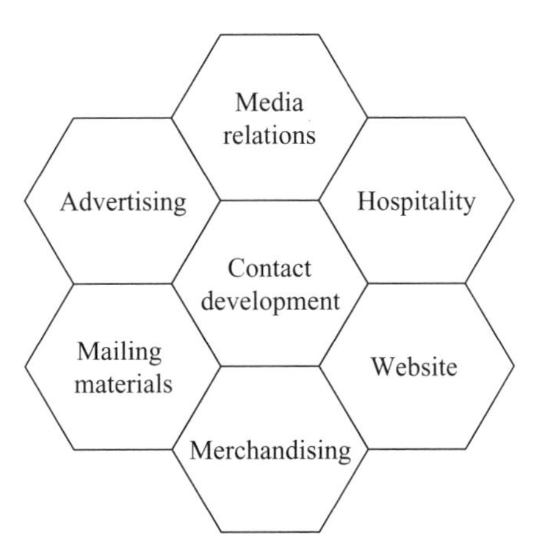

Figure 5.4 *Marketing support for contact development.*

marketing communications activity with selling activity, but detailed integration requires a lot of planning. As a sales manager, you need direct marketing materials such as demonstrations or presentations on the website to support the work of contact developers, and reassuring advertisements or "advertorial" (paid placement of articles) in trade magazines might also help to position your solution in the prospect's minds (Figure 5.4). It may even open doors. Working with marketing is covered in more detail in Chapter 10.

Sales promotions

Since the lifetime value of customers acquired by discount can be half the lifetime value of those who chose the supplier for other reasons, buying access to a customer's business is very high risk. Perhaps the nature of your business is such that lower profitability is acceptable because of marginal cost recovery enabled by volume of business. Perhaps organic growth at a lower profit is better than alternative business risks.

Since the lifetime value of customers acquired by discount can be half the lifetime value of those who chose the supplier for other reasons, buying access to a customer's business is very high risk.

As discussed in Chapter 3, although discounting your way on to a prospective customer's supplier list can jeopardize profit in the long term as well as the short term, potential new suppliers are usually challenged to discount as a technique to reduce the risk of change. Some element of trial purchase or piloting of a service may be necessary. In the case of some outsourcing contracts, there are extended handover periods, or an entire service has to be rebranded by the new supplier.

Outsourcing lead generation to an agency

Keeping salespeople productive and satisfied

Renee Botham, Chief Executive of Touchstone, a London agency specializing in customer acquisition for B2B clients, believes that salespeople are most productive and most satisfied when they can maximize face-to-face contact. "We are business growth specialists. Touchstone offers a dedicated new business team to clients. We will go as far along the sales process as is needed to set up a substantial meeting between the client and their prospect. We may attend that meeting in order to provide a handover. We have a role in conversion by progress-chasing the client to follow-up. We are selling, but we also think about the long term – building relationships."

Quoted with kind permission of Renee Botham, Touchstone
www.touchstonegrowth.com

Companies use agencies like Touchstone because of time pressures. They need a consistent focus on organic growth of the customer base, but do not want to waste expensive salespeople's time on prospecting, database development or contact identification. Of course, if you are planning to use an agency to develop prospective relationships, you need to choose carefully. You need to be sure that the agency's telephone sales team have appropriate levels of business knowledge, communication skills and share your brand values.

An agency like Touchstone also has its professional limits to ensure that it maintains its focus, and you need to respect that. They provide the time, skills and management involved in opening doors for your salespeople. Thereafter, they provide support and advice only. Ms Botham, says: "Most clients appreciate that. It gives the in-house salespeople the chance to be heroes and get recognition for handling the development and closing of the sale."

What sort of contractual relationships work best?

Some agencies work on a time basis, others manage to operate by requesting payment per lead generated. Others may have a sophisticated hybrid. Each approach involves risks for the sales manager as a client. However, the letter of the contract is not the issue in the success of client–agency relationships. It is important to get away from traditional views of agencies, where you, as the client, pay for tasks to be done and the agent operates strictly within the terms of the contract, offering an adequate enough service to get paid.

Anecdotal evidence, together with some rather specialist psychological research in game-playing, suggests that complex tasks are best completed in a cooperative setting. Rather than a contract, you and the agency might work more constructively together for the benefit of the prospective customers with a partnership agreement encompassing joint objectives and a joint business development plan. It is better still if that plan has been developed in a workshop in which you and the agency personnel meet and learn about each other.

Some agencies who focus on customer acquisition are desk and telephone based and can only develop the prospective relationship to a certain point. When the prospective customer wants to meet someone face-to-face for an in-depth discussion, most agencies feel that is best handled in-house. You then have responsibilities when you pick up the baton. The telesales agent that facilitated the meeting and the relevant salesperson need some time to prepare the call. Or you may pay the agency for the telesales agent to provide ongoing contact development by phone and do some progress-chasing, both within the prospective customer and with your salesperson. It is essential for the agent and you to share the prospect database so that you both know the stage the relationship has reached when speaking to the prospect.

> *"Clients say that we are their 'hidden weapon'."*
>
> Senior Account Director, Touchstone

There are also agencies that recruit contract salespeople for your specific campaigns. For example, a mattress manufacturer in Kentucky wanted to launch a range in 10 regional markets in the USA in six months. They used the services of a contract sales agency, on the basis that although it was not a cheap option, it was a fast one. Following the successful launch, 14 of the 25 contract salespeople were employed full time (Gruner, 1996).

Expanding internationally

> **Market entry performance**
>
> Tim Mutton has been involved in creating sales functions for companies entering specific segments of the UK high-technology market. Having managed the market entry, he then hands the customer base back to his client. He is reducing this risk for his client, as they are avoiding the cost of employing people and then trying to redeploy them if the project fails. Because of local expertise, he is also accelerating market entry performance. Tim recognizes that he has been trusted to build the right customer experience – an outsourcer has to reflect the client's culture and values.
>
> Case quoted with kind permission from Tim Mutton, consultant
> www.tpmmarketingandconsultancy.co.uk

The Thai study mentioned earlier noted that with a small local economy, a business services company needs to expand abroad to develop sufficient scope for long-term survival. In expanding internationally, you have essentially two options – to work with a third party or to recruit employees in the new market. Many companies have started by working through third parties and then establishing a local presence. There is more detailed comment about working with intermediaries in Chapter 6.

For companies that take the option to establish a local presence, they have a steep learning curve to adapt to developing business relationships in a new culture. There are many "war stories" about companies making blunders in new geographical markets, encompassing everything from poorly translated advertising slogans to inadvertently causing offence in meetings.

In my own career I have learned that punctuality is extremely important in Germany, that it is impossible to drink out of a Chinese "drinking boot" with dignity, and that, in Australia, I must pronounce a router a "rowter" rather than the UK English "rooter", which means something altogether different in Australian slang!

It is beyond the scope of this book to cover all aspects of international expansion. It is enough of a statement of the obvious to say that the principles of research, planning and training in advance must be applied.

Why can't companies drive their own organic growth?

It is all a question of focus. In small companies, no one is specifically tasked with business development, because all hands are on deck fulfilling the needs of existing customers, so cold calling is neglected. A bit of ad hoc activity such as mailings and networking does enough. Hiring someone to do business development is high risk. They are burdened with high expectations and the length of the sales cycle in B2B is such that they are constantly struggling to justify their salary check.

Medium-sized companies have a similar problem. Salespeople with territories have other things to do and cold calling is hard and potentially demotivating. Since most companies are under pressure to retain customers as well, working on retention has a higher priority. In-house telesales teams may provide leads, but given long sales cycles, prospects are inclined to complain that salespeople do not follow up or maintain contact persistently enough.

In larger companies, salespeople may feel that their hands are tied by internal politics. New salespeople may have been starved of leads by insecure senior colleagues, or be reporting to multiple managers whose rivalry is causing disruption, lost time and lost opportunities. With information not being shared, because information is power, prospective relationships are neglected because the right people are not developing contact with the customer. Dysfunctional things happen in sales departments. Academics call it "anti-citizenship behavior". Instead of working for the good of the company, salespeople begin to work for their own narrow interests because that is what everyone else appears to be doing.

Clearly, an astute VP Sales would nip such problems in the bud. But if you are a VP Sales inheriting a dysfunctional sales department with demotivated staff, feuding managers and a plummeting top line, you need a turnaround option. In order to get the top line moving in the right direction again, outsourcing is a viable option.

Outsourcing can also go wrong and you should not think of it as a quick fix to developing prospective relationships. Without the right brief, the right targets, the right relationship with you as a client and the right incentives, an agency will not succeed. As ever, research, planning and thinking space are required to build for the long term.

Without the right brief, the right targets, the right relationship with you as a client and the right incentives, an agency will not succeed.

Common mistakes in developing prospective relationships

There are many factors to balance when determining the best strategies. First, you must avoid setting "headcount" targets that focus salespeople on acquiring any business at any cost. Too often, such activity-based targets result in a fall in both revenues and profits. Even worse, they lead to an attrition of the best salespeople and begin a death spiral from which the salesforce may never recover (Rackham and Ruff, 1991).

We use the relationship development box to focus investment of scarce resources on acquiring new accounts where we believe that there is development potential for the long term. Although some new relationships may slip into the tactical box, the general view is that investment should focus on those heading for the strategic box. Focusing on the quality of prospective relationship is important, and measures must be found to reflect that.

Another common dilemma is the balance between recognizing the customer's need to minimize the risks of trying you – or switching to you – as a supplier, and recognizing that price offers are associated with lower customer lifetime values. Assistance with switching could be the provision of practical services rather than discount. It is also possible that the expectation of a better business relationship will overcome switching risk. What appears to be a price-driven situation may be more complex.

Price or relationship?

A survey of 109 companies who had recently changed their auditors found that the level of audit fee was the most frequently cited reason for going out to tender. Nevertheless, there were subsidiary factors affecting the decision, such as the influence of investors in the business or reorganization. Expectation of a reduced fee was not a top priority in selecting new firms to tender. And in choosing the new audit firm, the relationship between senior audit firm personnel and key company decision-makers was more important than the range of services.

Source: Beattie and Fearnley (1998)

Special training for salespeople and other staff working directly on prospective relationship development can be helpful in identifying the switching assistance that will preserve the long-term interests of both parties. In the study in Thailand mentioned earlier, the researchers noted a tendency for start-up companies to offer better prices than international companies, but it was really "state-of-the-art" knowledge that customers wanted and proof of their expertise might have had more leverage potential.

Overzealous pursuit of completely new business is also a weakness in many companies. In addition to the contacts of the Chief Executive, other colleagues and current customers, a rich source can also be found in former customers and unconverted past enquiries. Past enquiries may just have been distracted or may have taken longer than expected to allocate budget to solving a problem.

Former customers may be a higher risk call. Nevertheless, I have heard of salespeople going back to customers who had stopped doing business with their company owing to poor performance, and showing enough humility to get the purchasing manager interested. Sometimes, fortune favors the brave.

Conclusion

Every company needs to be proactive in developing prospective relationships with potential customers and new customers. Although organic growth is an ambition of most companies, it is surprisingly difficult to find companies that consistently achieve it. Of course, sometimes companies need to consolidate past growth, and it is the prerogative of entrepreneurs and company directors to decide if they think a company has reached its optimum size. But change is constant, so even a relatively stable company needs new customers to counteract the risk of losing existing ones.

There are a number of options available to you as a sales manager to ensure that your relationship portfolio has a healthy variety of prospective relationships in development. If ever it seems particularly difficult, consider that most agencies specializing in this area believe that many of the leads they generate for clients fade away because of lack of follow-up. It is therefore your responsibility to set the pace. In business-to-consumer (B2C) markets, the likelihood of converting leads from a direct response advertisement fades with every delay in call-backs and arranging appointments. The same is true in business-to-business. Prospective relationship development requires sustained effort, careful resource allocation, administrative support and the direction of a wise VP Sales.

6

Tactical relationships: the power of low touch

"From a standing start we quickly became the client's top sales team. We made 140% of target, carrying on doing the job through a period of immense change for them. Our remit changed four times in three years."

Mike Smith, Director, Tennyson, Chichester
Quoted with kind permission

We noted in Chapter 3 that the drive for low-touch or no-touch transactional buying has been with us for some years. Since Rackham and de Vincentis noted this in *Rethinking the Salesforce* in 1998, evidence has been growing that suppliers must do something to make it easy for customers to deal with them transactionally.

Peter Drucker (1955) defined tactical decisions as one-dimensional: "The situation is given and the requirements are evident. The only problem is to find the most economical adaptation of known resources."

You, the supplier, are a known resource to many customers who have a tactical decision to make about a low-priority purchase. You need to ensure that you are the most economical option for those customers, and that you are focusing on reducing the cost of the transaction to protect your own profitability.

Customers who buy transactionally are likely to see sales calls as an expensive waste of their time. The Head of Purchasing in a logistics company explained to a colleague, "When you consider the salary and overhead cost to us at the receiving end of a sales call, we are paying an average of $500 every time we agree to see a salesperson. Why should we pay all that to listen to a talking brochure when we already know what we want and the price we are prepared to pay for it?"

Being pragmatic about transactional relationships is a difficult task for a supplier. The temptation to offer service in return for higher status as a supplier is very strong, but it is not the best way to compete for the business of customers who are focused on reducing their costs and managing the associated risk themselves. Recognizing that these relationships do not justify salespeople's time can persuade the sales manager to ignore them completely, which also proves to be problematic. If all tactically oriented customers defected, many opportunities for profitable tactical business would be lost. The customer portfolio would be skewed toward large customers which, as Piercy and Lane have suggested, could be a strategic weakness.

The temptation to offer service in return for higher status as a supplier is very strong, but it is not the best way to compete for the business of customers who are focused on reducing their costs and managing the associated risk themselves.

It may sound contradictory to talk about "developing" tactical relationships, since the buyer does not want a relationship with the supplier. However, if the product is satisfactory and the service is very convenient, buyers may choose to habitually purchase from a particular supplier. Changing supplier every time the stationery cupboard needs restocking is not without switching costs or the potential for hassle. Therefore, by ensuring that the service is convenient, strategically minded sales managers can "develop" the potential of business with transactionally focused customers.

"Low-touch" options to satisfy transactional relationships

Other colleagues helping the customer to buy

"Order taker" is a term of abuse to salespeople, but to delivery drivers it may be a matter of pride to take responsibility for collecting orders from regular customers. It can make their job more interesting. In the UK, according to government research, for every person who says that they are a full-time salesperson, there are another three who say that selling is part of their job.

Like many companies, you may have a lot of customers on the database of whom you know very little, because their level of business is low. But they do receive goods occasionally or need services. It would not annoy them too much if a trusted engineer suggested a product upgrade.

Who in your organization might accept some selling tasks? Utilities companies encourage their engineers to talk to customers about additional products and services when they make maintenance calls; banks encourage staff in their branches to refer small business customers to new products and services. Auditors and consultants help customers to buy additional services from their companies. (A UK auditing firm won a national sales training award for its "helping customers to buy" development program.) Let's not pretend that delivery drivers, engineers, bankers or auditors want to become salespeople. They would hate the idea. Nevertheless, with training and reward, the inclination to think creatively about how their employer might otherwise help its customers can be nurtured.

Working with distributors or resellers

Despite a great deal of hype in the last few years about disintermediation of supply chains, distributors and resellers are alive and well. Some are very well known for their skill at providing services to producers and their customers. The idea of "sticking to your knitting" is a good one. If you are excellent at producing widgets, focus on producing widgets and let a distributor focus on getting your excellent widgets to the general marketplace.

Distributors, at the very least, "break bulk" for producers, transforming large quantities of product into the batch sizes that end-customers or retailers want. They may also mix them into assortments with other producers' products. They take on risks associated with stockholding and physical distribution. They also provide services to customers in terms of meeting their needs for convenience, e.g. specific delivery times, or even technical support. Distributors and agents may also have relationship levels with smaller customers that large producers could not sustain, particularly if they are expanding geographically and need help adapting to the cultures in their new locations.

Working with distributors to access a new market

In 2000, the market leader in high-horsepower generators in India was only a bit player in the low-horsepower market. Small retailers and farmers needed generators, because power outages were common. Each segment needed slightly different features, and the company could not afford to meet these needs directly. They developed lower-power engines with customization sets and supplied them to third-party distributors, who would fix the right feature to the engine per customer need. In this way, a hospital could have an adaptation to reduce noise, and a farmer could have an adaptation to protect the engine from dirt. By 2004, the market leader in high-horsepower generators also had 40% of the market for low-horsepower generators.

Source: Seely Brown (2005)

It is not just producers who need intermediaries. The IT industry has become a predominantly service-oriented business. Because of issues of scope, large players in the industry still need business partners. Even though software could be downloaded with a quick click, support is needed to implement it. Indirect sales account for more than 50% of revenue in high-tech sectors. Original Equipment Manufacturers invest in lead generation, partner portals, training, co-marketing and process integration to help to grow their top line with value chain partners (Schultze, 2004).

There are risks in working with intermediaries. Sales managers worry about channel conflict, because it undoubtedly wastes a lot of time, confuses the customer and undermines profitability as purchasers play the partner off against the direct channel (salespeople or Internet). Sa Vinhas and Anderson (2005) conducted some in-depth research in US and European companies and identified that there are circumstances in which channel partnering is not advisable. In low-growth markets, where opportunities are few, concurrent channels will pursue the same prospects and come into conflict. Where products are completely standardized, channels conflict, because the partner cannot add value to the customer.

However hard you try to prevent it, channels will fight. As one Director of Channels put it, "on a good day it's minor skirmishes, the rest of the time it's war". For many years the conventional wisdom for managing channel conflict was to set clear boundaries between channels to separate them as much as possible. Channels were separated by customer size, by product, by geography, by industry or by the old first bite principle of "Hands off! It's mine! I saw it first!". Setting up a clear set of channel allocation rules seems sensible enough and it also makes good economic sense. However, the idea has suffered from one minor disadvantage: it hasn't worked.

Left to themselves, customers have an inconvenient tendency to choose exactly the channels in which you least want them, and they refuse to be allocated to channels of the supplier's choosing. They expect channel choice. An increasing number of studies by McKinsey and others have shown that those companies that restrict the channel choices available to their customers end up with fewer customers and with a lower spend per customer. While it makes logical sense from a supplier's point of view to minimize conflict and interchannel fighting by keeping channels separate and watertight, it makes no sense to the customer.

Reducing channel conflict by building channel silos has made it difficult for customers to choose and move between their preferred channels. Increasingly, companies have abandoned the old rules of channel separation and, instead, looked for new ways to encourage cooperation between their channels. Today's sales managers can no longer treat channels as someone else's problem. To be effective, they must actively work with multiple channels.

Strong brands can reduce channel conflict. Resellers' customers value having "original equipment manufacturer" brands in the assortment on offer to them. But there are other practical ways in which producers can reduce the potential for channel conflict. In order to ensure clarity and reduce the potential for conflict, it is advisable for you as a sales manager to have close enough relationships with distributors and resellers to develop an understanding of each other's goals and common goals. Alongside that, Sa Vinhas and Anderson (2005) noted that differentiating the offering per channel was helpful. Having "rules of engagement" up front, rather than sorting out problems after conflict has arisen, was also valuable. And last, but not least, if you want to avoid channel conflict, reward all parties that participate in a sale. Although that sounds expensive, generating teamwork between direct

Generating teamwork between direct routes to market and channel partners looks good to the customer and does raise the probability of winning the business.

routes to market and channel partners looks good to the customer and does raise the probability of winning the business.

Table 6.1 gives a useful summary, based on the long experience of someone with sales management experience in an OEM and in its channel.

Table 6.1 *Comparing channel conflict and harmony.**

Cause of channel conflict	Policy for channel harmony
Territory wars with salespeople caused by a sales plan that rewards your salespeople only when channel partners are not involved.	Ensure teamwork between direct sales and your channel partners by designing team rewards.
Treating channel reward as an after-thought and squeezing it when the economy turns down. If you can't set a price that rewards the channel and represents value to the customer, you have a very commoditized product.	You should have looked at e-channels for shifting your tin. Work with channels where they can add service value to the customer and to you as a supplier.
Changing your channel strategy every year – and springing surprises. If your channel partners have invested in aligning their business to yours, they are not going to be happy with frequent changes.	If changes are needed, ensure a smooth migration.
Being precious about strategic accounts. You can't insist on a "no go" area for your strategic accounts, since channel partners are independent businesses.	Find ways to involve channel partners in key account teams.
Make it complicated No one likes complexity or bureaucracy. If your rules have the potential to deny or delay rewards to channel partners operating on tight margins, you could kill their businesses.	Keep channel management processes simple.
Offer no-support deals Tempting a partner with higher rewards to forego technical support seems like a quick win. But the customer at the receiving end of this game may suffer, and the product has got your logo on it.	Don't go there.
Inconsistent attitude to partners Some people think that channels are great, some people resent them. The channel partner does not know which person he is going to talk to when he calls.	Know why you are using channel partners and explain it to everybody who will be working with them. Encourage positive attitudes.

* Design based on an interview with Peter Bartlett of ValueCare Partners and reproduced with his kind permission.

Manufacturers' representatives

Since working with distributors can in itself be a relationship management challenge and requires the recruitment of "Partner Managers" for transactional business, further delegation may be desirable. In the USA, it is common for smaller producers to offer their products to the distributor/retailer market via manufacturers' representatives. These sales organizations employ staff who travel to distributors and retailers presenting products from a variety of manufacturers. They also provide field merchandising and store audit services, ensuring excellent feedback reports to their clients to support demand planning.

The justification for having an in-house sales team rather than using representatives is driven by breakeven analysis. But Ross, Dalsace and Anderson (2005) found that companies usually underestimate the value that external representatives provide. They noted a number of flawed assumptions in common cost models. For example, the costs of the direct salesforce are usually calculated without consideration of hidden administration costs, such as office space, time spent in meetings and vacations. The time cost of money is also overlooked – a directly employed salesperson starts costing money from Day 1, a manufacturer's representative does not get paid until sales are made.

The costs of the direct salesforce are usually calculated without consideration of hidden administration costs, such as office space, time spent in meetings and vacations.

The outsourcing option is usually costed without consideration of the financial benefits of better coverage of sales territories, the quality of selling effectiveness and the value of the representative's existing customer relationships. If you buy into a representative's existing customer base, the risk can be reduced. One of the market leaders in the USA has a multilingual telesales service that can reach 30,000 independent grocers across the continent.

Writing in *Strategy+Business*, consultants Landry and Pendrangi (2005) recommend a "syndicated" approach to medium-sized companies, using representatives for coverage and specific campaigns but also employing in-house staff to service large customers. They point out that agents can provide good management information such as feedback on consumer demand and retailer preferences.

For many smaller producers, especially in fast-moving consumer goods and associated sectors, controllability and predictability of costs in serving tactical customers are extremely important. Manufacturers' representatives are an attractive option. They let you avoid the risk of having too many salespeople or not enough. They can supplement your in-house team or provide part-time help.

They can also help you to avoid other risks. The average tenure of a field sales professional is five years in Europe and even less in Asia and North America, so most companies employ some new salespeople every year. Inexperienced salespeople can cost you money in their first few months (Cummings, 2004). They need time to become acquainted with the paperwork, the product or service they are selling, and the values of the company. In that time, they may make costly mistakes. Even if you recruit for work ethic and personality rather than industry experience, you would need to start new salespeople with monthly goals and ensure close mentoring.

In Asia, sales agents can play a similar role to the manufacturer's representative. A great deal of business is done on the basis of relationships (a system known as guanxi in China), and finding the best-connected agents is worth the considerable effort.

A great deal of business is done on the basis of relationships (a system known as guanxi in China), and finding the best-connected agents is worth the considerable effort.

The manufacturer's representative model is virtually unknown in Europe, but agencies do exist to help market entries into new countries where there are language and cultural barriers, and the emergence of sales outsourcing agencies is helping companies of all sizes to achieve flexibility in achieving top-line growth.

Outsourcing tactical relationships to a telephone account management agency

Outsourcing agencies claim to provide improved performance for their clients, not least because they can focus on the prospects or customers that the client has found difficult to serve.

Choosing a suitable outsourcing agency requires a great deal of concentrated research and discussion. Factors such as shared goals and willingness to partner should be considered. Achieving satisfaction is difficult for both parties, even where benefits can be proven. It is still common to have day-to-day operational problems, and outsourcing call centers can introduce new risks. In 2005 consultants Booz Allen Hamilton highlighted the reputational risk of data security violations that had blighted some US companies when they outsourced customer service processes. We might also note that offshore outsourcing of telephone communications has resulted in a backlash from employees, customers and local media (Anon., 2005b).

The outsourcing of particular categories of customer to agencies is a developing phenomenon. Some large corporates outsource their small company customers to telephone account management companies. This provides an alternative to using value-added reseller/channel partners to serve smaller customers, or recruiting an in-house team. With an outsourcer, you as VP Sales can keep brand control, behavior control and maintain your view of the customer (by sharing database information). You also have to give the agency some levers. They need some influence in customer service to be able to track and follow up sales activity.

With an outsourcer, you as VP Sales can keep brand control, behavior control and maintain your view of the customer (by sharing database information).

Telephone account executives in agencies have to be boundary-spanners between three sets of interests: the agency that is their employer, you as the client and your customer. It is of particular importance to you as the client that the agency staff can identify with your brand values. It is also important to establish that they are well-trained, accomplished salespeople. In theory, it is possible to enjoy flexibility of sales resource with an outsourcing company, while maintaining strategic and cost control. It is also possible in practice, but requires a proactive approach and agreement on cooperative goals.

In-house telesales

In-house telesales is also a route you could consider.

Telesales at Avaya

Before 2004, Avaya serviced its routine accounts through field sales and partners. Recognizing that they needed to achieve better coverage more cost-effectively, and to offer customers more choices, a telesales team was set up. This integrated coverage strategy yielded 40% of revenue through telesales, thereby creating a significant improvement in sales productivity of the field sales reps and partners, as well as increasing overall revenue and improving customer satisfaction. An in-house telesales team can also provide focused sales support to account managers working on strategic relationships.

Source: Information used with kind permission from Avaya

Global spend on call centers exceeds $300 billion (Gilson and Khandelwal, 2005). The companies that get most out of their call centers observe three critical success factors:

- *Having a customer service strategy that is not focused entirely on low cost* – If you overconcentrate on cost, it can have undesirable secondary effects. For example, if you encourage call handlers to get rid of callers by measuring them on average handling time, you can alienate the customer and eliminate the call-handler's opportunity to sell additional products. Training in improved sales technique would be a better investment.
- *Pragmatic use of technology* – One of the reasons that call centers continue to frustrate callers is that new technology is continually introduced and as companies try to install it, it has unanticipated knock-on effects on processes and the customer experience. Once the call center has been successfully integrated into the company systems, disruption should be approached very cautiously. Constant change can be confusing and irritating to customers. Continuous improvement is desirable, but as a sales manager you need to make sure that improving the customer experience is at the forefront of every change.
- *Investing in coaching and performance management for call center agents* – The average turnover of call center agents is 33%, and the average cost

of recruiting and training a new agent is $15,000. Coaching in the agent's first few months appears to have a positive effect on their length of time in the job, so it saves cost in the long run and can improve customer service (Gilson and Khandelwal, 2005).

A thought to consider about your telesales team is whether they are just call handlers, answering any random call as it is received, or whether your technology will facilitate telephone account management. Even if they are account managing 100 accounts, a regular relationship between an individual and customers can be satisfying to both.

A major manufacturer in the USA set up telephone account management in the late 1990s for customers who asserted that they did not have time to meet salespeople. Volume in those accounts increased by 69%, as the telephone account managers were able to maintain a higher level of contact with the customers that was less intrusive than a visit (Francis, 2001).

Doing business over the telephone is very acceptable for customers looking for a "low-touch" approach from suppliers. High telephone usage was driven by cheaper, better and faster connections. Cheaper, better and faster Internet technology has driven another revolution for the selling environment – transaction-seekers want to do business on-line.

Web-based relationships

Customers never complain about things happening too quickly. Customers who prefer web-based business transactions with suppliers do so because of the degree of control that it offers to them, and because the needs they are seeking to fulfill are straightforward and possibly quite urgent. By automating processes spanning different internal and external systems, transactions can be handled immediately, and up-to-date information should be constantly available. Customer self-service via an Extranet (also known as a portal) can virtually eliminate order entry errors, and it is possible to reduce overheads and satisfy customers by enabling them to track their orders.

Customers never complain about things happening too quickly.

Researching "ease-of-use"

An office supplies company conducted extensive usability studies when upgrading their website to encourage more on-line buying. Employees sat with customers in their offices and observed the way they used the site. They also asked them to sort the products on offer into logical "buckets". This enabled them to reduce office supplies and technology categories by about 20% each. The web was the channel of choice for customers in a hurry, so finding products easily was essential. The research enabled them to reduce "average time to locate" by two seconds. The redesigned site offered choice without overload, and eliminated clutter. An "easy reorder" feature was also introduced.

Source: Bannan (2005).

To deliver shorter lead-times, error-proof sales administration, responsive pricing and 24/7 up-to-date information is a challenge, but it is one that many companies are meeting. Many customer relationship management and supply chain management software providers are able to help their customers to achieve it. An alternative to packages and bespoke programming could be "agile computing" solutions that can integrate data across separate systems to accelerate internal value chains. If a supplier makes itself "easy to do business with", then transactional buyers will be satisfied, and costs can be designed out of that relationship. Of course, faster and cheaper must also mean better; but making bad processes faster is a risk.

Your website designers have to learn from Internet pioneers such as Amazon, who constantly innovate to incorporate new technology that keeps the customer interested.

Researchers Clarke and Flaherty (2003) noted three critical success factors for suppliers offering customer portals for on-line business. Each customer must be able to customize the portal so that they can design access and pathways that meet their particular needs. This element of convenience could generate a degree of loyalty.

Web-based customer portals must also be flexible, so that they can accommodate new technology easily and introduce new value-added services frequently. Although it seems very obvious, you also need to note that a portal must contain relevant and timely information! In the early stages of the Internet, companies were persuaded by agencies to embrace striking visual effects on websites. In more recent years, marketers have accepted what some web experts have called "undesign", to make websites simpler and more focused on the information needs of users.

Using web-based exchange sites

> **On-line exchange in healthcare**
>
> In 1987 in the USA, the first website was launched to enable hospitals to purchase supplies from several companies and to save administration costs for both suppliers and customers. There are now three exchange sites for medical supplies, including Global Healthcare Exchange, who achieved $25,500 of business in 2000, and by 2005 was handling $6.48 million. More than 50% of hospitals in the USA use an exchange.
>
> *Source:* Perrin and Conway (2005)

Something you can learn from B2C on-line commerce is the importance of communities of interest. The early days of the Internet saw the emergence of business exchange sites, some of which were discontinued or sold. The French company DDP launched the first European platform for electronic commerce, CitiusNet, in 1992. By 1995, the company was able to go global. In 1999, a new market entrant called Mondus was set up to provide a marketplace specifically for small companies to post requests for proposals to potential suppliers (Jelassi and Enders, 2005).

The concept of a global, virtual, multisector market enabling large numbers of suppliers and customers to interface was attractive. Joining an exchange could have enormous benefits for suppliers. You can reach companies that you would not otherwise have been able to service, saving considerably on marketing costs. You can buy into an existing IT infrastructure instead of building your own, and your customers can then buy from you more conveniently, reducing their administration costs.

Besides general supplier–customer exchanges, there are industry-specific exchanges. Covisint was set up by Ford, General Motors and Daimler Chrysler in February 2000 to be a supplier exchange for the automotive industry. The Federal Trade Commission investigated Covisint in March 2000, because legislators had concerns about the concentrated purchasing power of the major automotive firms. The European Commission followed suit. Despite the short delay, Covisint became a legal entity in December 2000, aiming to bring supply chain cost savings of $1,064 per vehicle to the industry, and offering facilities for on-line catalogs, on-line bidding events, quote management and asset management for selling scrap machinery (Jelassi and Enders, 2005). It has stood the test of time.

At the time of writing, Covisint is used by 30,000 companies in 96 countries and has expanded into the healthcare sector. But Covisint has its rivals, including Germany-based SupplyOn.com (8,500 companies in 30 countries) and general exchanges. Does a supplier have to join multiple exchanges? Some commentators expect that two leaders will emerge in most sectors, and membership of the top exchanges will be a "hygiene factor" in some industry sectors.

Rask and Kragh (2004) conducted extensive research covering 20 industries in 12 countries on the motivations for suppliers and buyers in joining exchanges. The buyers who join e-marketplaces have an "efficiency" motive. Getting lower prices is part of that, but identifying more potential suppliers and reducing the time and cost involved in procurement are also important. Suppliers are primarily driven by a "positioning" motive, a perceived need to be there in order to be competitive. "Legitimacy" is another important reason – they are there because some existing customers require them to be in their preferred e-marketplace.

Exchanges have their risks. Clearly the FTC had concerns in the early days of exchanges that some could become anti-competitive. Also in the early stages, many exchanges just failed or were absorbed into others. If you are hoping to improve your quantity of sales over an exchange you should also be aware that some are very focused on price competition. Customers posting requests for proposals often expect bidders to compete in reverse auctions, and you may not want your pricing to be transparent in that way.

Some more Web considerations

Whether developing your own site or joining exchanges, your company needs to have clear objectives for the web channel in terms of sales, profit, customer satisfaction and its relative efficiency compared to other channels (Chaffey, 2000). Some companies, such as Dow, have chosen to sub-brand their Internet channel to ensure that it focuses on its separate strategic objectives.

If you want it to improve sale performance, marketing will be needed to encourage customers to use the site for specific needs. It is widely expected that Internet business should be more profitable per transaction, but what is the knock-on effect? Banks found that the more their customers used Internet banking the smaller and more frequent their transactions became. If you have not retained distributor relationships to fulfill on-line orders, you have the cost of physically transporting the goods to the customer, perhaps in smaller, more frequent batches.

It is widely expected that Internet business should be more profitable per transaction, but what is the knock-on effect?

You need to pay attention to what the user wants. Simple design, relevant and straightforward content, ease-of-use, easy navigation, quick links, up-to-date information, responsiveness, security and privacy are all taken for granted. Customization, such as the helpful recommendations based on previous purchases provided by Amazon, is appreciated, and individualized customer portals are more welcoming. Of course, the beauty of technology is that if you want to track a customer's average path length, log-on frequency, page duration, page revisit frequency, etc., the analytical engine behind the website will do it for you.

You also need to pay attention to what legislators want. A website needs to be compliant with a diverse variety of laws from trade description acts to access for disabled people. Content management is essential, but can also stifle creativity and flexibility. You not only need to manage your content carefully, but protect it from corruption by hackers. If you thought salespeople were difficult to manage, a website can give you just as many headaches. Make sure that you hire a responsive information systems manager or e-commerce agency!

Using multiple channels to develop tactical relationships

Using multiple channels has many advantages in terms of coverage and customer choice. It also has the potential to generate conflict, between field sales and resellers, and between channel partners and direct telesales or web teams. Using the relationship portfolio to segment customers according to the nature of their desired relationship with you as a supplier is one step toward solving the problem. Beyond that, further segmentation may be achieved on the basis of their preferred channel. Customers will still switch from channel to channel, even within the same transaction, so a sophisticated customer relationship management system is necessary so that there is a single view of the customer accessible to all relevant personnel. A single comprehensive view of the customer's information can save a great deal of frustration for both supplier and customer.

Customers will still switch from channel to channel, even within the same transaction, so a sophisticated customer relationship management system is necessary so that there is a single view of the customer accessible to all relevant personnel.

An analytical engine ensuring that the customer gets the right promotional offers and information to enable them to make the most out of new channels is also essential. As multi-channel marketing expert Professor Hugh Wilson comments: "If a new channel proposition, whether revolutionary or evolutionary – is in the customers' interests, then it will happen sooner or later." He goes on to say that whether you are first to introduce a new channel – or a fast follower – may be debated, but you should not be much later than that.

Customer choice is important. Multichannel customers may spend as much as 20–30% more money than single-channel customers (Myers, Pickersgill and Van Metre, 2004). The downside, as we have noted earlier, is that incentives are necessary to keep all channels on board with transition. When a supplier of machine parts wanted to focus salespeople on prospective and strategic relationships, they were asked to train all customers on the Internet channel, so that tactical business was not lost. Salespeople were paid commission on sales regardless of the channel chosen by the customer. E-commerce sales boomed and the company gained market share (Myers,

Pickersgill and Van Metre, 2004). Savings were made, since salespeople were traveling less, and the top-line improvement was worth the incentive for the salespeople to change.

It works the other way, too. Dell, having been born as an Internet channel, soon found that they needed to recruit account managers to develop relationships with large customers.

The role of marketing communications in tactical relationships

Marketers may breathe a sigh of relief at the prospect of designing campaigns aimed at customers with transactions in mind. It may bring waves of nostalgia about the easy days of one-way messages, broadcast through the mass media to lots of people who needed to buy. Unfortunately, it is not so easy. Let's start with the messages. A message to customers who want to engage with you as a supplier at a transactional level must still be consistent with other messages going out to other customers. Brand values must not be eroded by activity in this quadrant.

The choice of media is problematic because of the fragmentation of the media across innumerable trade magazines and websites. And who needs to buy? Do you advertise to purchasing professionals, technical decision-makers, personal assistants or accountants? They all have choices and preferences, and the option to do nothing.

Tactical relationships are not reinforced daily at multiple touch-points like your strategic relationships, so they certainly need marketing support. The role of marketing communications is to differentiate, reinforce, inform and persuade (Fill, 2006), and you need to work with marketing to ensure that the messages and methods do that. You should be in regular discussions with your marketing colleagues about planning communication programs aimed at tactical relationships, and monitoring responses.

Making channel choices

We have already discussed how important it is in this quadrant of your relationship portfolio to control costs. If we look at Figure 6.1, we have a

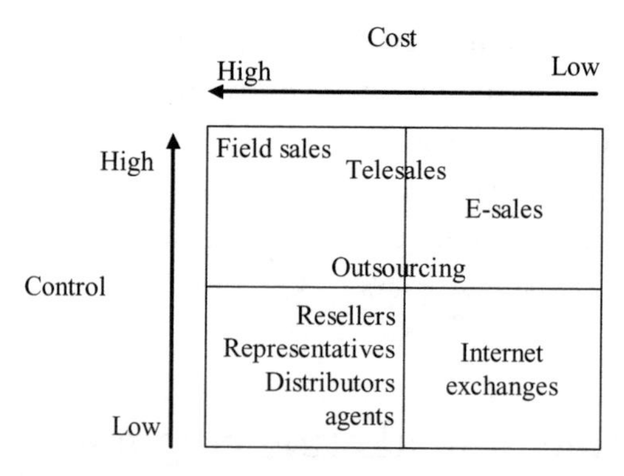

Figure 6.1 *Trade-off between cost and control.*

trade-off between lowest cost and control of the channel. In order to provide the easiest convenience for the customer, you will probably have to provide a combination of channels (e.g. order on-line and pick up from a reseller). When multiple channels are engaged, conflict has to be managed, usually by duplicate compensation, unless together with your colleagues in marketing and operations you can significantly differentiate the offer per channel. So what should a shrewd VP Sales do?

Your choices may depend on the nature of your industry, local business culture, or the size of your company. For example, a student from Martinique – a very small economy in the Caribbean – found in his research that while the use of IT was important for record-keeping, personal contact was still essential for doing any kind of business. Whatever context you have to work with, just ensure that you respect the principles of low-touch and least waste.

When do tactical relationships change?

There are a number of trigger points that you should feed into whatever system or systems you design to service tactical customers (see Kalyanam and Zweben, 2005). You need to know when a tactical customer purchases a new category of goods. That might mean that the customer's business is changing, or that the purchaser trusts your brand.

Building strategic relationships

Significant increases in volume are also of interest – is the customer growing very rapidly? I once interviewed a sales manager who had been approached by an accounts clerk pointing out that a certain customer kept exceeding their credit limit. He authorized her to make a visit to the customer with a sales representative to discuss the cause. It turned out that the customer was a relatively young company (therefore not highly rated by credit agencies), but growing very quickly. The purchasing manager offered to single source with that supplier if they would extend his credit limit. They did and a strategic relationship was born.

Equally, a drop in volume, whether sudden or gradual, is worth investigating. Perhaps the customer's business is changing or perhaps the purchasing manager has lost patience with poor service but has not reported it.

A change of contact name or company address should also be a trigger to talk to the customer in person. The new contact may not want to do business with you, or the new location may make delivery more challenging. In the latter case, you might want to negotiate your exit from the relationship.

Conclusion

Tactical relationships can be a source of opportunity for you as a supplier, and provide mutual value with a group of customers you might otherwise lose to competition. Few companies are big enough to constantly drive down their production costs, but sales can make a contribution to company profitability by working with marketing and IT colleagues to develop lower-cost channels for doing transactional business with customers. As with any strategic change, doing your own detailed research first will help you to make the right decisions. And remember not to trap small, occasional customers in channel silos. They may grow and need the flexibility to move to a different quadrant of the matrix.

7

Cooperative relationships

Cooperate (of things) – "to concur in producing an effect"

Oxford English Dictionary

What is a cooperative business relationship?

In Chapter 3 we defined "cooperative relationships" as those where your customer values you as a supplier, but the customer's value to you is low or medium. A typical cooperative relationship is one in which a supplier is providing parts and maintenance for a customer's obsolete piece of equipment. The customer is delighted that the equipment can be kept working, but maintaining old technology is non-strategic for the supplier.

Suppliers may also be caught in unprofitable cooperative relationships early in the product life cycle, particularly where a new and untested product has problems. A manufacturer of plastic pipes introduced a new material that was highly corrosion resistant and seemed ideal for making elbow joints that connected networks of pipes together. In the first few months it sold joints based on the new material to several customers, not realizing that the new material had poor flexibility and was inclined to crack. The use of more expensive raw materials solved the problem, but the supplier was locked into several long-term fixed cost supply contracts. Customers were happy, having gained preferential pricing, but the supplier barely broke even as a result.

Another common reason for a supplier to see less value in the relationship lies in geography. Customers who are on the edge of a supplier's territory are more inconvenient and more expensive to serve. The security system in a colleague's office is maintained by a company 55 miles away, making them the farthest customer. "Couldn't we pay you to go with a competitor?" the salesperson asked, having discovered that her company was making a loss on looking after the installation.

Does "cooperative" always mean friendly?

Not necessarily. In a famous television quiz show, it is in the interests of the better contestants to vote off the contestants who answer questions wrongly because the more correct answers the better the prize fund. But, of course, there is only one winner, so the better contestants sometimes vote to eliminate a rival for the prize fund in an early round.

Does "cooperative" always mean friendly? Not necessarily.

Psychological researchers who have devised games to test people's instincts when cooperation is in their best interests find that it is not necessarily a comfortable place to be, and negotiations are not necessarily cordial. For example, take two prisoners who are told that if they cooperate one or both will escape, and if they do not cooperate, one or neither of them will escape. Either one of them might prefer to take his chance and act alone.

So we have to accept that cooperation is not necessarily comfortable, which is true of many business relationships. Continuation of those relationships works for both parties, but one or neither want to put a lot of effort into it. For your customer, the purchasing manager might see that they are in a "bottleneck" situation, feeling that even though you are good at what you do, they do not want to be stuck with you. Or maybe they feel in a strong enough position to bargain hard on price in return for volume or long-term contracts. As we have seen from the SCEB research discussed in Chapter 3, "the least profitable 20% of customers represent only 11% of volume of orders. But these are large orders – over 20 times the revenue of the average order, and they generate large losses." There is a correlation between size of order and lack of profitability.

You as a supplier may feel that the customer is worth keeping, but is not a candidate for strategic investment. Or perhaps things are not so definite.

Perhaps there are some business relationships in your portfolio that are simply "in limbo". Perhaps some will be invigorated by external events at some later stage and become strategic; others may slip into the tactical box over time (Figure 7.1).

Perhaps there are some business relationships in your portfolio that are simply "in limbo".

One of the most neglected topics in all that is written about buyer-seller relationships is the dysfunctional but essential relationship. Suppliers and customer can respond to the challenge of strategic and prospective relationships; they are indeed interesting and even exciting to work on. Being efficient in mutual tactical relationships also has its psychological satisfaction as results can be achieved in short timescales.

One of the most neglected topics in all that is written about buyer-seller relationships is the dysfunctional but essential relationship.

But when I give talks to salespeople starting their vocational studies, one of the most frequently asked questions is "What do we do about the relationships that aren't strategic to us, but the customer thinks they should be?" Every salesperson knows how dangerous this territory is. You cannot afford to invest lots of resource in a non-strategic relationship, but a customer that offers volume of business to keep marginal costs low, or long-term loyalty,

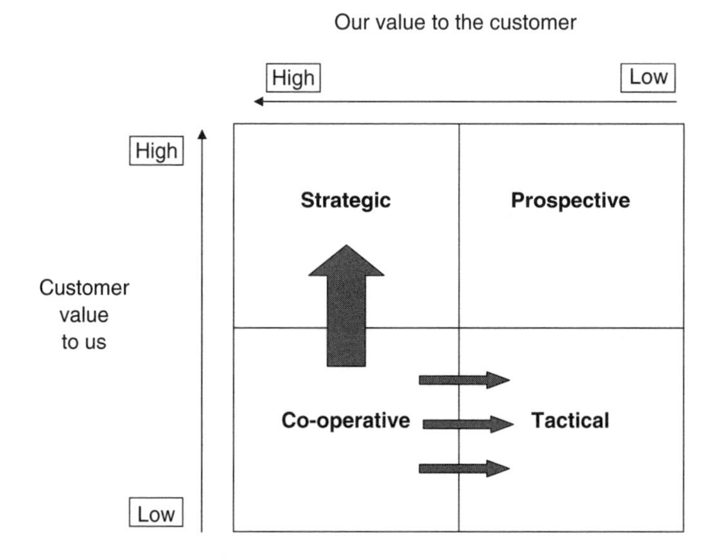

Figure 7.1 *The co-operative quadrant.*

is worth keeping. These relationships are often referred to as "keep" from the supplier's point of view, to distinguish them from "key". Purchasing professionals have the same dilemma. Remember the APQC benchmark research that shows that marginal returns diminish if you try to have too many strategic partnerships with suppliers.

But, does that mean that the box is wrong about the customer valuing us as a supplier? No. They value you as a supplier, but may not be prepared to behave in a way that makes them strategic to you. These interorganizational considerations can become tricky. Purchasing managers know that they can only afford to invest time and money in a few suppliers where joint product development or process integration yields returns. They need many other suppliers for different reasons. Contingency suppliers might be in the "tactical" box, but other suppliers are going to be needed every day. Their performance against core criteria might be admirable. But because the purchaser is putting you in the "manage risk" or "leverage" quadrant on their portfolio, they should not be strategic to you.

Distinguishing between "key" and "keep" is a factor of the objectivity of the "customer attractiveness factors" and scoring system chosen by the sales management team when designing their axis of the relationship development box. You perhaps might not like to admit that much of your business sits in that "cooperative" quadrant. But it does. Relationship development boxes tend to have a natural balance within them. When I have been working with companies on their boxes and they end up with too many key accounts, I make them park the other three quadrants and segment the "strategic" box into four to examine different degrees of "strategic" relationships (Figure 7.2).

The aim of the box is to help you to allocate scarce resources. So choices have to be made about "more strategic" and "less strategic", one way or another. When "keep" accounts are treated as "key" accounts, you open yourself up to waste and risk. If a customer wants lots of your product regularly but is not developing their use of it, or if they are price-obsessed about it, or if their business is in decline due to industry conditions, they are "keep" customers. There are also customers who want your product but also want to abuse their power as a large customer. They are also "keep" rather than "key".

Irish playwright Oscar Wilde said that "a man who knows the price of everything and the value of nothing" is a cynic. Of course, we all need

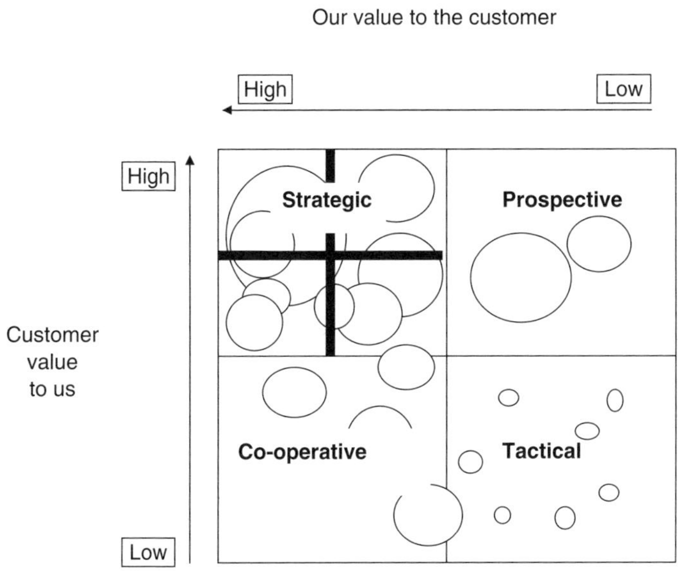

Figure 7.2 *Examining different degrees of "strategic" relationships.*

awareness in business in a way that makes us feel cynical at times. The awareness you need as a sales manager is that if the discussion with a customer never varies from price, you had better treat them as "cooperative" and watch the profitability of that relationship very carefully. Risking profit in prospective relationships is acceptable. Cooperative relationships should at least break even.

Who should manage cooperative accounts?

Cooperative relationships still require extremely careful account management approaches from a supplier. Account managers of "keep" accounts tend to feel that they have low status and that reflects on their status and career prospects. This should not be so. The person who interfaces with customers in cooperative relationships is doing an extremely important job. Some of these customers can be a delight to work with; they know that they are not going anywhere with your category of product, and are satisfied with good core product and service. They are perhaps the minority in this segment. It is almost inevitable that in the "cooperative" quadrant, we find the most potential for frustration and conflict between suppliers and customers. This is the box in which your large but adversarial customers must sit.

Each difficult situation probably requires a unique solution, which is why researchers find it difficult to study and make generalizations about cooperative relationships. Each relationship probably needs a different personality as an account manager – perhaps a project manager for cordial ones and a pragmatic negotiator for adversarial ones. The sales executive focused on a relationship in this category needs problems-solving training and a great deal of symbolic and tangible support from you as their sales manager. Boundary-spanning in a dysfunctional relationship is the most difficult thing that you can ask a salesperson to do. It is at best routine and at worst, very stressful. If you have an hour to spare for coaching at the year-end and you have a choice between spending it with the account manager in a strategic relationship or an account manager in a cooperative relationship, bear in mind that the person in the cooperative relationship is more likely to be scouring the job advertisements in January if you overlook their needs.

Boundary-spanning in a dysfunctional relationship is the most difficult thing that you can ask a salesperson to do. It is at best routine and at worst, very stressful.

Recognizing "cooperative" relationships

A traditional view of cooperative relationships between suppliers and customers would be that they are relationships that operate well at a basic level. The triadic balance of price, quality and delivery that you offer as a supplier is acceptable to the customer, perhaps even admired by the customer as the best in the buying category. The customer therefore classifies you as a preferred supplier, and contracts may be designed to last for a long period of time. Although there are frequent communications and exchanges of information, the customer maintains other sources of supply, or expects considerable discount for bulk or for length of contract.

That generally holds true, but there are subcategories in this relationship quadrant.

Cordial cooperative: "keep" suits us both

Some relationships may involve trust and single sourcing, but not be going anywhere. You cannot afford to invest resources in the customer, but the

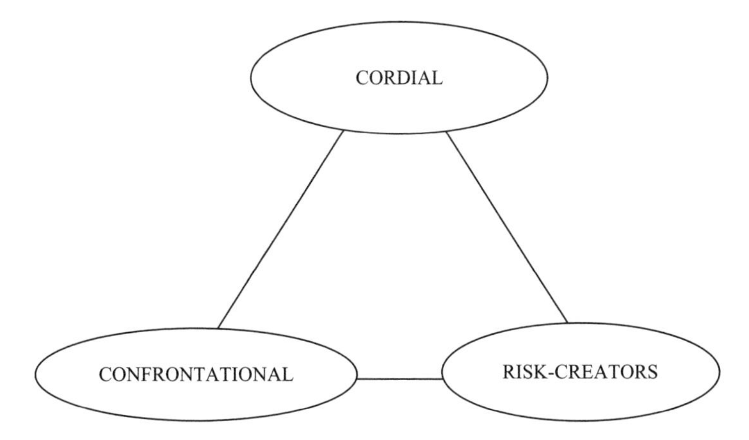

Figure 7.3 *Categories of co-operative.*

customer is confident in your capabilities and happy to have a regular relationship with your company. This may be a development of a tactical relationship that has progressed from random one-off transactions to regular business.

A risk in this kind of benign relationship is that it may drift into complacency. Often, because the relationship lacks conflict, it may become routine and salespeople may fail to uncover new opportunities. A study carried out in Kodak in the 1980s took a group of 45 accounts where salespeople assessed that, while the current level of business would continue, the accounts were "dead" in terms of profitable new opportunity. Interviews with customers showed that, in almost 40% of these accounts, significant new business opportunities existed. These had not been discovered by salespeople because the account was in the "keep" mode (Rackham, 1989).

One technical manager who was the main decision-maker in a buying category in a food company told me that he preferred one of his suppliers much more than their nearest rival, but he still occasionally bought from the rival to ensure competition. The product was very important, and he liked the service he received from the preferred supplier, but there were no opportunities for mutual strategic projects. It was a classical cooperative relationship. The customer is not necessarily generous, even in "keep suits us both".

Confrontational cooperative

Do you have any large customers who offer little by way of profitability or loyalty, but expect special service and investment? Who doesn't? These relationships are a fact of business life, and it seems as if they are particularly prevalent in the automotive and consumer goods demand chains. Consumers cannot have very cheap jeans and cars that last for years without some stresses and strains among the companies aligned to serve their needs.

These relationships are extremely difficult, and need to be constantly monitored because they operate on a cliff-edge in terms of return on investment. Some are bound to be unprofitable, at least at times. Some suppliers in manufacturing supply chains are used to relationships being unprofitable for many years before returns are realized, but the question of viability must always be raised with the aggressive large customer. At what point does doing business with them become a worse scenario than exiting the relationship? One textiles company that had been dealing with a retailer for many decades exited the relationship when the retailer was in decline and was negotiating very hard on price. Doing business at the price demanded was not worth it.

Risk creators

These are the most awkward of business relationships. How dare a customer come along and put your whole business at risk for the privilege of doing business with them? They dare because you want the volume they offer. Risk creation is usually present when large companies are dealing with smaller suppliers, and some customers purposefully generate high levels of supplier dependency. One British retailer had such a policy for decades, until they hit financial problems in the 1990s and rationalized their supplier base. Loyal suppliers had to resize rapidly when they lost the retailer's orders.

Customers can make unreasonable demands

Sometimes big customers give smaller suppliers little control over their business. One case study in the automotive industry examined how a large car company chose a supplier in a tendering process because of the superiority of their product, but then nominated the second- and third-tier suppliers that they were to use. The customer had instantly shown lack of trust in their new supplier, who assumed that the nomination of second- and third-tier suppliers was to ensure price transparency. The new supplier did not find it easy to deal with the suppliers nominated by the customer, finding that they withheld information and circumvented them in communications. The car manufacturer was also dual sourcing. The supplier felt that, despite their superior product, the customer was showing no trust or reciprocation. The company did adapt to working with that customer, but with a very close eye on the cost/benefit analysis.

Source: Johnsen and Ford (2005)

In summary . . .

The cooperative quadrant could be called the sales manager's headache – can't live with them, can't live without them. You can probably see how easily cooperative accounts can suck resource, especially management time, from strategic relationships. Your challenge is damage limitation. Give some time to the people issues, such as the stressed out account manager at the year-end. And remember to reach for your exit plan every time an unreasonable demand comes in, so that you can make a considered judgement about whether or not to continue the relationship.

How each customer scores on your attractiveness matrix will depend on how much you weight each attractiveness factor that is strategic to your company. I have noticed that weighting "partnership approach" and profitability reasonably highly tends to distinguish "key" from "keep" quite well.

How can "cooperative" relationships really work?

Cooperative relationships can work, and have a useful role in any portfolio. However, you should never forget that many suppliers have managed to survive when a big customer stopped doing business with them. It is all really a matter of risk management. Recognizing the risks inherent in these relationships means that they can be minimized and contingency plans can be put in place. Cooperative relationships may last a long time, but the expectation of exit or threat of exit is a more regular aspect of the supplier–buyer communications. Successful approaches to managing these relationships can be classified as reactive, wrestling match and balancing act.

Managing cordial cooperative: Reactive

Where the relationship between your company and your customer is cooperatively non-key, a reactive approach is one where business-as-usual is generally good enough, but extra response may be necessary at times of stress. The purchasing decision-makers in the customer recognize that their business is not the golden egg in your basket, but do rely on you fulfilling their contract terms effectively and cheaply.

In the Pearl River Delta in China, there are a number of clothing suppliers with large customers who do not necessarily make long-term strategic commitments to working with them. They focus on providing a good-quality standard for a low price and reliable delivery. They have strong local supply networks and focus on operational performance.

In order to operate a portfolio approach at all, suppliers need to identify what has been called a "lean backbone", a low-cost standard business model which reduces sales and general administration costs such as order-handling, delivery and invoicing and automates basic information exchange and customer service (Baumgartner, John and Naucler, 2005). Effectively that means that for cooperative relationships, you need to take your tactical business model and add to it some specific services.

A high volume cooperative relationship deserves some "high-touch" overlays, such as face-to-face contact with an experienced account manager. However, the account manager might have quite a number of customers to visit and be supported by what some companies call a "desk-based account manager" who provides telephone back-up to deal with customers' day-to-day needs.

A high volume cooperative relationship deserves some "high-touch" overlays, such as face-to-face contact with an experienced account manager.

Assuming that your company is operationally efficient, that should mean that the account manager who provides the personal contact in the relationship with a cooperatively "non-key" relationship would enjoy pleasant communications most of the time. However, their problem-solving skills will need to be finely tuned when things go wrong. You should have a robust complaints-handling process (see "Conflict resolution" in Chapter 8), but even a great process can be rather impersonal. The account manager needs to intervene and sort things out for the customer. Responsiveness will ensure that the relationship is kept.

A mature and steady account manager who is responsive and likable can handle this type of relationship. He or she needs to maintain good telephone contact, backed up by occasional visits. This conciliatory role may sound trivial, but it is important. In Japan, customers are greeted with a bow, shown respect, given a pleasant business atmosphere and treated to occasional social events, such as games of golf. It is all part of the supplier's obligation to provide the customer with "ashinkan" – peace of mind. The nice treatment of customers who are prepared to be nice in return is not optional in any culture. Many marginal relationships survive problems and suppress competition because buying decision-makers develop a certain amount of personal loyalty toward the account manager.

Many marginal relationships survive problems and suppress competition because buying decision-makers develop a certain amount of personal loyalty toward the account manager.

Because it is unlikely that you will want to respond to every request for service from a customer in a cooperatively "non-key" relationship, the account manager has to act as a true customer advocate. If a customer request is not worth your attention, the account manager's role is to get the service from elsewhere. Most companies have a network of connections with smaller suppliers of complementary services. This is certainly the case in the IT industry, where there are innumerable small specialist suppliers who can do bespoke software or services, and ex-employees of the large companies run many of them. Contacts between the large companies and the "eco-system" of supportive smaller companies may be formal or informal, but they can certainly be leveraged for a beneficial win-win-win on a service request.

If a customer request is not worth your attention, the account manager's role is to get the service from elsewhere. Most companies have a network of connections with smaller suppliers of complementary services.

Managing confrontational cooperative: Wrestling match

> **Customers can force suppliers out of business**
>
> A case study in the Finnish forestry industry highlighted the problems facing small forestry companies after the government abandoned fixed fees in the industry in 1992. Each small firm that fells trees has to sell to large paper mills. The study mentions one entrepreneur, who battled alone in the annual price negotiations with a number of buying decision-makers who claimed to understand his problems, but still wanted keen prices and more services. He saw his income eroded year on year.
>
> *Source:* Alajoutsijärvi, Tikkanen and Skaates (2001)

Business academics like to talk about the old days of adversarial negotiations being dead and buried. I have said it myself, then a good friend brings me back to the real world. There are still certain relationships where personalities or the nature of the industry require protracted negotiation of acceptable, time-limited deals. We can talk idealistically about principled negotiations, and of course that may be the outcome. More often the concessions come slowly as both sides need to "keep face" and tread carefully so that they do not send false messages to each other.

Each company's opening positions will change over the course of the negotiation, and each expects that. Nevertheless the process of exchanging concessions is sensitive. Concessions cannot be made too easily; that might make the original negotiating position look flimsy.

This is not a book about negotiating techniques. There are very good texts that focus purely on that stage of the sales process. However, the role of concessions is particularly important in adversarial cooperative relationships. If you want to keep a customer but avoid overcommitting resource to them, you have to negotiate thoughtfully. Concessions cannot be made too easily, and that might make the original negotiating position look flimsy. An open approach would be to state the benefits of concessions alongside an explanation of cost to the supplier. A tactful suggestion that the customer should withdraw a demand that adds cost to the deal may be acceptable.

Some deals are inherently difficult to cost. Some types of information systems projects carry high risks of overrun, scope drift and the need for rework. They need to be conservatively priced because the unexpected always happens. If you absorb an extra cost within such a deal, it is always necessary to tactfully expect reciprocation from the customer. Perhaps they can be more flexible on their deadline; perhaps they can provide more information or take on some extra activity.

Trust is usually low in situations where the wrestling match approach is appropriate. Therefore, there is often a focus on contingency concessions – I can do *x* if you do *y*, or concessions can be made in instalments. Concessions delivered over the course of a contract are likely to maintain some goodwill and make the supplier look flexible.

When terms are agreed, it does not mean that trust has been established. Suppliers need to check for contract drift, where customers ask for extras for no additional payment after the contract has been finalized. There may also be contract breach by stealth, for example, where a customer takes too many days credit. In an adversarial relationship, boundaries have to be set and kept. Any breach of contract terms must be countered. This takes a particularly hard-skinned individual, and may mean years of uncomfortable meetings for them. Nevertheless, customers do not generally leave relationships with suppliers whose core product or service is good, just because additional demands are not met.

Retailers are, by tradition, tough negotiators and you need talented salespeople to deal with them. Large retailers are also famous for forcing price concessions, shifting inventory risk to suppliers, demanding just-in-time delivery and taking extensive credit. Media commentators accuse them of pushing problems up the supply chain, as their suppliers then start to penalize their own suppliers. From the retailers' point of view, they are responding to consumer demand and helping suppliers to improve their competitiveness.

Large branded goods manufacturers may have the market clout to negotiate back, but before small companies can become bigger they have to deal with large retailers, and they have little to work with. Their need for profile may encourage them to make price trade-offs in return for joint sales promotions and merchandising.

A milestone study in 1995 by Kalwani and Nayarandas of Harvard Business School established that long-term relationships could be advantageous for manufacturers in terms of quality improvements, process performance and cost reductions. Even where a customer forces price reductions and lower gross margin, long-term relationships can still be profitable if you and your colleagues can lower discretionary expenses dedicated to the relationship.

What if you are in the position of our Finnish lumberjack, or a small farmer dealing with a major supermarket, or a small specialist manufacturing company dealing with a gigantic car company? The Finnish researchers recommended that the small forestry firms should consider setting up a cooperative marketing organization, which would be allowable under European law. This would enable them to share in the focused effort of specialized negotiators.

Alternatively, they could lobby the government to renew the role of the Trade Association that previously fixed prices for timber, and make sure that major buyers of timber are not keeping prices artificially low (Alajoutsijärvi, Tikkanen and Skaates 2001).

Small companies in many countries have the option to complain to a statutory Competition Commissioner about large corporations abusing their market dominance. Of course, as no small supplier wants to be de-listed because they were the only one to complain to a regulator, investigations are relatively rare.

Generating public sympathy with the help of the popular media is also possible, and may have direct diversification benefits. In order to show support for small farmers facing the might of major supermarkets, affluent UK consumers flock to Farmers' Markets, which have returned to town centers decades after supermarkets drove them into obscurity.

Managing the risk-creators: Balancing act

Do you remember watching the tightrope walkers at the circus? As I can barely balance myself on a bicycle, watching people with a great command of balance is wondrous to behold.

I think of those tightrope walkers when sales managers ask me about improving relationships with the risk-creators. If you are skilled enough to keep your balance, you can do it, but it takes so much nerve. You can't afford to fall, because risk-creators can take your whole business away when they withdraw their orders. Largely, what they bring to you is the leverage of their brand. So leverage it – to develop some more promising relationships!

It never seems right that a supposedly independent business should be just a sidekick of a bigger organization. Tax authorities perceive that the larger organization is just avoiding vertical integration of its supply chain. And history shows us that they will definitely discard you as a supplier when times are difficult, no matter how loyal you have been.

There is, however, another angle. Some years ago I was mentor to a young entrepreneur who had a good small specialist service business. He was offered a deal by a large well-branded service business that would have made his business a satellite of theirs. We discussed the advantages and disadvantages. He refused it; it wasn't the way forward that he wanted. For another individual, at a different point in their career, the opportunity of such a deal would have outweighed the risk.

One dominant customer can offer medium-term security and such a relationship can be endured if you use it to open other doors.

One dominant customer can offer medium-term security and such a relationship can be endured if you use it to open other doors.

Managing customers who have slipped from strategic

Dealing with the customer that was once strategic, but has dropped down your attractiveness league table is a sensitive issue. Maybe their position in their industry has slipped, in which case, their purchasing manager may be sympathetic to a reduction in service levels. What will probably be more difficult is that your account manager may have asked you for a transfer to another account, and the change in personnel might cause resentment. As a sales manager, you have to ensure a smooth succession. A very experienced account manager with one eye on retirement can be an excellent "safe pair of hands" in this situation.

If the purchasing manager has changed and has a new perception of you as a supplier, renegotiation of all terms will be up for grabs anyway, and it might be easier to get a new account manager to do it.

Conclusion

Cooperative relationships deserve to be studied far more than they are. Each month I review new articles about sales management from academics, consultants and practitioners, and while customer retention occupies many column inches, there is little exploration of what "keep" might actually entail. We know that some business-to-business relationships are occasionally unprofitable and non-strategic, but the nature of those relationships and how they are managed has not been easy to generalize. We know that it is pointless to waste investment where there is no obvious prospect of return, and we know that the contraction caused by the loss of a substantial regular customer is painful. You, as VP Sales, have to live with those risks. The discussion in this chapter should be useful in helping you to think about your options with your specific cooperative relationships. In the next chapter we consider your options when your exit from the relationship has to be managed.

8

The end of relationships

"We had 50% of our gross revenue disappear in one phone call . . ."

Business owner quoted in the *Dayton Business Journal*
With kind permission from the editor

Twenty-five percent of business relationships are expected to fail. Whether it is called breakdown, withdrawal, exit, disengagement, uncoupling or dissolution, it happens. Nothing is written about it in sales books and relatively little is written in research journals. Nevertheless, in relationship strategy, one of the strengths of an organization is its ability to terminate business relationships that are not mutually beneficial, and to do it constructively. Every sales manager must have some doubtful relationships in their portfolio. They are time-consuming in a negative way, and you just have to work out what to do with them, and/or be prepared when they do it to you.

Certainly the length of a relationship may be some indication of strength to both supplier and customer. But long relationships can also be long histories of dissatisfaction and conflict.

I do not hold with the often-quoted mission statement of companies that "we aim to delight all our customers". It is a vain hope, not a realistic objective. Any business relationship involves stress, conflict and the risk of breakdown. Some techniques to measure relationship quality or strength are suggested elsewhere in this book and revisited in this chapter, but they are rarely formalized in practice. Certainly the length of a relationship may be some indication of strength to both supplier and customer. But long relationships can also be long histories of dissatisfaction and conflict.

Conflict normally arises from some form of dissatisfaction for either party, often triggered by neglect. Whether or not a business relationship survives may depend upon how good you and your customer are at conflict resolution. Good conflict resolution can strengthen perceptions of value. Unsuccessful handling of conflicts almost always leads to the end of the business relationship.

Relationship stress can build up over time for both you and your customer – an accumulation of negative experiences, or things not meeting expectations. The stress usually emanates from the perceptions of the individuals who are most significant in the relationship – on the customer's side this may be the purchasing manager or the operational manager closest to your product or service in use. There are unpleasant aspects of long-term relationships, including complacency and neglect. You or your customer can make a business exit by reducing relationship investment or an emotional exit by reducing social contact from the relationship as mutual benefit declines. As relationships are analyzed and re-analyzed over time, some drift into being more of a burden than a benefit.

Relationship stress is almost unavoidable. Conflicts and the occasional bit of chaos are normal in business relationships. Although everyone assumes that things should run smoothly, they don't, which is why the salesperson (and the purchasing manager) frequently adopts the role of progress-chaser, trying to make things happen that should have happened and didn't. Purchasing managers may pride themselves on attention to detail and enjoy the progress-chasing aspect of the job, but salespeople generally do not. This is why salespeople suffer from "role conflict" or "role ambiguity" as they try to see both the supplier's and the customer's points of view on minor issues and try to broker some resolution.

Causes of conflict

There are a number of possible causes of stress between suppliers and their customers, and the items in Figure 8.1 have all been observed in research and/or the business press over the past 10 years.

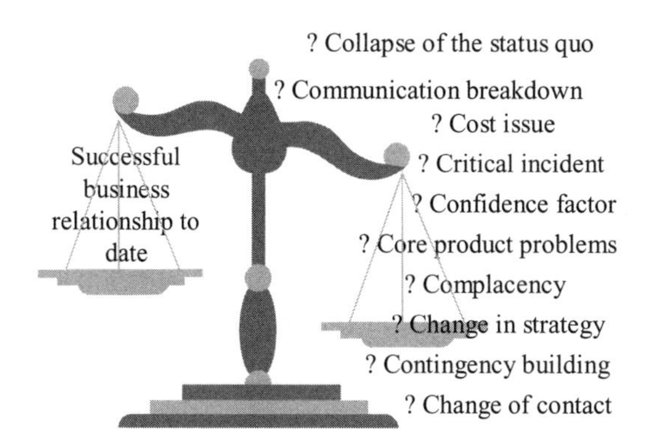

Figure 8.1 *The 10 Cs of relationship conflict.*

Cost considerations (or price?!)

Professional purchasers cannot ignore significantly cheaper sources of supply as the world economy makes them more and more accessible. Although most IT professional services buyers in the USA say that they prefer to buy from a US company with local resources, most have experience of off-shore providers, good and bad. In the case of commoditized products – as we have seen in earlier chapters – you have to adapt to cheaper supply models, or die.

Professional purchasers cannot ignore significantly cheaper sources of supply as the world economy makes them more and more accessible.

Companies who are over-reliant on a single customer may find themselves in trouble when the customer decides to test the market on a new product design. Allegedly, one European company, whose Number 1 customer represented over 25% of turnover, lost out to its own Chinese manufacturing partner when that customer decided to go out to tender globally, because price competition for the bid was intense.

Critical incident

When something major goes wrong, it is brought to the attention of senior managers. It affects the careers of the buying decision-makers who chose you as a supplier when you fail. Any negative occurrence provokes stronger reactions than positive events. It is remembered for a long time and creates a significant negative weighting on future decisions. The need for blame results in scapegoats, and suppliers are easy targets. No amount of hard data will override a management perception that Supplier X makes mistakes.

It affects the careers of the buying decision-makers who chose you as a supplier when you fail.

I once did a review with a key account manager whose customer (a pharmacy chain) had been left with empty shelves without warning due to a production problem. She negotiated a civilized handover of the business for that product category to a competitor in order to protect the company's business with that customer in other product categories. She recognized that there was no point trying to be defensive about the mess-up, and was able to minimize the loss of business.

Core product/service or process problem

Buying decision-makers take so many "hygiene factors" for granted that failing to meet one of them is likely to result in the termination of your contract. If a product or service fails to keep pace with market standards, or if there are performance problems, your customer will be checking for alternative sources of supply. One buying decision-maker told me that he had noticed that his supplier's product hadn't kept pace with competitors' offerings. He said that he couldn't refuse better technology just because he liked the account manager.

Problems with a basic product are not tolerated, and problems with special customer-specific products are even more likely to raise questions about corporate competencies. Process excellence and quality customer service and technical support are also often expected as a minimum. More generally, if both you and your customer are monitoring the benefits received from the relationship overall and start to notice deterioration, it may be time for an exit strategy.

Suppliers must get the basics right

Businesspeople normally assume a cultural preference for a personal relationship approach to business (guanxi), in the Far East. However, a study in Hong Kong of the relationship between companies and their advertising agencies found that decision-makers focused on the core service when rating them. Long years of association did not seem to improve satisfaction levels. Even after 10 years, many companies stated that they still had to check their agency's work and chase deadlines. With the average tenure of advertising agencies decreasing, a focus on closing the gap between customer expectations and agency performance is critical to avoid losing customers.

Source: So (2005)

Communication breakdown

Neither party to a business relationship welcomes shocks. If you are about to miss a deadline, a delivery, or any other sort of routine obligation, your salesperson should let the customer know in advance. Equally, you can be faced with a crisis if a customer suddenly reduces a monthly order. It is important to anticipate situations and discuss them. Whether customers are important enough to warrant a significant quantity and quality of face-to-face meetings, or whether they just receive e-mail bulletins, simple communications lapses can lead to dissatisfaction and demotivation. Keeping up the momentum on major and minor communications is a constant challenge. It is not just the responsibility of your account manager (or the purchasing manager from the customer point of view); it is a company-wide responsibility.

A purchasing manager in process manufacturing told me about his utmost frustration with a supplier whose product was good, but whose staff failed to communicate with his. For a process manufacturer, keeping the factory running is critical. If a supplier delivers less goods than promised, or all the order a day late, it causes the purchasing manager considerable stress. He commented that it was not the fact that the delivery was wrong or late, but that he had not been informed and so could not adjust for it. Despite the language difference between the two companies, he felt that they should try harder. He said that even though he liked the product, he was looking for an alternative supplier.

Confidence factors: breach of trust or abuse of power

A breach of trust is the most frequently quoted reason for customers to end a business relationship. Losing confidence in your word as a supplier soon leads to a loss of confidence in your ability. This is also the case where a customer's promise, e.g. to pay on time, causes you to lose confidence in the value of their business.

A breach of trust is the most frequently quoted reason for customers to end a business relationship.

If inconsistent performance is persistent, or a single critical event is handled badly, a breach of trust can be said to have occurred. This is probably most easily explained through examples. A technical manager in a food-processing company told me about a problem he had with a supplier's ingredients that caused his company to lose production. He asked the supplier to visit to discuss the matter and said that they started behaving aggressively, telling him that his staff could not have been using their product properly. Needless to say, their business relationship was over at that point.

Customers can also breach trust. Misusing supplier information is a common cause for concern, and unilateral changes to contracts at short notice also create supplier resentment. And then, of course, there is the perennial problem of late payment.

The owner of a small logistics firm sent his trucks to blockade the headquarters of a supermarket chain because they were taking months to pay his invoices. He felt that he had to create bad publicity for them in order to negotiate on equal terms.

Complacency

Customer expectations of innovation do not reduce over time. The longer a business relationship continues, the more difficult it is to sustain a high level of attention. For example, if you introduce long-established customers to new products after an advertising campaign using those sexy new products to attract new customers, your loyal customers will feel neglected. In one piece of research I did with a company that prided itself on customer focus, it transpired that although their customers were very satisfied, most of them would still search for the best value at the next decision point.

Suppliers must be proactive

In a study of advertising services in 2004, the researchers found that when the customer demanded "value changes" such as additional information, the customer was acting on a belief that the supplier was slacking. The supplier knew that they had to respond to reduce tension and avoid dissatisfaction. In relationships where the supplier was coming up with ideas and suggestions for value improvement in the relationship, the customers felt more motivated to stay. Proactive value generation on behalf of the supplier led to stronger relationship bonds, even when it was a case of repairing a relationship damaged by complacency. Complacency on either side was expected to lead to the deterioration of the relationship.

Source: Beverland, Farrelly and Woodhatch (2004)

Change in strategic direction

Sometimes the strategy or values of organizations in business relationships are not in alignment. Sometimes it is the people operating on a day-to-day level with the other party who can see this more clearly than senior managers, hence the need for internal teams. Some companies have difficulty relating to organizations of a different business culture; for example, some companies are bureaucratic and others are entrepreneurial. In fast-moving consumer goods markets, suppliers with strong brands are reluctant to deal with supermarkets that might not treat their brands with the respect the supplier feels is appropriate. Volume potential may be offset against those strategic considerations.

New chief executives and/or new strategies can spell trouble for business relationships. Usually it is customers who initiate supplier rationalization or change to cheaper sources of supply. You may then be left arguing over compensation.

Another trigger for changes in a business relationship is the merger or acquisition of either party. Once again, suppliers are particularly vulnerable. The customer base of an acquired company is an asset; the supplier base is a target for cost-cutting. Mistakes are made because, in the short term, mergers and acquisitions rarely add to shareholder value. Nevertheless, they are part of the business landscape. Merger or acquisition is going to happen to some of your customers sooner or later.

When a major retailer terminated a long-term agreement with a computer services supplier after only a year, they claimed that the company had not met required service levels. IT industry watchers felt that the merger of the retailer with a rival had more to do with it, and the changes of management that followed.

Contingency building

Customers fear that if they are over-reliant on a single source of supply, they may end up at some stage with no source of supply. For example, a fire at a supplier's plant severely disrupted a major auto manufacturer's production worldwide.

Suppliers suffer if they are heavily dependent on a small number of customers. Although there is little choice other than to operate with a few large customers in some industries, as discussed elsewhere, a diverse portfolio is generally better. Business is about risk, and despite many companies having a risk-averse culture, risk cannot be minimized out of existence. Risk reduction activity often shifts risks to another aspect of the business where it may cause more damage.

Business is about risk, and despite many companies having a risk-averse culture, risk cannot be minimized out of existence. Risk reduction activity often shifts risks to another aspect of the business where it may cause more damage.

This compensating factor can be observed in human behavior. In a study of construction workers' responses to safety measures on building sites, researchers found that awareness of a particular risk was reasonably high before a safety measure was suggested to address it. It was also high when the measure was introduced and was being publicized. After a period of time, it was forgotten and the construction workers were taking other risks because they felt protected from the original problem (Aranda and Finch, 2003).

Therefore, if there is risk in developing a relationship with a particular supplier or customer, it is better to acknowledge it, explore it and manage it through contingency plans. This requires both parties to agree on the possibility of certain high-impact scenarios such as an interruption in raw materials extraction due to an earthquake. It also requires a planned approach to circumventing possible problems.

Change in key contacts

Relationships between suppliers and customers ought to operate at several contact points. However, it would be foolish to ignore the importance of the personal relationship between your salesperson and their main contact in the customer. Sometimes it is all that holds the business together. If either leaves, the customer is presented with an ideal switching point. I once met a purchasing manager who was transitioning from a multisourcing to a single-sourcing policy. He was having problems deciding between two suppliers of a certain commodity, both of which seemed to be very good. The salesperson of one company left, and so the purchasing manager decided that that would be the time to place all the business with the other supplier.

> **Account managers must give professional advice**
>
> Buyers who like their relationship with the salesperson of a particular supplier, perhaps because they believe that it is based on fair, honest and open communication, are more likely to be satisfied and even committed to the business relationship. Some purchasing managers admit to relying a lot on the professional advice of an individual account manager. Their perception of the value of salesperson means that they perceive switching costs to be higher.
>
> *Source*: Johnson, Barksdale and Boles (2001)

On the other hand, if the relationship between your salesperson and their contact deteriorates for any reason and action is not taken, switching can occur. Sometimes, a change in a personal relationship is just a matter of personal chemistry. There are also some rational reasons why a change in key personnel causes problems. The buyer may perceive that your new salesperson is less skilled or less responsive than the previous salesperson. Your salesperson may believe that the new buyer has a price-driven approach that threatens the value that has previously been supplied, or that the buyer is less inclined to discuss strategic matters.

If a competitor recruits a popular salesperson, the buyer may be persuaded to consider the competitive offer out of personal loyalty, especially if the buyer observes that the original supplier is losing a lot of key staff. Or perhaps the relational stress may just be temporary, for example if your salesperson is sick and colleagues do not provide adequate cover.

Although the buyer–salesperson relationship is very important, in most close business relationships there are also bonds at every level from operations to the Board. A fallout among senior managers at the golf course may cause stress. Or perhaps a maintenance engineer from the supplier is rude to a receptionist at a customer's branch office and her complaint escalates. Ideally companies aspire to a "corporate personality" so that personal qualities can be assigned to the organization and many stakeholders can say, "Company X always employs nice people". But humans are humans, and anyone's bad day can have knock-on effects.

Collapse of the status quo

If a customer suffers a financial crisis or a dramatic loss of market share, you must retrieve your exit plan from your filing cabinet. I have heard key account managers of faltering market leaders express the desire to switch to more exciting up-and-coming accounts. Customers also worry when you have a public relations disaster, or lose external focus because of internal reorganization. When discussing mutual risk management, embarrassing "loss of face" factors tend to be avoided. That's a mistake; frank and open conversation of difficult issues is usually a better approach. Sometimes when there is flux in the market, it affects everybody.

A textiles company that had been producing clothing for a retailer for over 30 years was in serious trouble when, due to the financial problems of the retailer, they terminated the contract. The adjustment costs included redundancy payments and asset write-downs. The company had to develop new relationships with smaller retailers quickly.

Rebuilding relationships after economic upheaval

The most dramatic example of wholesale changes in business relationships was in the aftermath of the fall of Communism in Eastern Europe. In the Soviet planned economies, firms were not free to start or finish business relationships. Success was judged by achievement of the State Plan. Consequently, supplier–customer relationships were weak (they might never meet) and there was no knowledge of alternatives.

Most of the customer and supplier relationships of a regional printing company disintegrated when the Russian economy was liberalized in the early 1990s. Its biggest customer was the Soviet Post Office, which found regional suppliers to save on transport costs. Local electronics firms went bankrupt. The company had to rebuild from a core customer base of local newspapers.

The company's main suppliers had been government agencies, acting as intermediaries. It was suddenly able to buy paper directly from producers, but after a few years preferred to use distributors who were able to focus on the quality they required. The company had to change technology from zinc printing blocks to photopolymer plates as sources of zinc in Poland failed. The awareness of alternatives enabled new relationships to be built.

Source: Hallen and Johanson (2004)

In summary, there are at least 10 possible triggers for a business relationship to fail. Being aware of them is the first step in managing them.

Next steps

You need to think ahead about what to do about a relationship is in crisis. You have four choices, depending on the nature of the problem. If the customer is angry with you, but you want to keep them, you need conflict resolution. Ideally, conflict avoidance should be in place with most accounts so that things don't get this far. Your contingency plan should be to accept and rationalize a customer-initiated exit. Perhaps they will let you tender for their business again in the future.

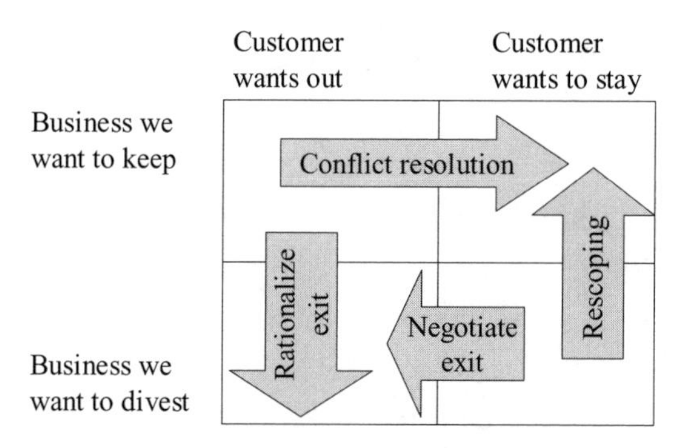

Figure 8.2 *A relationship in crisis. (Adapted from Professor Neil Rackham.)*

You also need conflict resolution when you are tired of the customer's business, but they want to keep you as a supplier. It is likely that complacency has caused the situation, and that can be avoided by positive tactics. If it is too late for avoidance, you need to rescope the business to breathe some life back into it. If rescoping is not possible, then you need to initiate and negotiate withdrawal in a way that avoids bad publicity.

Conflict avoidance

There are a number of commonsense safeguards that you need to put in place, particularly in the case of strategic accounts:

- Succession policy for salespeople/account managers must be carefully handled. Some companies put a junior sales recruit into account teams to handle some administration and progress-chasing for the account manager, but also to act as a continuing point of contact should there be an interruption in the leadership of the team.
- Communications should be open, honest and proactive at all levels.
- You must constantly achieve on "hygiene factors" in the relationship – meeting the specified levels of product and process quality.

Beyond that, there is still some work to do on a regular basis to identify specific causes of stress in particular relationships. It is not relationship stress itself that causes business relationships to end, but how that stress is managed. Ask your salespeople to try to detect relationships that are at risk. Perhaps periodically they should "audit" stress levels by asking how buyers recall previous negative incidents, and finding out whether or not they are still resentful about those problems.

Ask your salespeople to try to detect relationships that are at risk. Perhaps periodically they should "audit" stress levels by asking how buyers recall previous negative incidents, and finding out whether or not they are still resentful about those problems.

One of the surest ways of avoiding future conflict is for your salesperson to identify problematic situations and events in regular planning with customers. In order to understand their view of what is critical and what is less critical, criteria can be agreed. Your salesperson can also discuss contingency plans so that there will be less panic when something goes wrong.

In the most vivid training exercise I ever experienced, I was involved in a scenario planning exercise at the university. A number of small teams had to play the role of a critical incident task force in response to a flood at a student hall of residence. Other members of staff played the roles of distressed parents, investigative journalists and disgruntled students. I really felt the pressure and learned a lot. Emergency service workers frequently practice responses to terrorist attacks, plane crashes and extreme weather, to enable them to think clearly and know what to do when such things occur. Although supply interruptions or a virus taking out half the customer service department for a week are not as serious, a little bit of planning goes a long way.

If all else fails, make sure that you have a robust conflict resolution procedure for all categories of relationship.

Conflict resolution

Conflict resolution is not just a matter of observing a correct procedure, but of demonstrating a commitment to resolve problems and misunderstandings. The principles are:

Accessibility

- Customers must be given clear information about how they can complain, where, and to whom.

- Every customer should have equal access to relevant senior managers when they need to complain.
- The supplier must provide advice and assistance to customers who wish to pursue a complaint after the initial complaint-handler has failed to resolve their concern.

Ideally in a business-to-business relationship, the customer should also have a mechanism that allows the supplier to raise concerns.

Simplicity

- Procedures must be checked with customers by consultation. They should be "user-driven".
- Efforts must be made to resolve issues "on the spot" (i.e. no buck-passing).
- Managers must speak in straightforward language when dealing with customers.
- Staff should be fully trained in conflict resolution.

Speed

- Reasonable targets must be set for acknowledging and responding to complaints. Frequent updates on disputed matters are also essential.
- Ideally, complaints should be handled "on the spot" by front-line staff, but it is a senior management responsibility to monitor the company's performance on complaint-handling.

Fairness

- Complaints should be welcomed and taken seriously.
- The company should commission internal and external reviews/audits of its procedures and performance.
- Staff dealing with disputes need to be supported as well as the customer who has raised the problem.

Confidentiality

- Appropriate precautions must be taken to ensure that complaints are handled securely.

Effective compensation

A suitable process of compensation might be:

- Immediate apology and explanation of how the problem occurred.
- Solving the problem.
- Financial compensation, if appropriate.
- Calls should be made after apparent resolution to check if the customer was happy with the process.

Tracking progress

- Formal AND informal problems must be recorded, monitored and analyzed.
- Information should be exchanged throughout the organization so that departments and professionals can learn from each other's experience.
- There should be regular feedback to strategy-makers.

If you can achieve all that, then most conflicts can be resolved amicably and no conflicts need to fester for months and years.

Avoiding the complacency trap

Dissatisfied customers do not always switch to a competitor, which means that suppliers can be lulled into a false sense of security. In most cases, customer dissatisfaction is not about a one-off incident, but has been simmering for a few months. Dissatisfied customers usually report that they have complained to the supplier. In a study in Australia in industry markets, nearly half of the

Nearly half of the customers who complained said that they were dissatisfied with the recovery action taken by the supplier, or the way the complaint had been handled

customers who complained said that they were dissatisfied with the recovery action taken by the supplier, or the way the complaint had been handled (Yanamandram and White, 2006).

Nevertheless, those customers had not switched to a competitor. The main reason given was that they thought that alternative suppliers might be just as bad, although clearly the possibility of switching had been researched. Switching costs and switching risks also concerned buying decision-makers. Personal loyalty to the account manager can be a factor in staying with a supplier. Sometimes customers believe that it is better to stay and rectify problems if there is some sort of goodwill and the supplier seems to be working to resolve their issues.

Some buyers admit their own inertia. Switching would mean hassle, so the pain from a supplier not performing would have to be very great in order to make it personally worthwhile to manage the change to another. Buyers also have some idiosyncratic switching barriers such as patriotism and reciprocal purchasing.

A relationship of convenience can last a long time, but you cannot rely on switching barriers, because the "retained" customer might spread negative anecdotes that would become a barrier to customer acquisition.

How does negotiated exit take place?

Customer initiates exit

As we have seen, customers can be reluctant to discard suppliers. A history of successful transactions gives the buyer the reassurance that working with a well-known supplier will reduce effort in today's transaction. Expected future business encourages cooperation today. Investments have already been made when firms share a common past. A shared past is worth more than the recommendations that an alternative supplier might be able to offer.

There are huge costs involved in relationship exit, including lost investment, the costs of searching for a replacement supplier, the costs of negotiating with that supplier and negotiating out of the previous relationship, set-up costs of the new relationship, litigation costs, loss of rewards or benefits, the possible impact on end-customers, the risk of choosing a non-performing new partner (out of the frying pan, into the fire), and so on!

Nevertheless, professional purchasing managers do initiate relationship exits. They may do so for any of the reasons listed earlier in this chapter, or others. Unfortunately, for you as a sales manager – with the knowledge that buyers face costs in a relationship exit – the costs for your employer are also going to be a great shock to the organization.

You need a contingency plan for switching resource quickly to generate replacement business. The contingency plan should also identify how you can quickly generate cash flow from company resources that were previously tied to that business relationship. It may mean subletting office space, contract manufacturing, and loaning staff to other divisions in your company.

Supplier initiates exit

> **When is a customer too unprofitable?**
>
> Some suppliers tell researchers that a large proportion of their relationships with customers are not profitable. Seven percent of respondents in one study in Germany in manufacturing industry said that less than 25% of their relationships were profitable – but only 34% of companies in that study had any minimum requirements for customer profitability and only 21% had any sort of policy on handling unprofitable customers.
>
> *Source:* Helm, Rolfes and Günter (2006)

There is general agreement among supplier decision-makers that unprofitable relationships should be terminated, but despite concerns about the value of some business relationships, supplier-initiated exit is not common. Suppliers with strict financial criteria for customer relationships have been known to terminate unprofitable ones, without fear of other customers losing trust in them. For others, there are reasons to stay with an unprofitable customer, just as there are reasons why customers stay with unsatisfactory suppliers.

Many of your unprofitable customers may be newly acquired, and there may be reasonable expectations of future profits from the relationship. Even if they are long-established relationships, the investment required to replace old customers with new ones might not be appropriate. In particular, why bounce an apparently contented customer into the hands of a competitor when they are at least making some contribution to cost recovery? The costs of readjusting to lower volumes are significant and include reconfiguring operations and making staff redundant. A parting can be public and make you look vulnerable. Also, unprofitable relationships are a common feature of some markets, such as process manufacturing. Low profitability is expected when costs to serve are high and capital investment is high. Therefore in these markets the need for long-term relationships is keener.

Sometimes there are policy reasons. For example, you cannot preach customer orientation and then dump customers because of a low contribution at a given point in time.

Staying too long with an unsuccessful business relationship is more common than you would expect (Horn, Lovallo and Viguerie, 2006). Is your account manager willing to "exit" their own job or those of colleagues? Are you willing to admit to a wasted relationship investment?

Once they feel that a relationship should end, suppliers can resort to "grave dressing". This means that they try to exit by indirect means, such as reducing investment, increasing prices, or fewer communications. This does not go unnoticed by the customer's decision-makers. It causes resentment and sabotages the potential to revive the relationship at a later date.

How to leave

Any contract should have legally binding exit provisions. These should be flexible enough to cover a variety of possible termination circumstances. When entering into a business relationship, you need to be clear about who can terminate it, in what circumstances and when. It should also be clear in advance how jointly owned assets will be shared, who will work for who if staff have to be reallocated, and how mutually developed intellectual property will be managed. It is also useful to understand in advance how any transition from one party to another will be implemented, and who will pay for the transition.

As previously mentioned, you and your customer should include the anticipation of negative scenarios in your regular joint planning, and document the contingency plans. Exit strategies require parties to work together. A legal situation of allegation and counter-allegation will not help either of you to readjust. Some researchers recommend a periodic "state of the relationship" review. It is also suggested that people new to both companies should take part, so they will not be swayed by the shared past. They should be able to avoid the "sunk cost fallacy" – unrecoverable money spent in the past does not justify spending more unrecoverable money now or in the future. However, these participants need to have some accountability for the outcome of the review.

Both consultation and compensation should ensure that broken relationships will not cause loss of trust elsewhere in the supply chain network. A negotiated exit also ensures the possibility of rebuilding a relationship at a later date.

Both consultation and compensation should ensure that broken relationships will not cause loss of trust elsewhere in the supply chain network.

Conclusion

None of us likes to spend time focusing on negative possibilities. But I hope that I have convinced you that some time spent on worst-case scenarios is worth your while. First, having been there in thought, you can be assured that life is rarely as bad as we can imagine. Second, having thought through bad scenarios, you should be better prepared and able to minimize damage if one does occur. And, last but not least, some bad situations are worth initiating to stem losses and free resources to create opportunities elsewhere.

PART III

Strategic Focus for 21st-Century Sales Management

These four chapters have been written to address four weaknesses observed in the management of sales functions. They have been chosen because of innumerable studies that have identified them as areas that need improvement.

So here is a discussion about how to get better at:

- Reputation management
- Working with marketing
- Leadership
- Process management.

9

Reputation management

"In law, a man is guilty when he violates the rights of others. In ethics, he is guilty if he only thinks of doing so."

Immanuel Kant, 18th-century German philosopher

Corporate reputation management has become the new "CRM" of the early 21st century. Following some major corporate scandals, the US government decided to legislate to raise the profile of accountability on Board agendas. The Sarbanes–Oxley Act has had repercussions worldwide, affecting all companies doing business in the USA and businesses that are part or wholly owned by American corporates. The principle of the Sarbanes–Oxley Act (affectionately known as SOX in some quarters) is to restore public trust in corporations by promoting ethical business practice and encouraging an open information culture within companies, which should ensure the completeness of external financial statements. But this is not just for accountants and IT managers. And it is not just a matter of double-checking your representatives' expense claims.

Salespeople are boundary spanners, juggling customer expectations with the performance expectations of their employers. They encounter ethical uncertainty every day. They know the situations that cause problems between supplier and customer, and they know the guidance they need to protect the company's reputation and their own.

The issue of ethics is particularly important in very large accounts. An IBM, a General Electric or a Hewlett-Packard, for example, has huge corporate accounts each generating several hundred million dollars of revenue per year. Every one of these accounts is a business in its own right that is as large as the average public company. Who should oversee the business practices of these very large relationships? The customer? The supplier? It's not always clear. And who takes responsibility in the event that there are ethical violations? Best practice companies take an active interest in the ethics of very large account relationships. They have introduced the idea of "governance" and set up review and compliance processes to ensure that these accounts are well managed. As one senior manager in a global corporation put it: "In the future we will have many more of these very large sales relationships. The account manager of tomorrow must understand corporate ethics and governance in the way that they understand sales process today."

As with all legislation, compliance is not necessarily a threat; it can be an opportunity to identify new angles of competitive advantage. The professionalism of salespeople and sales management is critical to the overall impressions of excellent corporate governance. You should also bear in mind that research in real estate indicates that if salespeople acquire professional qualifications they can develop high ethical standards alongside higher performance (Izzo and Vitell, 2003). There is therefore potential "win-win" in the SOX challenge.

As with all legislation, compliance is not necessarily a threat; it can be an opportunity to identify new angles of competitive advantage.

Apart from the legal considerations that have brought corporate reputation management to the fore, there are many more reasons to concentrate on it. In my examination of supplier–customer relationships in the mid-1990s, "breach of trust" was quoted as the single most likely cause of the disintegration of a relationship. "Integrity" was the quality that purchasing decision-makers most wanted in the key account manager and the supplier as a whole.

There is also a reinforcement effect. If the company has a good reputation, it helps salespeople to get appointments with potential customers. If those salespeople demonstrate high behavioral standards, then that feeds back into the good reputation of the company and its sales performance. Reputation is the impression that stakeholders have of the firm's performance over a period of time. The UK Institute of Directors, among other influential bodies, has noted that a corporate reputation is a valuable intangible asset. Research shows that a favorable reputation attracts shareholders, the best staff, and customer retention. It is also associated with superior financial returns (study by Rosa Chun, 2006).

Research shows that a favorable reputation attracts shareholders, the best staff, and customer retention. It is also associated with superior financial returns.

So where's the problem? Surely it is just plain common sense to take care of your company's reputation, which takes years to accumulate but can be lost overnight? But "common sense" is not particularly common.

Why does sales have a problem?

A salesperson's personal values are under fire from many competing influences, as shown in Figure 9.1, and reconciling all these competing interests is not easy. Research and anecdotal evidence suggests that many people fail to reconcile them and get trapped into sub-optimal behavior patterns, perhaps without even realizing that it has happened to them.

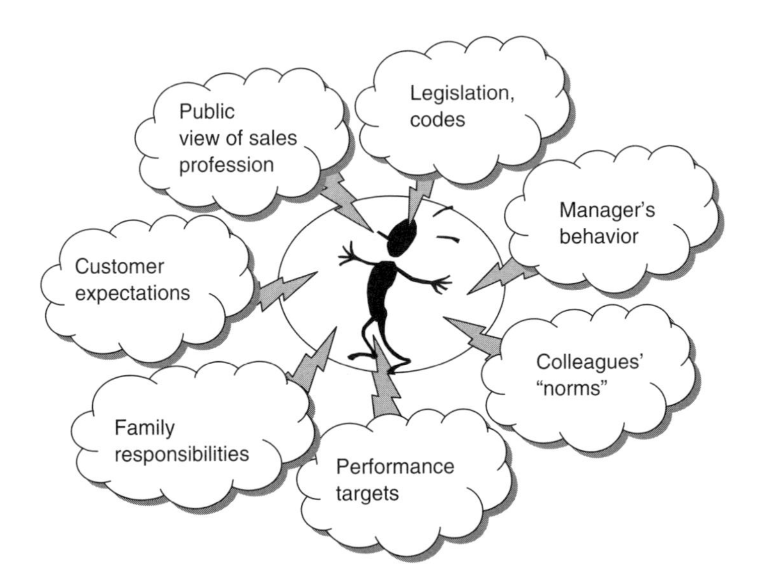

Figure 9.1 *A salesperson's competing influences.*

In a seminar some years ago, I explained to the salespeople attending that purchasers thought integrity was rare, and a differentiating factor among suppliers. Many were quite indignant. "How dare they think that we lack integrity?!" was one reaction.

What researchers call "deviant" or "anti-citizenship" behavior occurs in all professions. But if a company has an accountant with an explosive temper, it is less visible to customers than a sales representative so desperate for the sale that they offer a substantial gift to seal the deal. A salesperson's ethics affect customer relationships. Most purchasing decision-makers say that they consider it in every buying situation. Salespeople's behavior is also very public, and the public has a very bad image of salespeople.

A fascinating study by Katherine Hartman (2006) of media images of salespeople since the beginning of the cinema in 1903 found that "depictions of salespeople and the sales occupation have been overwhelmingly unflattering and negative". Having studied 281 plot summaries, she found that there were "significantly more negative and very negative descriptions of salesperson characteristics than expected by chance". Of course, stereotypes have to be recognizable to audiences, so film and television scriptwriters would point out that they are just reflecting cultural norms that assume salespeople to be overbearing, unpleasant and dishonest. Despite knowing these stereotypes, I was still shocked when, in a social situation, someone vehemently accused me of "lying for a living" when I mentioned that I worked in sales. These public perceptions do have a knock-on effect on purchasing decision-makers in businesses.

It is very demoralizing to feel that your profession has a low social status. A study at St Cloud University, Minnesota, led by Dennis Bristow (2006), showed that even business school students who have completed sales courses believed that salespeople were not customer-oriented. They were also convinced that the general public saw salespeople as untrustworthy and dishonest. We may know from our own experience that the stereotype is unfair. In fact, there is research to support the view that this stereotype is inaccurate. But it has persisted for many years, and it will take time to change it.

> *"People of the same trade seldom meet together, even for merriment and diversion, but conversation ends in a conspiracy against the public."*
>
> Adam Smith, Scottish philosopher, 1776

The problem with changing the poor public image of salespeople is that the profession still has some problems with its own image and its contribution to corporate reputation management. It was reported recently (Jelinek and Ahearne, 2006) that 60% of sales managers have found a salesperson cheating in some way, and 36% believe that bad behavior is getting worse. "Deviant" behavior covers aggression, avoiding work and resisting rules. You would be an angel if you never got cross or tired at work, or frustrated by the rules, but a minority of salespeople do make a habit of bad behavior such as disrespecting colleagues, exaggerating their expenses and exaggerating to customers. And the more that behavior is tolerated, the more their colleagues will try it.

Where does bad behavior come from?

There are a number of identified causes of bad behavior. Where a high proportion of someone's income is variable, paying this month's bills easily overcomes an ethical concern. Aside from the conflict between responsibility to feed the family and the firm's reputation, salespeople are confused by mixed messages from within the firm, including rivalry between departments. A small minority of managers are known to encourage "deviant" behaviors, if they think that it will help their bonus or ego. If honest people perceive that their manager considers bad behavior to be normal, they may copy it to survive.

If salespeople think that company rules are not equally applied, or that managers are selective in their application, they are tempted to ignore such rules. If a manager reprimands someone in public for an infringement usually overlooked, they may even provoke sabotage. Salespeople are also affected by the assumption of distrust. Systems that seem to be excessively controlling can create retaliation. (For more information see: Jelinek and Aherne, 2006; Litsky, Eddleston and Kidder, 2006.)

Salespeople are also affected by the assumption of distrust. Systems that seem to be excessively controlling can create retaliation.

All the above can create bad behavior in any profession. If you are working in a dysfunctional firm, expect your employees to contribute to its dysfunctionality. As VP Sales, you should be particularly worried if salespeople are indulging in bad behavior. Because they feel responsible to customers and stockholders and are in the public domain more than many other colleagues, salespeople are more subject than other professions to job stress caused by role conflict. That stress can lead to bad decisions in a significant way that can reflect on the whole firm.

Salespeople usually say that most of the pressure prompting bad behavior comes from their own company demanding performance in the face of reality, such as customer downsizing or economic recession. Perhaps as a sales manager you are caught in the middle – between economic reality, representatives that you want to succeed, and senior managers with short-term aspirations. Sales management is not an easy job, and will test your relationship with your own integrity. That is a good reason to read this chapter in full and work out some "what if" scenarios you might need.

Of course, we must not forget that the purchasing profession is exposed to high pressure to save costs, which also exposes them to ethical issues. Purchasers have the opportunities to draw salespeople into unethical situations, and never is the interface between purchasers and sellers more complicated than in the context of international business. The interplay between business cultures and country cultures is complex and sensitive, requiring a great deal of research of all aspects of both (see Figure 9.2).

If you were thinking that business conduct codes were a waste of time, the international challenge should make you think again. Marketing, with

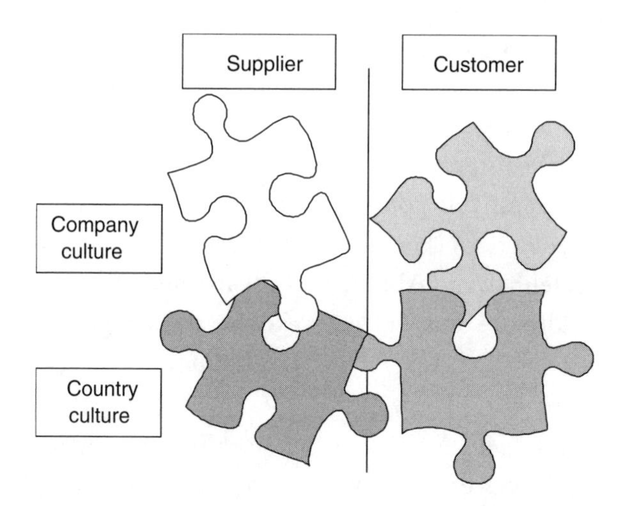

Figure 9.2 *The interplay between business and cultures.*

HR, should do the homework for salespeople in international situations and provide guidance on issues such as: giving and receiving gifts, which is expected in some regional cultures; table manners in different countries; and what to do if you are refused access to a plane unless you pay extra. Is the company going to excuse a bit of bribery to ensure your personal safety?

No shortage of guidance

There are a variety of sources of guidance for companies that wish to (a) formalize their understanding of what is regarded as ethical practice and (b) create their own policies.

Legislation

There are many interpretations of any law, but I have come to a few conclusions about the contribution that company law generally requires sales managers to make to ensure good corporate governance:

- Business strategy promised to shareholders must be reflected in sales strategy, such as a profitable sales mix. Incentives and training will have to be adjusted accordingly.
- Salespeople have updates on the commercial law and regulatory codes in which they have to operate.
- Customer information is treated as a corporate asset, not a salesperson's personal property.
- Sales administration procedures are robust enough to ensure traceability of decisions and actions.
- It is clear where authority and accountability lies, e.g. on issues such as discounts and hospitality.

Beyond accounting accuracy, company law requires companies to mitigate risks to shareholder value. Most commentators on Sarbanes–Oxley believe that it includes a requirement for ensuring ethical business conduct. The Federal Sentencing Guidelines in 2003 extended the compliance standard to address the ethical culture of a company.

There are other legal standards that companies need to observe. Sales representatives taking professional examinations often struggle with the variety of laws they need to know. I have heard many sales diploma-holders say that the examination paper on legal compliance is the most difficult. Plain contract law and "sale of goods" acts are difficult enough. The law relating to misrepresentation is scary, especially when there are industry-specific additional statutes (e.g. in pharmaceuticals and financial services), as there are in some countries. A salesperson also has to be aware of privacy and data protection law, employment law and equal opportunities law.

Arguably, there is too much law. But law is usually a response to public demand. If there is a law about it, customers have expectations of good practice. So it has to be learned and applied – in the spirit of the law as much as in the letter of the law.

Business and industry codes

The business community has been discussing corporate responsibility for many years, and has established some institutions to provide guidance. For example, the Caux Round Table is a body of business leaders from the United States, Europe and Japan "committed to energizing the role of business and industry as a vital force for innovative global change".

Company code of conduct – example

The Caux Principles, originally drawn up in 1994, state that: "Businesses should recognize that sincerity, candor, truthfulness, the keeping of promises, and transparency contribute not only to their own credibility and stability but also to the smoothness and efficiency of business transaction, particularly on the international level." They also state: "we have a responsibility to treat our customer fairly in all aspects of our business transactions". They urge respect for rules and avoidance of illicit operations such as bribery.

The Caux Principles apply to customer behavior as well as supplier behavior. They state that suppliers should be treated fairly, honestly and with respect. Customers should consider their long-term stability and should pay them on time.

Source: Quoted with kind permission from the Caux Round Table

There is also a Latin American Corporate Governance Roundtable. Its Companies Circle brought together organizations with practical experience of improving stockholder returns from the adoption of corporate governance reforms in 2005. Circle members have been proactive in sharing best practice in the region.

Clearly, companies can gain competitive advantage from applying high standards of corporate responsibility. Since these codes are voluntary, the opportunity for differentiation exists.

Industry codes

Financial services and pharmaceuticals are heavily regulated industries, but also have their own codes in order to ensure the highest standards of behavior in selling and other company functions.

There were an estimated 80,000 pharmaceutical salespeople in the USA in 2004 (Wright and Lundstrom, 2004) operating within the constraints of the industry codes (which are set internationally and amended to reflect national markets). Sales representatives in pharmaceuticals have to give accurate information about drugs and other medical products to doctors, who have the authority to write prescriptions.

The codes that govern the pharmaceutical industry around the world are very detailed. The Association of the British Pharmaceutical Industry has a code incorporating the principles set out in international and European codes and law, and the World Health Organization's ethical criteria for drug promotion. The code is rigorously upheld, with companies being publicly rebuked or even being suspended from ABPI membership for breaches of the code.

Extracts from ABPI code

Guidance given states that representatives must:

- Be given adequate training and have adequate scientific knowledge to enable them to provide full and accurate information about the medicines they promote.
- Maintain a high standard of ethical conduct.

Representatives must NOT:

- Offer any inducement to get an interview with a decision-maker.
- Inconvenience health care professionals in the way that they seek and use time with them.
- Mislead health professionals about their identity or the identity of the company that they represent.

Companies must:

- Ensure that any sales-related commission that representatives receive is not an "undue proportion of their remuneration".
- Prepare detailed briefings for representatives. (Copies of briefings must be made available to the Medicines and Healthcare Products Regulatory Agency.)

Companies are responsible for the activities of their representatives, even if they are acting contrary to given instructions.

Summarized extracts from the ABPI Code of Practice (ABPI, 2006), produced with kind permission from the Prescription Medicines Code of Practice Authority

Even with strict industry codes, doctors around the world are telling researchers that they have less time to spend with representatives, and are less satisfied with the value they receive from the interaction. It is virtually impossible for them to keep up to date with new treatments via the medical journals, so they rely to some extent on information from the sales representatives, but there have been legal cases prompted by salespeople incorrectly specifying product capabilities.

Company reputation is important. Doctors are believed to rate pharmaceutical companies on commitment to research and development, credibility and educational orientation. Ethical behavior on behalf of the salesperson is an essential element of credibility. Understanding physician's needs and explaining the product capabilities to meet those needs is one thing, but doctors expect salespeople to exhibit values as well. They need to believe that the salespeople will serve their long-term interests and the interests of their patients (Wright and Lundstrom, 2004).

Professional codes

The United Professional Sales Association (UPSA) is one of the fastest growing non-profit membership organizations in the sales profession. It has headquarters in Washington DC and voluntary Chapters throughout the USA and in Brazil, Hong Kong, the UK and South Africa. UPSA's website provides information and guidance on many aspects of professional selling, including an extensive ethical guide. One element of this guide is the business card sized member's code of conduct:

Extracts from UPSA member's code

As an individual engaged in the selling profession, UPSA members pledge to uphold and abide by the following:

I will maintain high standards of integrity and professional conduct
I will accept responsibility for my actions
I will continually seek to enhance my professional capabilities
I will sell with fairness and honesty
I will encourage others in the profession to act in an ethical and professional manner

Source: Reproduced with kind permission from UPSA
www.upsa-intl.org

The code also offers 12 rights for professional buyers. The right to:

- have their needs put first
- information in the manner requested
- facts (benefits and drawbacks of a solution)
- a fair price and negotiation in good faith
- respect

- confer with others on the buying team
- objective advice
- confidentiality
- professional competence and integrity
- expedient service
- comfort and confidence
- exit.

Clearly, UPSA members know where they stand when it comes to their day-to-day selling activities. A code such as this can be very helpful to you when you are involved in designing and updating conduct guidelines.

However, salespeople also have rights to expect standards of conduct from buyers, and as VP Sales you should advise salespeople on the sort of behavior they should expect from their counterparts in purchasing, so that they can identify if something is wrong.

Professional associations representing buyers have codes of conduct. For example the member's code of the Purchasing Management Association of Canada includes the following:

Extracts from the PMAC code of behavior

Members should make decisions based on the following values:

- Honesty/integrity
- Professionalism
- Responsible management
- Serving the public interest
- Conformity to the law.

The norms of ethical behavior expected by PMAC include:

- Putting the interests of the company first
- Being receptive to advice from colleagues
- To buy without prejudice
- To seek increased knowledge and skills

- To work for honesty in buying and selling
- To be prompt and courteous.

The rules of conduct encompass:

- Declaring personal interests
- Observing confidentiality
- Ensuring fair competition
- Not accepting gifts, other than "items of small intrinsic value"
- Acting without discriminating against or harassing others
- Being aware of environmental issues.

The PMAC code also includes enforcement procedures.

Source: These extracts are reproduced with kind permission from the Purchasing Management Association of Canada (www.pmac.ca)

By raising salespeople's awareness of the behaviors expected of professional purchasers, they will be better able to identify and challenge any unusual requests from counterparts. We assume so many things when we send people into meetings. We assume that life has taught them how to deal with all kinds of things, and that may not be reasonable. Most commentators on the subject are agreed that the best way to teach ethics is by role-play. That's how we learned at IBM many years ago. Even in role-play, it was very difficult to cope with the "customer" behaving strangely. Real customers were never so scary as senior colleagues playing at being customers. So, when we trainee IBMers were allowed out to meet buying decision-makers, we were competent, prepared, and very relieved.

Corporate codes

Each company needs its own distillation of all the guidance available on best practice business conduct (see Figure 9.3).

As a trainee in IBM, I was expected to learn the Business Conduct Guidelines. Some customers might have joked about the "clones" that called on them from IBM, but they knew that they could expect certain standards

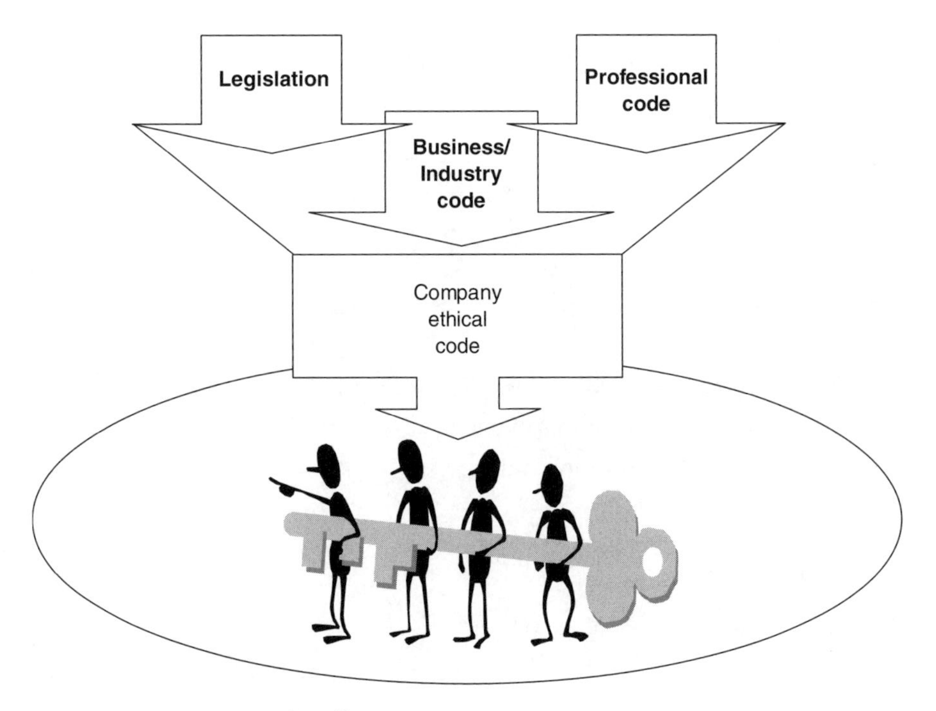

Figure 9.3 *Best practice codes of business practice.*

of behavior from IBMers, and that provided IBM salespeople with a framework of which we could be proud.

Many companies are very open about their guidelines, to ensure that all the stakeholders in the company, and legislators, can see that reputation management is taken seriously.

Code of conduct at Dover Corporation

In a statement from the Chairman at the beginning of Dover Corporation's Code of Business Conduct and Ethics, he writes, "An uncompromising adherence to ethical standards is integral to creating and sustaining the necessary strong foundation on which Dover's success is built and which Dover can grow and prosper."

The detail includes a position on gifts that applies to both salespeople and purchasing staff. Salespeople are advised not to denigrate the competition or make false claims about the performance of Dover products.

The code covers many other things, including legal compliance, workplace safety, records retention and avoiding conflicts of interest.

Employees can report ethical violations anonymously to the legal department, and it is clear that violations of the code will be dealt with seriously, and could even result in dismissal.

Source: Quoted and referenced with kind permission from Dover Corporation (www.dovercorporation.com)

Although a code in itself cannot ensure that employees and salespeople know what is expected of them, or that customers can feel reassured, it is an excellent starting point.

If it can go wrong, it will . . .

Of course, an ethical code will only work if it is trusted, and if ethical dilemmas can be discussed in a constructive environment. I have noticed that some sales managers have on their desk a plaque saying, "Don't bring me the problem, bring me the solution." It makes it easy to guess what reaction they would have if one of their reporting team walked in to discuss a problem. In fact, I've seen it happen. The manager starts to rave about "not wanting to hear about problems!" They have missed the point. Unless you understand the problem, how will you know a good solution when you see it?

Unless you understand the problem, how will you know a good solution when you see it?

As VP Sales, you have to act as a role model and help the salesperson to deal with ethical questions through coaching. You also have to apply discipline if one of your sales team breaks the code. Researchers have noted that it is extremely important when a salesperson violates the ethical code that all employees are made aware of the actions taken against them. At IBM, a lot of war stories circulated about what had happened in the past to people who had not observed the guidelines. The code of ethics must have some bite.

Unfortunately, studies at Arizona State University (Bellizzi and Hasty, 2003; Bellizzi and Bristol, 2005) show that neither a tighter and more equal corporate ethical code nor more training seems to stop the tendency of sales managers to treat high sales performers more leniently than others when they breach ethical codes.

The sales managers in these studies may have believed that they were strict enforcers of company rules, but the evidence was that their use of discipline was affected by the past sales performance of the individual concerned. In my informal discussions with sales managers on this topic, some have confessed to being lenient with their high fliers. They are worried that if they chastise them, they might flip from being great performers to being disruptive, which is probably worse than if they left the company.

You can work out what happens next. This leniency toward high performers immediately convinces other salespeople that their manager is not fair, and therefore it is perfectly acceptable for them to get their own back in some way. So what can you do? Maintaining the trust of all requires some superhuman effort to be seen to be truthful, to keep promises and to be fair. It also requires you to be seen to be conforming and setting an example. If exceptions are justified, put yourself out for any of your reporting team, not just the high fliers. If you stand up for them, look after them and make sacrifices for them, they might be more inclined toward self-discipline and accept your discipline when you need to exercise it.

A word of caution, however: it's important for sales managers to distinguish between ethical violations and violations of procedures that don't have an ethical component. Research into effective sales managers shows that good managers let their top salespeople break procedural rules all the time. "She's my top performer," explained a Xerox manager, "and if she doesn't want to come to work on Mondays I'm not going to make her." But that same manager would never allow any salesperson to break the Xerox code of ethics (Rackham and Ruff, 1991).

The effects of an ethical climate on the salesforce

The good news is that a strong ethical climate in a company has many more benefits than just ensuring that directors and vice presidents don't go to jail. A recent study led by

The good news is that a strong ethical climate in a company has many more benefits than just ensuring that directors and vice presidents don't go to jail.

Fernando Jaramillo at the University of Texas, involving 138 salespeople found that a strong ethical climate leads through lower role conflict to higher job satisfaction, higher job performance and better commitment to the job and the employer (Jaramillo, Mulki and Locander, 2006a). Therefore, a company with a strong ethical climate should expect happier and more productive salespeople and lower salesperson turnover, which saves a lot of money on recruitment and induction.

The researchers also found that clarity about ethical issues reduced stress among salespeople, who become concerned if they feel that their employer's values are out of alignment with their own. Clarity suggests that "the ethical climate" needs to be very well communicated, and sales managers need to reinforce ethical expectations on a day-to-day basis to reassure salespeople.

The other good news from a study in Spain by Sergio Roman and Salvador Ruiz at the University of Murcia (2005) is that ethical behavior plays a positive role in building customer relationships; in fact, they describe its role as "major". Their study involved interviewing 630 bank customers, 26% of whom were business customers. There was a very significant correlation between the customer's perceptions of the bank salesperson as ethical and their satisfaction and commitment.

It would appear, therefore, that a code is a good idea, but there are a few other things that you need to align to make sure that your sales team are getting consistent messages.

- Is your reward system aligned with your reputation management objectives?
- Is your training externally benchmarked to ensure best professional practice?
- Does your code travel across all the channels that you use, including the Internet?

Rewards and reputation

One sales manager in a small firm told me that his company's sales presentation mentioned the fact that his salespeople were not paid on commission, because it got the prospects' attention and they seemed to like it. Certainly, in the IT industry, that was unusual and a differentiating factor. Nevertheless, a majority of employers use a combination of salary plus commission to motivate salespeople, and how that is applied can affect a company's reputation.

It has long been assumed that money is a great motivator and it has been widely applied in motivating salespeople. It also works for purchasers – many get bonuses based on how much money they save their employer. And rewards linked to outcomes do have a positive effect – where they are perceived to be "fair", where the individual can actually influence the outcomes, and where they do not fluctuate widely. Many salespeople resign after a bad month or quarter, proving that competitive pay systems can create losers as well as winners. Desperate salespeople who have had a bad month, or disgruntled salespeople who feel that the system is not fair, are the people who might be tempted to stray into ethical minefields.

Ensure that variable pay does not distort performance

Ken Teal is a performance management enthusiast with a varied background – armed forces, manufacturing and service provision – who is currently working with inventors to commercialize their innovations. He has wide experience of taking waste out of activities and encouraging behaviors that contribute to organizations' real objectives. Ken believes that sales payment systems can have a dramatic effect on customer relationship development and corporate reputation management.

While acknowledging that variable pay associated with sales revenue has a role, he cautions that companies must ensure that it doesn't distort performance. Systems must avoid creating temptations to play games – for example, getting distributors to take goods "on trial" (channel stuffing) or manipulating delivery dates to improve the end of quarter results (sandbagging). These devices mess up other parts of the company by skewing production schedules and generating waste. Ken believes that fixed monthly/quarterly targets are too vulnerable to short-term manipulation. Many sales managers would benefit from using longer term, rolling performance measures that reward consistent performance linked to a variety of bonuses tailored to achieving long-term corporate objectives.

Source: Quoted with kind permission from Ken Teal, South Hampshire Enterprise Agency

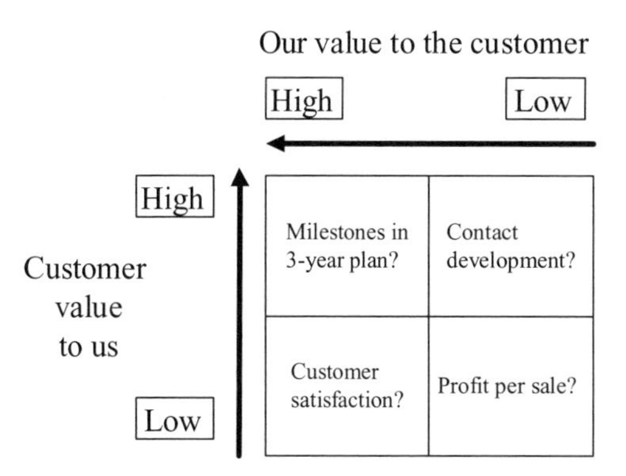

Figure 9.4 *Supplier/customer value matrix.*

Nobody would argue that the sales function has to be focused on the top line. Top-line, profitable growth is the critical contribution that sales make to shareholder value. Nevertheless, the sales function is also responsible in part for customer satisfaction and company reputation (as its standard bearers). The sales function should also be an incubator for future leaders of the company.

There are a variety of performance measures that companies may use to vary the triggers for variable pay so that these other contributions can be rewarded – for example, contract renewals, results over extended periods of time, increase in share of customer spend, customer satisfaction ratings and personal objectives. And since salespeople are often leading teams, team-based incentives also need to be considered.

More importantly, rewards should vary according to the type of business relationships that the salesperson is developing (see Figure 9.4). The reward triggers and the amount of reward appropriate for a key account manager developing a strategic relationship will be quite different from a telesales person working on prospecting or processing tactical business. In this way, rewards can be more realistically linked to what the individual can reasonably achieve (Ryals and Rogers, 2005).

Training to professional standards

A study in real estate in three US states in 2003 found that education for a professional qualification and accreditation improved salespeople's ability to reason ethically, and their job performance. Qualified professionals were likely to stay longer in the industry. There was a consistency with the customer's expectation that real estate agents with a professional designation would have higher levels of ability and demonstrate higher standards of sales behavior.

Most companies provide some training for salespeople. Product training is essential, and perhaps some communications skills updates. In recent years, perhaps because it is no longer possible for a company to offer much long-term job security, leading employers have started to link their in-house sales academies with external qualifications, so that their salespeople acquire transferable skills and a professional grounding that transcends the employer's interests. If companies want accountants and engineers that are professionally qualified and certified by a professional body, why not employ or develop professionally qualified salespeople?

In the UK, the government has developed "National Occupational Standards for Sales", which are the basis for the certificates and diploma of the Institute of Sales and Marketing Management. A professional association can provide a framework enabling companies to start from basic training for recruits and design a development path to best practice.

> *"The National Occupation Standards for Sales reflect all the important aspects of sales competencies including behaviors, skills, knowledge and understanding."*
>
> Dr Chahid Fourali, Chief Executive
> UK Marketing and Sales Standards Setting Body
> Quoted with kind permission

Do customers care? Most purchasing professionals are members of their national professional institutions. Almost all vice-presidents of finance around the world are qualified and required to maintain membership of a recognized accountancy body. When there are still so many unqualified salespeople around, having qualified salespeople could give you a reputational advantage with buying decision-makers. Will you lose some of your training investment because other companies offer jobs to your qualified salespeople? You probably will, but many more will choose to stay with you because they like your company values better than the values of the poacher.

Are your channels in tune with your reputation?

Some of the most successful outsourcing arrangements are based on the outsourcers understanding the importance of taking on their clients' brand values and guarding their reputation. Distributors and retailers will be more keen on their own brand values than those of any single producer, so that may be a point to debate when making channel choices (see Chapter 6).

And then there is the Internet ...

If it is difficult enough managing corporate reputation through people, it is equally challenging to manage your corporate reputation on line. Suppliers take the bulk of responsibility for protecting customer data from hackers and fraudsters. Network security is a never-ending arms war. For smaller companies, the outsourcing of networks to managed service providers who employ security experts is an attractive option. Security also needs to be built into e-commerce applications so that unusual activity can be identified and investigated.

Privacy regulations vary from country to country and from state to state in the USA. European legislation is comprehensive, and even in business-to-business markets, permission must be obtained for Internet or telephone contact with individuals in organizations. Your Privacy Policy has to be displayed on your website. Proactive approaches to permission-seeking for various types of customer contact, and encouraging feedback, both contribute to reputation-building. (For more information, see Rogers, 2003b.)

Best practice includes:

- Easy access to your privacy statement from every page on the site.
- Enabling browsers to visit your website without identifying themselves.
- Enabling users who are registered on the site to access and update their own information.
- Stating what information is gathered on the site and how it is used.
- Stating whether information is shared, and if so, with whom.
- Giving users choices about sharing their information.
- Enabling users to opt out of e-mail contact.
- Explaining how the data of website users is kept secure.
- Making it easy for website visitors to contact relevant members of staff.

As with everything on the Internet, ideas about "best practice" on security, privacy and on-line reputation move fast. Working with specialists in this field should help you as VP Sales to keep ahead.

What's the alternative?

Risky arrangements do not contribute to shareholder value.

There are still a few old stereotypes left out there, like the person who claims to have influential power in his company who suggests to one of your sales team that he will only give him orders if he takes him to a strip club and pays for lots of drinks. Neither supplier nor customer could be transparent about such an arrangement, so it has no corporate relationship-building value. Indeed, it puts both companies reputations at risk. Bear in mind that individual investors and institutional investors are increasingly interested in your company's "social responsibility". Dodgy arrangements do not contribute to shareholder value.

Even if the questionable deal appeared to offer some short-term gain, the competitor's sales representative might know a better strip club and the advantage might be very short-term indeed! Save your expenses budget and put this customer firmly in the "tactical" box of the customer portfolio matrix until you can find a way to have a rational discussion with the real decision-makers.

10

Working with marketing

". . . if marketing and sales do not co-operate, the company's strategy will be inconsistent and weak; and execution will be flawed and inefficient." Shapiro (2002)

Quoted with kind permission from
Professor Shapiro, Harvard Business School

Why don't sales and marketing get along?

There is a feeling among salespeople and marketers that sales and marketing just don't get along together, and that the conflict between them is harmful to shareholder value. Nor does it help customers very much. From the outside looking in, customers think that marketing and sales share the responsibility for creating a positive image of the company and communicating its value.

In practice, sales and marketing are usually separate kingdoms in companies. Perhaps they are separate in yours. Many companies claim to be customer-driven or even "customer-obsessed", but the organization of sales and marketing seems to create an environment for disputes. Most Chief Executive Officers have traditional views about marketing being responsible for demand generation and sales being responsible for converting leads into revenue. When a company is small, the need for a dominant sales orientation is obvious, and marketing will be aligned with sales to generate volume. As a company becomes established, marketing's interests diverge, while sales stays focused on volume. Marketing and sales develop different worlds, reinforced by separate training and different backgrounds.

Some work by Dewsnap and Jobber in 2000 on the relationship between sales and marketing was blunt in its comment. They stated in their conclusion that "the sales–marketing interface, while strongly interdependent, is reported as neither collaborative nor harmonious". In fact, it is characterized by "lack of cohesion, poor coordination, conflict, non-cooperation, distrust, dissatisfaction and mutual negative stereotyping".

Research by sales guru Neil Rackham and marketing guru Philip Kotler (Kotler, Rackham and Krishnaswamy, 2006) indicated that there are two sources of friction between marketing and sales. One is economic, focused on how budgets are allocated between the two departments. The other is cultural. Marketers are generally focused on analysis rather than action, and on the long-term plan rather than individual customers' short-term demands.

In an on-line discussion that I conducted recently with some marketing and sales opinion leaders – followed up by a workshop held at the Chartered Institute of Marketing – the vast majority thought that it was likely or very likely in an organization that sales and marketing will perceive their interests to clash. Twenty-seven suggestions were made for the cause of that conflict. As in the 2006 study by Kotler and colleagues, responses clustered around differences over the expertise or effectiveness of each other (cultural rivalry) and concerns, or even disputes, about targets and budgets (economic rivalry). The culturally-oriented disputes were about relative status, ownership of the customer relationship and the implementation of strategy. Clashes over expertise, effectiveness and status suggest that mutual disrespect is a common experience among sales and marketing professionals.

I asked about the source of conflict, and received a clear message that blame should be shared, if not just between sales and marketing, with others. Given that the response boxes offered (as the source of the conflict) were "sales", "marketing" or "other", it was noticeable that most people responding ignored the boxes and replied "both sales and marketing" or ticked all three boxes. Some specified "other" as "senior directors". So the conflict appears to be, in the experience of sales and marketing professionals, an organizational dynamic that is fuelled by both functions and others, not least of which is a lack of resolve at the top of the company.

Why should sales and marketing get along?

The bottom line

To the world at large, sales and marketing look alike and they are both perceived to be focused on the customer.

> *"Nowhere is the need to work together more important than in the twin customer-facing functions of marketing and sales"*
>
> Shapiro (2002)

Research findings from integration studies suggest that collaboration, including information sharing and working collectively for common goals, has a positive effect on business performance outcomes such as the success of innovation. Opinion is weighted heavily toward the desirability of integration and the assumption that it would have a positive impact on business performance.

> *"We believe that a 20% or more gain in profits can be realized by companies that improve a poorly working marketing/sales relationship into a better one."*
>
> Kotler, Rackham and Krishnaswamy (2006)

A majority of the participants in my discussions on the sales/marketing interface felt that, in their experience, they had seen the clash of interest between sales and marketing having a negative effect on business performance; some had not and others gave a qualified "no". Among those who gave a qualified "no" there was an observation that it had been seen in some companies but not in others, and another that they suspected that there might be some negative impact but cause and effect are too far apart to track. So, conflict is expected to damage business performance, and other research tells us that integration should improve business performance. It is hardly surprising that, when asked in my study whether or not it is desirable for sales and marketing to integrate, a majority of both marketing and sales professionals gave an enthusiastic "yes"!

The brand

Branding is an important area in which marketing contributes to sales. In B2C markets the brand may be the single most powerful sales tool – ask Coca-Cola or Pepsi. But brand communication is also very important in B2B markets. Some of the biggest brands in the world are B2B (e.g. IBM) or have B2B divisions (e.g. Mercedes, Sony). Being a "brand" can provide reassurance to a prospective customer about a company's reputation. In B2B markets, the brand must have functional characteristics, but it can also generate emotional expectations that a salesperson, as the standard bearer of the company, must represent.

Buying decision-makers do take into account intangible things when they are reviewing potential suppliers.

- Do they consider the company, and its personnel, to be trustworthy?
- Does working with this supplier attract any prestige?
- Could this supplier help me to achieve my career objectives?

In the 1970s, there was a saying among data-processing managers: "No one ever got sacked for buying IBM." This may never have been completely accurate, but it contributed to IT managers perceiving the company as a low-risk supplier in terms of their personal career prospects. IBM has continued to promote their image for security, e.g. an advertisement that showed a pillow embroidered with the IBM logo and the headline "What most people want from a computer service company is a good night's sleep".

Branding in B2B markets contributes to developing opportunities for value creation, sustaining prices, ensuring customer retention and enabling differentiation. Buying decision-makers are interested in the values of suppliers and potential suppliers and the brand can provide a shortcut to understanding what they are. The trust and credibility of the brand must matter to all stakeholders, as discussed in Chapter 9.

Personal selling is the dominant communication tool in the marketing communications mix in business-to-business markets. Successful selling is dependent on salespeople's behavior. The buyer experiences the company's brand values through the behavior of your salesperson. The salesperson must adapt messages to the buyer's communication preferences to improve customer satisfaction, but going off-message is risky for all parties. Some researchers claim that the very success of the sale is dependent on compatibility of style and content of communication. Salespeople generally have considerable freedom to adapt brand messages to accommodate the buyer's frame of reference.

The brand ambassador role of the sales representative is a sensitive one. He or she needs to walk the company talk. As a sales manager, you wouldn't want branding to be an external activity, developed by an agency and imposed from on high. In the 21st century, it is recognized that branding is dependent on employees (and that includes salespeople) understanding it, valuing it and committing to it. Employees have to be brand ambassadors long before customers will be convinced to provide references for a supplier. If salespeople, in particular, are fulfilling their role as standard-bearers, they must be in tune with brand values.

In the 21st century, it is recognized that branding is dependent on employees (and that includes salespeople) understanding it, valuing it and committing to it.

Marketing clearly plays a dominant role in the identification of brand artefacts such as the logo, slogans and advertising imagery. A lot of consultation should take place to ensure that these images are acceptable and, in particular, that salespeople are pleased to identify with them.

How should sales and marketing get along?

Looking at our B2B relationship box (Figure 10.1), with its focus on rational allocation of resources, you would expect marketing to take a leading role in driving tactical business, and a major role in the early stages of prospect development, plus perhaps a reinforcement role for cooperative business. However, there are going to be lots of occasions when the line becomes blurred.

Step 1: Definitions

If the roles of marketing and sales are not defined in your organization, you must define them. Essentially, the definition includes a description of the role of the department, the value it is adding and what activities it leads.

Most dictionaries describe selling as the exchange of goods or services for money, but that does little to explain how the sales profession views itself.

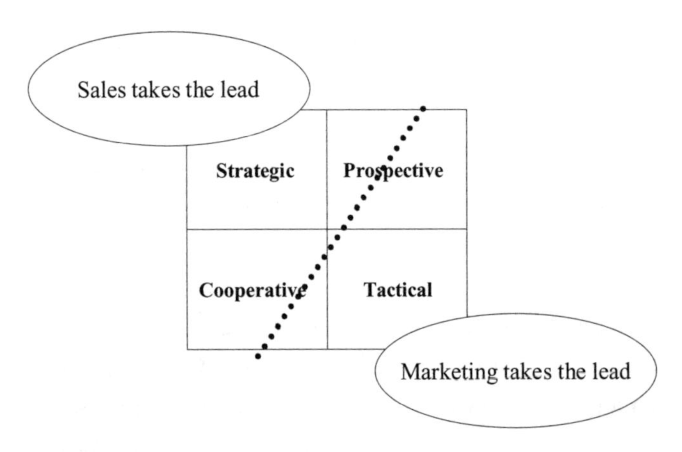

Figure 10.1 *Sales focus: marketing focus.*

The UK government's vocational sales standards are helpful in giving a flavor of the pride inherent in professionally qualified salespeople.

> *The key purpose of selling is described as "to create, build and sustain mutually beneficial and profitable relationships through personal and organizational contact".*
>
> Marketing and Sales Standards Settings Board

Marketing has for many years tried to be defined as a profession. It is sometimes seen as just about advertising or communications, and it also gets confused with selling. Once again, we can borrow from the UK government's vocational standards to see how marketers view themselves.

> *The standards for marketing proclaim that the key purpose of marketing is "to advance the aims of organizations by providing direction, gaining commitment and achieving sustainable results and value through identifying, anticipating and satisfying stakeholder requirements".*
>
> Marketing and Sales Standards Settings Board

It is instantly clear that although there is a difference in scope in these definitions, there is some overlap. Marketers tend to claim that they do strategy while sales is an operational function that should be implementing marketing strategy. Sales managers often feel that marketing strategy is remote from the realities of day-to-day contact with customers. The first challenge any company faces in integrating sales and marketing is that both functions will take some time to develop mutual respect. In that learning process, some joint agreement about who does what and why will be necessary. Each company needs its own definitions.

How marketing evolves

Start-up companies do not have marketing departments, but they do need to make sales. Salespeople have to do their own market development work, and the entrepreneur who owns the company may be heavily involved in prospect and customer contact. As a company grows, either a marketing agency or a marketing employee is used to provide lead generation services to sales. As a company develops from small to medium-sized, marketing will be involved in market development encompassing segmentation, targeting and positioning, setting promotional strategies and getting involved in product, price and channel strategies. Large companies that are dependent on maintaining a strong brand, such as fast-moving consumer goods, may have marketing-led business strategy at the highest level.

Source: Kotler, Rackham and Krishnaswamy (2006)

Step 2: Interaction

The next stage is called interaction by many commentators on departmental integration such as Kenneth Kahn. It has also been called alignment by, for example, Kotler, Rackham and Krishnaswamy (2006).

As a bare minimum, information exchanges and meetings between sales and marketing departments are essential to the smooth running of the company. There is a balance between too much interaction, which can inhibit productivity, and too little, which can result in hidden costs caused by misunderstandings between departments. If marketing fails to interact sufficiently, it has been found that this affects other departments' perceptions of the usefulness of their output, and the same is probably true of sales. Interaction has a positive influence on each department's success, the company's success and each department's satisfaction with the others.

Interaction support is also helpful. For example, an Intranet-based sales support resource including presentation materials, competitor updates, in-company news, personal links and marketing material can be a valuable resource for salespeople.

Types of interaction

Meetings

Kotler and colleagues insist that you must schedule regular meetings between sales and marketing. The joint meeting may be monthly or quarterly depending on the amount of activity in a company. Meetings that are regular and routine tend to create less emotion than special meetings caused to discuss an issue, and so create time for constructive discussion and even exploratory discussion. Meetings are also needed when particular circumstances occur, such as a particularly large opportunity with a customer, or when marketing material is updated.

Working together

Respondents to my discussion were keen to see sales and marketing people understanding each other's jobs. They even went so far as to suggest swapping jobs for limited periods. Certainly, many companies encourage marketers to go on sales calls and listen first hand to customers' opinions. It is less common to find a salesperson in a meeting between the marketing department and the advertising agency, but it would help the agency to hear about how a campaign can assist field activity.

Another example of working together is what I have heard called "sales-ready marketing". By working with sales, marketers can get beyond awareness to providing credible proofs in marketing material. Marketing messages can be tailored per industry type and per decision-maker. The professional purchaser will like to know that a product is cheaper in the long run because the user needs less of it. The line manager will like to know that the same product reduces their hassle factors because the users find it easier to use. The user wants to know that it is easier to learn and helps them do their job.

When marketing throws messages "over the wall" to sales, you can hardly be expected to catch all of them correctly. Producing a call brief together is an integrated way of exploring and consolidating what needs to be said to the customer.

Call brief

Product/Service: Security Services

Overview

We provide remote and on-site support to enable customers to concentrate on their core business whilst we ensure their physical premises are safe from intrusion.

Fact-finding/setting the scene

How many locations need protecting?

Do they have varying priorities (e.g. low risk branch office versus high risk warehouse)?

What security measures do you have in place at the moment?

Do you have closed circuit TV installed?

How many staff are involved in security at the moment? Do they work shifts?

What service levels (availability, response times) do you guarantee?

Identifying challenges

Are you able to meet your service levels regularly?

What is the biggest recurring challenge in meeting service levels?

How much time is absorbed in issue resolution e.g. when delivery drivers have wrong documentation?

Do staff turnover, redeployment or unexpected staff absence ever cause service level exposure?

How much management time is absorbed in security issues?

Identifying the impact of challenges

Is how much you can achieve in a day affected by security issues?

Is the stress of security management a cause of staff turnover?

Usage scenarios

Would it be helpful if . . .

. . . you could reduce the risks associated with physical security?

. . . you could feel confident about next month's service level reports?

. . . you could reassure staff about their personal safety?

Pay-off questions

How much would it be worth if . . .

. . . you could reduce "shrinkage" by x%?

. . . you could reduce the damage caused by thieves and vandals?

. . . you could reduce insurance premiums?

Examples

Results we have achieved for customers:

Reduced internal theft by 85% at customer X.

"I have found •• to be a top-tier service provider," said Joe Bloggs, Operations Manager of customer Y.

Reduced insurance premiums at Customer Z by 15% in first year.

Possible objections

Some customers may be concerned about loss of control.

Others may be concerned about cost-savings being marginal.

Quality of contracted staff is often an issue.

Overcoming objections

Nominated managers can have access to control data and CCTV views at any time via an Internet portal.

The cost advantages of security services include avoiding hidden costs, and ensuring cost predictability.

Customer can be involved in vetting individuals who patrol their premises.

Call to action

Arrange a visit to a reference account.

Arrange a visit to our demonstration centre.

First published by the author in *Sales and Marketing Professional*, 2004 (now *Winning Edge*). Reprinted with kind permission of the Editor (www.ismm.co.uk)

To make messages actionable and consistent, marketers can work with salespeople to take the thinking behind the company's offer right to the customer's desk. In Box 10.2, a call brief has been worked out to establish the customer's pain points so that the need for the solution can be identified, verified and quantified before the introduction of the solution.

In one company I worked with, call briefs were symbolic evidence of enhanced relationships between marketing and sales colleagues.

Feedback

Your salespeople need to know who in marketing they should contact when they have heard something important about a competitor or a customer has mentioned a new project. In some companies, a secretary might take responsibility for forwarding information between sales and marketing personnel, but a direct understanding of who does what in both departments would be valuable to them. In general, marketing are regularly using a lot of general data about markets, while salespeople gather a lot of "word of mouth" stories and anecdotes from customers. Data is useless without context, and stories are useless without evidence. The combination of data analysis and anecdotal examples that will happen when sales and marketing exchange their information should develop insight that can be actionable.

Opportunities for informal interaction

Some supporters of integration between departments recommend that they should be physically located close to each other. It seems that grumbling about the weather or soccer at the same water cooler can also lead colleagues to solve some of their business problems at that water cooler. If it isn't possible to put the desks of marketers and salespeople close together, then having lunch after joint meetings becomes an important opportunity for informal communication.

Step 3: Collaboration

Although interaction is a prerequisite for it, a major study by Kenneth Kahn and John Mentzer on the topic of integration (1998) found a very strong connection between collaboration and successful performance, but the link between interaction and performance was relatively weak. Collaboration is a big step beyond interaction. It involves shared processes, shared goals, shared values and win-win behavior.

Collaboration is a big step beyond interaction. It involves shared processes, shared goals, shared values and win-win behavior.

Studying social interactions, psychologists have found that the way in which people believe their goals are related affects the outcome of their behavior. For example, if goals in games are perceived to be interdependent, each player will believe that if one player makes progress, all players will make progress. Each player will want all players to act effectively and expectations of trust will build. They will collaborate to share information and try to understand each other's perspectives. They will communicate effectively using higher quality reasoning. They will exchange resources and be supportive. Where collaboration exists, the individuals believe that what is good for the group is also good for each of them in the long term.

> *"The shadow of the future provides the basis for cooperation, even among egoists."*
>
> Quoted with kind permission from Professor Robert Axelrod, author of *The Evolution of Cooperation*, 1984

Assumptions about collaboration in the workplace assume that we are rational beings, but usually we just adapt to circumstances. We have to see collaborative strategies generate success before we adopt them. Senior managers find it challenging to create a collaborative culture – it needs devolved decision-making, and it requires a lot of individuals to cope with some role ambiguity. It also requires training and coaching, and takes time.

Aspects of collaboration

Joint vision, values and goals:

> *"The typical company rushes along from year to year in frenzied activity, without a clear vision of the future, and lacking distinctive or superior propositions."*
>
> Davidson (2000). Quoted with kind permission

But it doesn't have to be like that. . . .

> *"To take a sprawling, stumbling conglomerate and reshape it into a keenly focused, highly profitable company in the vanguard of one of the world's fastest growing industries is the stuff of management dreams."*
>
> Carnegy (1995) Finnish telecommunications company Nokia described in the *Financial Times*

Marketing and sales have big roles to play in conveying the vision and values of the company to customers. Both departments also have a responsibility to the company to anticipate and work towards the revenue growth that the company needs in the future in order to satisfy all its stakeholders. Generally, if you just carry on doing what you have always done, other companies will come along and do it better.

Marketing and sales may feel that they share the "big picture" target (see Figure 10.2), but they also need to share responsibility for targets in the short term. That means that they have to be judged by related metrics and accept complementary rewards based on those metrics. Sales may take primary responsibility for growth in "share of purse" of existing customers, and marketing may take primary responsibility for acquisition of new customers. Both have a role in customer retention, which is an important element of profitable growth, and both may have incentives based on working within tight budgets to reduce operating costs.

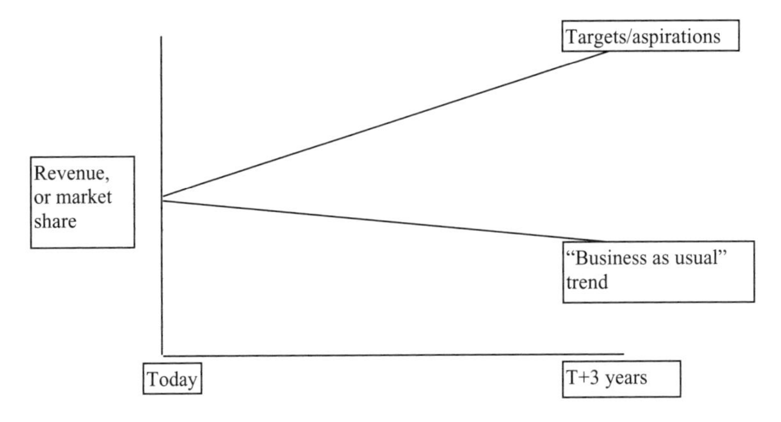

Figure 10.2 *Gap analysis.*

Teamwork

Marketing and sales should be planning together. Marketing analysis for marketing planning overlaps with planning for strategic relationships, and joint planning with customers should be feeding into the marketing plan. Assessing customer needs that have been expressed for that joint planning should lead both marketing and sales, together with other colleagues, to design interesting value propositions.

Promotional campaigns also require teamwork. Marketing can generate creative input, but your salespeople know the practicalities of what customers want to read about, and the sort of images with which they identify.

Mutual understanding

In a poll of sales and marketing executives undertaken by researchers by the Center for Business and Industrial Marketing at Georgia State University, marketers thought that salespeople should understand: the factors that drive their markets; branding and other aspects of marketing strategy; strategic planning; profitable pricing; and channel optimization. Meanwhile sales executives thought that marketers should understand: account management; questioning for customer needs; solution selling; and territory management. They all felt that marketers should meet buyers (Donath, 2004).

I have found similar responses in talking to both. Many sales opinion leaders feel that marketing people should have sold at some stage of their careers. Marketing opinion leaders say that "salespeople should be trained in marketing techniques and marketing should be integrated into the operational (sales) process". Both advocate a "shared understanding from doing each other's jobs".

This mutual understanding, both through training and working together (see "Step 2: Interaction" above) can enrich both. For example, a power tools company recognized that product training and negotiation techniques were not enough to enable salespeople to succeed. Their training covered how their B2B customers responded to the brand values (Lynch and de Chernatony, 2004).

Shared information

Marketers are expected to play a deeper role than sales, gathering information from within the company on strengths such as product advantage, process efficiencies and specialist knowledge; then designing campaigns to promote them. Meanwhile, they also commission market research to identify what "the market" wants. Such research has had its frailties in the past, but the application of technology to customer/prospect information and communication can enable granularity of analysis about customer motivation, behavior and needs. Attitudes to products and services can be explored.

Meanwhile, salespeople visit the customer decision-makers in their own environment, and can gather a great deal of circumstantial and informal information, which adds considerable quality to the quantity of information that might be gathered from transaction histories and feedback questionnaires. Customer service also plays a complementary role in capturing what customers enquire and complain about.

As mentioned earlier, data is useless without context, and stories are useless without evidence. Rather than just exchanging information, marketing, sales and customer service need to be operating from the same system. It is amazing how many islands of automation there can be in companies, but the technology exists to integrate them so that information can be accessed by all who need to use it, when they need to use it. The one proviso is that no one should get information overload. Relevance is key.

Shared process management

The whole sales process, from market definition through to proposal presentation, implementation and relationship development needs to be mapped indicating where marketing leads, where sales leads, where they cooperate and where they are both supporting operations or finance (Figure 10.3).

Although the sales process is normally drawn in a linear manner, the interdependence of activities within it is more obvious when it is drawn as a circle. The interdependence does not just involve marketing and sales; technical staff and support staff are also involved. Nevertheless, marketing and sales have to lay firm foundations for operations with a customer to succeed and for payment to be secured through customer satisfaction.

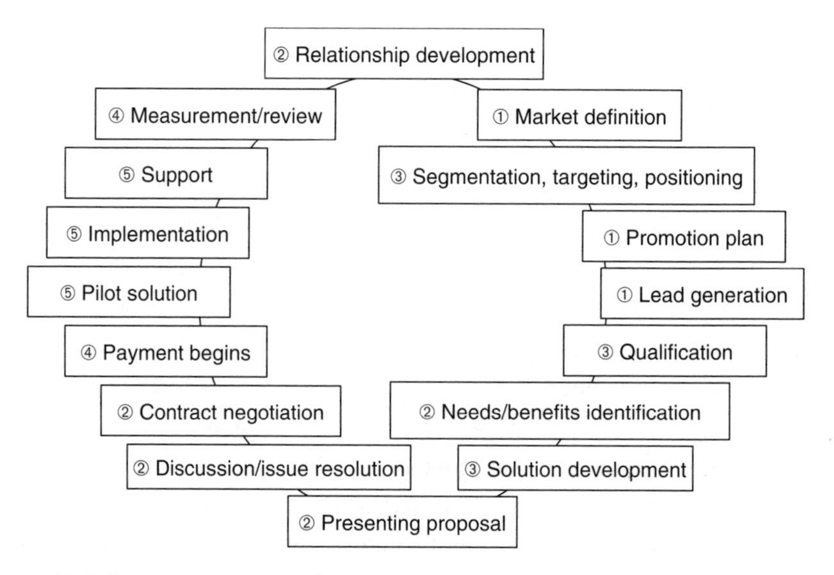

Figure 10.3 *Revenue generation cycle.*
Key:
① *Marketing lead*
② *Sales lead*
③ *Marketing and sales collaborate*
④ *Both support finance*
⑤ *Both support operations*

Marketing may take the lead on market definition, but sales have to share their understanding. Definitions of "leads" from cold to warm to qualified have to be agreed. Marketing can support you in preparing the call to establish needs and benefits sought. Marketing and sales work together with technical and finance colleagues on solution development. The sales function takes the lead in presenting the proposal and refining the proposal in negotiation with the customer. Within all that, a lot of learning is acquired. This can then be fed back to marketing.

What else is needed?

Senior management leadership

Chief Executive Officers have a role in promoting integration within the company to focus on value delivery. They have an interest in ensuring that strategy is interpreted consistently across departments. They are also responsible for designing reward systems that ensure consistent motivation and implementation. Some respondents in my discussion looked for strong leadership from the CEO. For example, one hoped for "top-driven understanding of what customer-driven means in all facets of the business".

Getting the CEO to spend time with customers

Philip Lay of The Chasm Group (in 2003) argued that revenue generation requires the leadership of an executive with cross-functional authority. Since analysts and investors want to know how the company is performing with major customers and new deals, it is good for the CEO to have direct experience of both. The CEO spending more time with customers would "set the right tone" for revenue growth.

Quoted with kind permission of Philip Lay, Managing Director
TCG Advisors LLC (www.tcg-advisors.com)

A Chief Customer Officer?

"Organisational structure is a natural beginning, but most people expect too much from it."

Shapiro (2002)

In many smaller businesses, the title "Sales and Marketing Manager" is common. One person has to manage both. In larger companies, the idea of combining sales and marketing under one manager is relatively new.

Researchers Johnson and Schultz discussed "the Chief Customer Officer" as a source of integration, whose role is "to maximise the value of the firm's customer relationships" in an article in *Marketing Management* in 2004. The first CCO was appointed in the US utilities sector in 1995, and supervised all customer-facing activities including sales, service, billing, marketing communications and the contact center. Other examples have followed. In some companies, the role covers sales and services to retailers. In others, the CCO covers marketing, sales and business-development-related services, or marketing, sales and innovation. A major US retailer took the view that the roles of CCO and CMO should be combined, so their CCO covers advertising, branding, communications, and marketing strategy as well as customer service, contact center and customer relationship management. In service industries, it is common to see the full range of marketing, sales and service functions under the CCO.

Kotler, Rackham and Krishnaswamy (2006) preferred the title CRO – Chief Revenue Officer. "The CRO's responsibility is planning and delivering the desired revenue the company needs to meet its objectives." He or she therefore needs control over the functions affecting revenue.

Half of the respondents in my study were initially suggesting that combined leadership at Board level would be helpful for integration. Comments about how sales and marketing might be integrated included:

- "a Sales and Marketing Director with no tolerance of a silo mentality";
- "a Marketing and Sales Director with training and experience covering both areas";
- "have both reporting to a business unit director";
- "Sales and Marketing Director who really understands both";
- "combine both functions at board level";
- "a new function/title and ensure that whoever leads (it) has first class experience and belief in both professional sales management and strategic market-led business transformation";
- "a very strong business director who oversees both".

When I followed this up, consensus was less clear. The suggestion that a CCO might be desirable was certainly thought-provoking and some answers that I received were very long. A global account manager in a manufacturing company described the importance in his company of the "customer influence interface" which certainly drove integration between customer service and sales. Strategically, a reputation for excellent service can be a sustainable competitive advantage and command a price premium, therefore parts and service, technical design support and new sales sit well together with operational marketing (i.e. promoting the service differential). However, strategic marketing in his company was closer to product development.

An experienced sales manager felt that having one senior person to decide on the balance between long-term customer satisfaction and short-term sales targets was an excellent idea, but it would take strong leadership to manage the sales and marketing departments. In his experience, the people who are good in leading combined teams have to be good leaders. The only "must" in terms of experience was sales, but finance or business management would be an advantage. A good leader would be able to learn and accommodate other disciplines quickly.

A sales consultant felt that while sales and marketing needed to be brought together, it might not be so wise to add in customer service. If the Chief Executive Officer delegates all customer-facing activity to one director, might that person lose sight of the importance of their own role in leading customer focus? Another respondent commented: "In most cases a CEO should do his job and not need a CCO."

So, although the idea of sales and marketing enjoying common leadership at Board level is popular, merging functional silos into one big customer focus silo is not necessarily the answer. Companies have to be wary of creating a title without power and responsibility, or a function without strategy, measurement or incentives.

Conclusion

Whatever the state of sales and marketing integration in your organization today, there will be opportunities to improve: from the basics of joint meetings and tokens of "sales-ready marketing" to complex planning and process integration. As there are huge political power plays at risk, the support of the Chief Executive Officer is important. Since he or she is unlikely to see disengagement as desirable, being the VP Sales who initiates some co-operation between sales and marketing should enhance your career.

11

Leadership

"The influence of each human being on others in this life is a kind of immortality."

John Quincy Adams, Sixth President of the USA, 1767–1848

Every management guru since Peter Drucker has given us a visionary role model of the manager coaching his valued team to success. In the ruthlessly competitive global markets of today, that is perhaps hopelessly idealistic. After all, careers are not what they used to be. Employers cannot offer the same job security as previously. Nevertheless, it is crazy to contemplate the alternative – that your role as a manager would be to help people to fail. Throughout history, leaders who have helped their people to fail have ended up as smashed statues.

"She was 300% of quota year after year," explained one sales VP. "But she crashed when we gave her the manager's job. She was a great sales rep but she was a useless leader." With minor variations, versions of this story exist in every company. You cannot work in sales without hearing stories about great salespeople who were promoted to become lousy sales managers. Ken Blanchard, of *One Minute Manager* fame, says that the primary reason for the failure of new sales managers is that they don't understand leadership.

You cannot work in sales without hearing stories about great salespeople who were promoted to become lousy sales managers.

A few years ago, alumni and students urged me to redesign the Portsmouth MA in Sales Management to devote a significant proportion of it to leadership. They argued that the greatest challenge of account management and sales management in the 21st century is that you have to achieve results through other people. Management may vary in style, but in order for you to succeed you have no alternative but to help others to succeed.

Psychologist Dr Raj Persaud (1997) describes the three Cs of best mental health (Figure 11.1) as:

- *Commitment*: A sense of purpose and goals in life
- *Control*: The belief in your own ability to influence your future
- *Challenge*: Accepting risk and being excited by change.

We need this as individuals and we need it in our workplace. Risk-averse decision-making, lack of motivation, cynicism, and fear of change are often found in organizations where managers are not leaders, and it affects employee morale. Businesses that demonstrate poor corporate mental health are not likely to survive for long in highly competitive markets.

How, therefore, can a sales manager inspire commitment, control and challenge? How can account managers in charge of account teams do the same, especially as they do not have formal line management authority?

Understanding the nature of leadership, how to exercise different styles and diagnosing when to use which, are all important. Ideally, sales managers

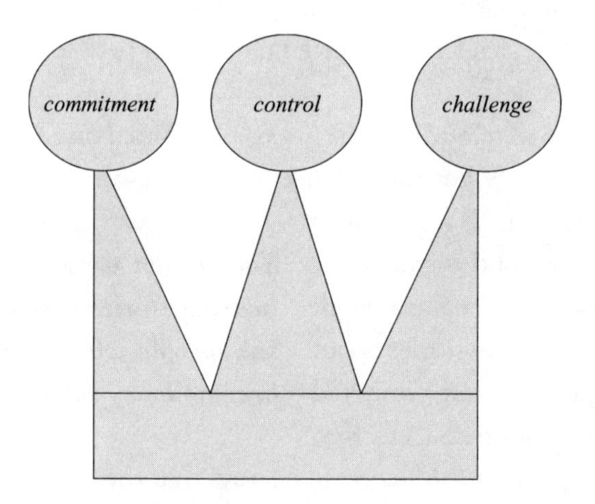

Figure 11.1 *The three Cs of mental health.*

and key account managers should have some defined formal influence, but formal influence is a luxury in modern organizations. The next generation of professionals do not automatically trust someone's judgment just because they have formal power. Without the skills to demonstrate leadership, managers of any function will struggle to get the best out of their reporting staff. The challenge is particularly acute for sales managers.

What's the problem?

Sales managers have usually been promoted from sales, where they have been responsible for meeting their own targets. Achieving results through others is unusual territory. In an insurance company investigating huge differences in divisional performance, sales managers focusing on helping their salespeople to succeed through coaching were on average doing 20% better than those who continued to focus on selling (Beaujohn, Davidson and Stacey, 2006).

A study in Australia indicated that 50% of salespeople considered that they had received inadequate leadership support in some areas, and an additional 20% complained of lack of support in most areas of their work (Wilkinson, 2006). A study with 426 participants in Europe, including some global brand companies, revealed similar trends (The Communication Challenge Ltd, 2006). Leadership was the weakest area of performance across the sales function in the majority of companies. Citing leadership as one of the five key drivers of sales performance, the researchers found that there were several areas where salespeople felt that there was room for improvement. Their managers were weakest on spending time on coaching. Balancing the long term with the short term was another weak area. The third weakest area was setting a strategic direction.

Of course, we should all spare a thought for the complexity of the challenge of leadership of the sales function. Salespeople are traditionally independently minded professionals who are not naturally in tune with "followership", so managing salespeople is frequently compared to herding cats. Many sales managers believe that experienced salespeople

Salespeople are traditionally independently minded professionals who are not naturally in tune with "followership", so managing salespeople is frequently compared to herding cats.

do not want "leadership support". However, if they do not monitor their activity, they cannot give meaningful feedback on improvement. Of course, salespeople need to feel empowered about how they meld their personal objectives with the objectives of their employer and motivate themselves to do their job, but there is a balancing point. Sales managers who leave their salespeople to "do their own thing" can find themselves, instead of herding cats, trying to keep track of "lone wolves".

Lone wolf salespeople are not unproductive; they devote energy to their customers. Their singular self-reliance means that they do not value assistance or advice from colleagues or managers, in fact, they are motivated because of their lack of trust in others (Dixon, Gassenheimer and Barr, 2004). They do not like working in teams, and research suggests that they have low commitment to their employer. They will not fulfill work commitments to colleagues, and in the worst-case scenario, may sabotage team efforts.

What is leadership?

Pele, who captained Brazil in three Soccer World Championships, is widely quoted as having attributed his outstanding ability to wanting to be "where the ball is going to be".

Pele was an inspirational leader to his team and also to generations of soccer supporters. We all have our heroes. There are some big egos in selling, but most of us find it difficult to imagine that we could ever emulate the people who inspired us. But nor should we assume that we cannot improve our leadership capabilities.

Leadership is often described as the ability to influence a group of people toward the achievement of goals. People usually assume that leaders are born, not made. Research about leadership over the past 80 years suggests that there are certain characteristics associated with leadership, such as intelligence, dominance, self-confidence, high energy levels and task-relevant knowledge. Do people become leaders because they have leadership characteristics, or do they become leaders and acquire the characteristics as a result? In World War I, many soldiers saw their officers being

Do people become leaders because they have leadership characteristics, or do they become leaders and acquire the characteristics as a result?

shot as they led them out of the trenches, and leaders emerged from among the men to take their place, men who appeared to have the natural instinct to do something bold. But the eighty years of research also includes teachers asking quiet children to take a responsibility and observing them becoming more confident. Performing a leadership role successfully clearly reinforces leadership behavior.

Perhaps too much emphasis is put on personality traits as indicators of leadership qualities. Justin Menkes in *Executive Intelligence* (2005) says that an individual's ability to think clearly and intelligently is what largely determines success as a leader. The ability to absorb information and make good decisions is important, and also requires a certain amount of humility. It is not necessarily a matter of high IQ, but "common sense". As Voltaire noted in the 18th century – common sense is not actually that common. It is rare, and we could all do with more of it. In order to acquire this type of "executive intelligence", managers need training in problem-solving.

Certainly some kind of facilitation is needed when you first accept a management role. Leadership through authority alone is rarely successful or long-lasting in companies. No modern professional gives their manager the benefit of the doubt because that person is the boss. The expectations of the millennial generation are high. They have had highly trained school and university teachers focused on facilitating learning rather than imposing knowledge. All their "buy in" has to be won by consultation and persuasion, which might suggest that you should adopt a democratic style of leadership.

But life is never so easy that one style will do! Different situations require different leadership styles and the person who can adopt both directive and democratic styles, and some in-between, is most likely to succeed.

Figure 11.2 is based on a matrix called the Blake/Mouton managerial grid, which demonstrates the interrelationship between concern for people and concern for the task in hand. "Concern for the task" means defining roles and structure, organizing activities and planning progress toward the achievement of goals. "Concern for people" means focus on generating trust and respect.

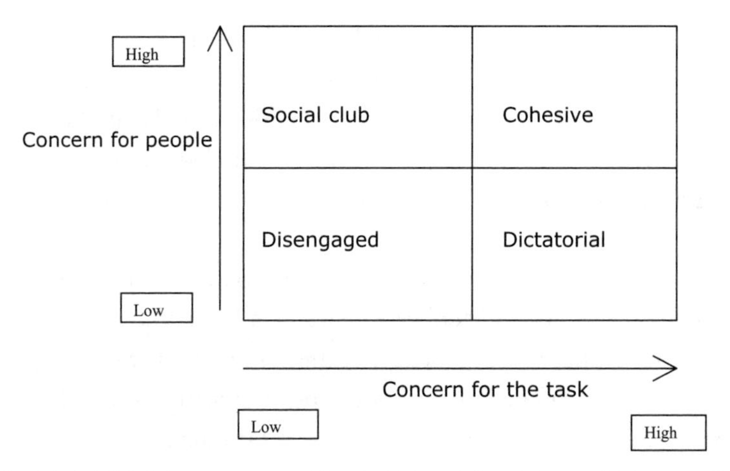

Figure 11.2 *The Blake/Mouton managerial grid. (Adapted from Blake and Mouton, 1964.)*

The "cohesive" option is usually believed to be the most desirable, but there are many challenges in the workplace that require something else. For example, when there is a panic about a potential overrun on a project, concern for the task requires primary focus. The "concern for people" approach is consistently associated with greater follower satisfaction, but it is not always associated with higher productivity! Consultative leadership may be ideal for achieving the "buy-in" of followers (assuming the leader is good at it), but it can be time-consuming.

An organizational behavior specialist (Fiedler, 1967) identified that leadership is strongest where relationships are good, tasks are structured and the leader has positional power (in other words, control of rewards and punishments). This is something you can achieve as a sales manager. Where a manager only has an informal position, such as one of your key account managers in a team-selling situation, researchers Hersey and Blanchard (1982) suggest that success will depend on the maturity of the followers. Those who have job maturity (ability, experience) and attitudinal maturity (motivation) are more likely to respond to informal leadership than those who are inexperienced, lack confidence or lack motivation. You need to bear that in mind when negotiating with colleagues about which of their reporting staff should take part in key account teams.

Robert House (1971) summarized his findings about leadership in his "path-goal" theory. Leaders set goals and then help followers to achieve them. They show the way forward and help to remove obstacles. They are directive, supportive or participative depending on the maturity of the follower and the task environment. Note that he identified "removing obstacles" as critical. Your salespeople will think that you are great if you eliminate a process step or open a previously closed door in their account.

Leaders set goals and then help followers to achieve them. They show the way forward and help to remove obstacles.

So, leadership in general can mean different styles for different situations, and that is also undoubtedly true of sales management. But specifically for sales management, I am going to suggest a model I have called the "three fives" of sales leadership (Figure 11.3).

The first list of five is the familiar five criteria for SMART objectives – specific, measurable, achievable, realistic, and timed. The last list of five is the key stakeholders in the business who require results from your leadership – stockholders require profitable growth, your company's brand requires desirable sales behaviors from your team, customers want satisfaction, your salespeople want career development, and you want career development as VP sales.

In the center we have the five leadership tools that you need:

- Awareness, incorporating self-awareness and awareness of others
- Framework – strategy and values
- Extensive communications
- Coaching and development
- Trumpeting.

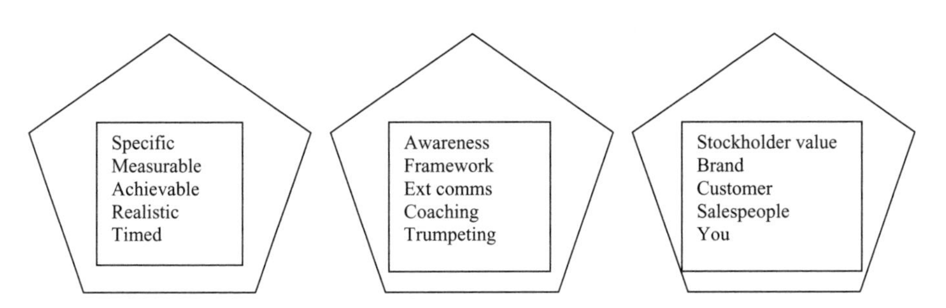

Figure 11.3 *The three fives of sales leadership.*

The five tools of sales leadership

Awareness

Self-awareness

> *"The higher the rank the more necessary it is that boldness should be accompanied by a reflective mind."*
>
> Carl von Clausewitz, Prussian General (1832)

Many of us think that we can do this leadership stuff. But how do we know? Who tells us?

Some time ago, I reviewed material for a sales management diploma course and was surprised by the amount of time devoted to self-awareness. Then I realized that the course designers had allowed that time because self-awareness is a prerequisite for improving our leadership behaviors. Instead of "hooray-hooray" motivational sessions, the ability to motivate ourselves and others starts with reflection and deep thought.

Instead of "hooray-hooray" motivational sessions, the ability to motivate ourselves and others starts with reflection and deep thought.

> **Extract from "If"**
>
> If you can dream – and not make dreams your master,
> If you can think – and not make thoughts your aim;
> If you can meet with Triumph and Disaster
> And treat those two impostors just the same . . .
>
> *Source:* Rudyard Kipling (1909)

The advice to "know thyself" goes back to the ancient world – the priestesses of the Oracle at Delphi who were consulted by kings before they embarked on wars. Daniel Goleman in *Emotional intelligence* (1995) tells the story of a samurai who asked a Zen master to explain heaven and hell. The Zen master replied with an insult, which sent the samurai into a frenzied fury. "That is hell," the master explained. The samurai realized how the monk had taught him something through his own reactions. He calmed down and thanked him. "That is heaven," said the monk.

We need to be able to observe ourselves, recognize thoughts, feelings, values and our needs as a prerequisite to changing what could be better, and then we can help others to do the same. Self-awareness is related to self-control. People who are overwhelmed by their emotions or are unwilling to change their moods are unlikely to be successful leaders in the long term.

Self-awareness can take a long time to master, and in business we need short cuts. Occupational psychologists have provided a variety of structured questionnaires, or psychometric tests, for people to use to check their perceptions of themselves. The tests can cover measures of knowledge, skills, attitudes and personality.

Reputable psychometric tests are supported by research findings demonstrating their reliability and validity. National professional bodies for psychologists offer training for the human resources staff who are responsible for administering and interpreting the tests. Research findings and opinions on the use of psychometric tests are very mixed. Nevertheless, used prudently, they can do a number of things for individuals such as:

- indicate strengths and weaknesses;
- suggest what motivates and demotivates them;
- explore how they react under pressure;
- indicate work styles that may affect those they team with.

The tests may be over quite quickly, but time should be allowed for debriefing with an HR colleague, and wider discussion if the tests are being undertaken in peer groups.

Self-mastery

"The essence of leadership is recognizing, discovering and identifying with one's true self."

Would-be leaders should get to know their own inner dynamics to enable them to lead themselves before presuming to lead others. Each person is the owner–manager of his or her own mind and emotions. We all exist by feeling and must know what we mean when we say "I". Detachment allows us to master ourselves.

Source: Parikh (2005). (Dr Jagdish Parikh is an internationally recognized author and speaker on the topic of leadership and a director of four major companies in India.)

Awareness of others

As a leader, you need to talk with conviction about the front-line experience – the experience of the front-line employee and the experience of the customer. You need to think about the thoughts and feelings of others and create meaning and clarity of purpose for them. You need to tune in to their values and personal emotional needs. You need to help others to develop their own ability to overcome doubts and difficulties.

We have known for a long time that change causes stress (Figure 11.4), but scientists now believe that because it engages our conscious mind and makes us sensitive to differences between expectations and reality that causes "intense bursts of neural firing". It provokes emotional and instinctive reactions (Rock and Schwartz, 2006). Managers have tried many tools to motivate people to change: rewards, threats and persuasion. We can all think of many examples in which colleagues have been unwilling to change, even to improve their own performance and rewards.

The brain is capable of change when we focus our attention on change. You can help your team to rewire their mental maps by provoking them to change their attitudes and expectations. We all need "moments of insight" to see alternatives and their benefits in a vivid way. These alternatives need to be internally generated rather than given to us as conclusions. For example, weekly or even daily meetings on process improvement have helped employees in many companies to focus on quality.

We all need "moments of insight" to see alternatives and their benefits in a vivid way. These alternatives need to be internally generated rather than given to us as conclusions.

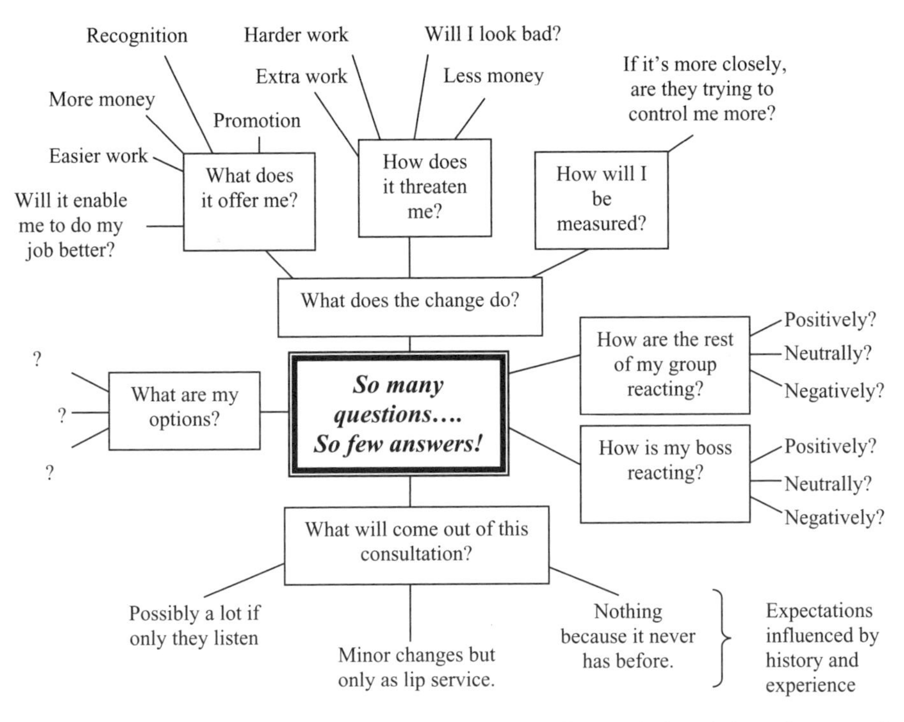

Figure 11.4 *An individual's challenges when faced with change. (Adapted from Corner and Rogers, 2005.)*

You can also use psychometric profiles, or people's learning styles, to plan the individual training and development that they need to succeed in times of change. Knowing their work styles and learning styles can help you to anticipate how individual team members will respond to change. They may need reassurance about their status; they may be concerned about the implications for their relationship with the customer; they may be anxious about the pace of change; or they may be probing to make sure that the strategy has been thoroughly considered and is clear.

Awareness of self and others is a prerequisite for successful leadership. Finding out how people in your team "tick" helps you to frame the way in which their SMART objectives can be achieved.

Framework – setting

Strategy

> *"Strategy can . . . never take its hand from the work for a moment."*
>
> Carl von Clausewitz, Prussian General (1832)

As a leader, whether in a military or a business setting, you need to equip your team with a framework for achieving their objectives, usually known as strategy, although many other things are also given the name "strategy". The framework must include the expected deliverables. For example, if the company wants to achieve its objectives through innovation, make it clear that sales of new products are required, or salespeople might think that they can just continue to sell their familiar products. Set milestones and make it clear what will be tested and at what stage.

Although plans are important to prepare people's minds for the future, real strategy happens in real-time. Risk must be accepted, anticipated and managed. Staff should be picking up on feedback from "the field" and advising senior managers when the market is demanding a response, or just hinting at one. Many start-up companies ended up with strategies that were completely different from those they had started with. It is not weakness to change course when circumstances require it, but a monitoring system with some trace between cause and effect is needed to inform the strategy.

Value frameworks: Setting standards

If you search on "leaders" and "the power of personal example" on the Internet, you find references in business, voluntary effort, military sources, and political and religious settings. It is a universal requirement.

You need to take responsibility for high standards. It is the old-fashioned notion of "setting an example", and demonstrating personal values in alignment with the company's brand values. No one will give a bit extra for a customer if you do not give a bit extra for a customer when it matters. A leader is human, and will admit mistakes. A leader also takes responsibility for their team's mistakes, but will also act quickly to put things right.

Salespeople do notice the behaviors and attitudes of their managers, and appreciate it when their manager "walks the talk" of company values, so that they can follow that example. Salespeople lose respect for sales managers who do not behave in a way that reinforces what they say. By observing a role model, salespeople can form ideas about how they can change to be more like their model.

Once again, this is backed up by research. There is a positive association between sales managers with "role model" styles and sales performance (Rich, 1998). The content of role modelling includes:

- Personally demonstrating appropriate sales behaviors
- Being on time for meetings
- Being honest and moral
- Appropriate personal appearance for work
- Listening
- Being a team player
- Never asking someone to do what you would not do yourself.

If you want respect, you have to earn it. And if you want implementation, you have to communicate – extensively.

Extensive communications

> *"We know that communications is a problem, but the company is not going to discuss it with employees."*
>
> Popular quote, allegedly originating from a senior manager in an international telecommunications company

It is often said that half the reason for something not getting done is the lack of communication. The characteristics of top communicators include empathy alongside decisiveness, and supporting alongside leading, but above all clarity and openness. In addition to communicating with the top team, shrewd managers build direct links with everyone, including the cleaner and especially the receptionist. Seeking direct feedback from customers and business partners is also essential.

As a leader, you must be able to express yourself clearly, consistently and convincingly in person and in writing, internally and externally, using all today's communication methods. You need to ask good questions, so that your presentation can be adapted to the needs of the audience. You must argue rationally, with evidence and with reasons. You need to conclude your interactions with a shared understanding of what has been agreed.

Sometimes, the best communications start with questions. It makes the people you are addressing feel important. We know this when we are dealing with customers, but do we always remember it when we are dealing with colleagues? We need to demonstrate our appreciation of others. Don't ask people to change before you have thanked them for what they are already doing. When we are asking for change, we must appeal to people's rationality and emotions. We need to ask for change in a clear, direct and tactful manner. We need to encourage thought about the reasons why not changing would be a bad thing. We need to say please.

In our communication, we should consider giving pleasure by making what we say interesting and entertaining as well as informative. We also need to allow time to show that we are listening. There are many good books and courses on successful communications. For the purposes of this book, I will just repeat what I tell students to remember when they are writing or presenting for an assessment. If they want to get good marks they have to clearly communicate:

- What it is that they are talking about (the business concept)
- Why it is important
- How it can be successfully applied

> *"The major problem in communication is the illusion that is has occurred."*
>
> Albert Einstein

We often make assumptions about change. We assume that people will adapt to change because they have had the benefits explained to them. Some sales managers even think that everyone in the salesforce will put the interests of the company above their own immediate interests. It is not even certain that a manager will always put the interests of the company above the immediate interests of their department. Senior managers often assume that different functions share a common view of the best interests of the organization, but they do not (Corner and Rogers, 2005).

Positive thinking is a great thing, but to be successful you need to address the realities of how people react to change. The invalid assumptions that something has gone wrong become more and more difficult to remedy as time passes. The following valid assumptions are more useful:

- People are more interested in change when they can see that there is something in it for them.
- People tend to adopt new ways of working more readily when the opinion-leaders within their work-based peer group are in favor of them.
- People do not believe what you tell them just because you want them to believe it.

Consultation assumes that you are asking more than telling – and telling has to be carefully styled. For most occasions, you will need a "coaching style" and a budget for training and development.

Coaching and facilitating development

If your team members are going to learn from the training and development that you plan for them, they must have answers to basic questions such as: "Where am I going?", "Where am I now?", "How do I get where I am going?", "How will I know when I get there?" and "Am I on the right track?"

The Kolb learning cycle tells us that learning requires involvement in new experiences, followed by time and place to reflect, followed by forming and reforming ideas, followed by experimentation with the new understanding to solve problems and make decisions in new situations (Figure 11.5). In other words, we learn through activity, reflection, theorizing and applying.

Kolb (1984) argues that all four stages are required for effective learning to take place. However, we all have different preferences as learners. Most salespeople are "activist" learners, who are focused on learning by experimentation. They like new experiences and new problems and expect learning to be exciting – role-play and simulation exercises suit them well. When a utility company wanted to convince their field and customer service staff about the advantages of new systems, the company designed several training

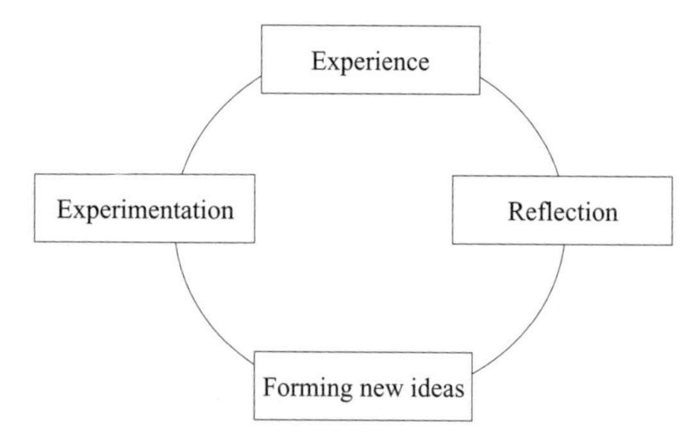

Figure 11.5 *The learning cycle. (Adapted from Kolb, 1984.)*

sessions called "a day in the life", where the staff lived their working day with the new equipment and information.

Instructor-led programs require a lot of preparation with the training providers, and consultation with participants. Sometimes salespeople seem reluctant to attend courses, and have their minds and mobile phones focused on their next deal. The company's investment in their skills is a significant career benefit; therefore you need to work with the trainers to ensure that the individuals understand the advantages for them in return for the effort they will have to put in. Your participation in the training is also a strong indication of commitment.

Empathy training – example

For over four years, a US engineering company has spent nearly $11 million on training to help the salesforce identify with customers' situations and feelings. All salespeople had four weeks "empathy" training in the first year of the program. The training includes psychometric tests and exercises that put them in their customers' shoes. They are asked to list thoughts triggered by a picture of a yellow rose, and how it feels to fire someone.

One sales executive, who went into the training describing it as hogwash, realized its benefit when he won some business with a company that he had been unsuccessfully prospecting for four years. He began to realize that they wanted much more detail from him than he had given before.

An influential customer was so impressed with the improvement in attitude that he recommended the chip-maker to other divisions in his group. "They are sympathetic and sensitive to the issues we have," he said.

The CEO of the engineering company believes that the training, instituted after a dramatic loss of turnover, turned the company around to achieve sales growth of over 11% per year.

Source: Edwards (2006)

Since most salespeople are activist in their learning style, role-play is a valuable element of training. Extensive objective research and anecdotal wisdom indicates that preparation through simulation helps anyone to have more confidence and perform more effectively in real-life situations. If role-play or at least "what if?" discussions are a regular feature in internal meetings as well as training, then the anxiety of the situation is reduced and the learning points are more likely to be absorbed.

Role-play is not always about objection handling over price, quality, delivery or payment terms. It can be used to cover the whole sales cycle from planning with the internal team, information-gathering meetings, presentations, and negotiations, closing and follow-up.

No instructor-led role-play would be complete in the 21st century without the option of audio or video recording and play-back. It is often difficult to believe that the body language, hesitation or confusion on the play-back are really ours! Professionals of all categories are subject to constantly "raising the bar" on every minute aspect of their presentation, and salespeople should be at the vanguard of that. So we have to keep squirming and learning!

Perhaps the most telling comments come from the participants. One training company told me that their evaluation database, which captures the post-course thoughts of trainees, is full of remarks such as, "Would have valued even more role-plays and case studies."

PC-based tools can also be helpful in enabling salespeople to work through "what if?" situations. They can contain high-quality content, presented in an interesting way. Usually they are broken up into short modules that can be accessed when participants have a suitable breathing space in their working day. They may incorporate video clips or animation. Each module is likely to be supported by examples and an exercise. They are much better than "just reading stuff" as distance learning used to be. It is a training method that is very useful for companies with a geographically widespread salesforce. It is also very useful for companies who, for whatever reason, need to ensure that training messages are standardized. Whatever other training methods are being used to introduce new learning, PC-based tools, whether "off-the-shelf" or customized, are ideal for providing reinforcement, revision and ongoing support.

There is still some fear in companies that if you train a salesperson then that person will leave, taking those newly acquired skills to the competition. But business is about taking calculated risks, and the risks associated with untrained salespeople can be even higher. For example, the salesperson may fail to communicate effectively with the customer, leading to lost sales or mis-selling. They may waste time on unpromising prospects or neglect key customers. And anecdotes about salespeople who "sell down" to commodities because they are not confident enough to sell high-value solutions are common.

No Chief Executive Officer would think it a good idea to save money on training and updates for accountants or engineers. But it is salespeople who represent the company to customers and therefore bear a significant burden of risk, and they need development to manage that risk. Corporate governance directives are beginning to drive that message up the Board agenda.

Reflection and reinforcement via coaching

Your feedback is an extremely important influence on the job satisfaction and performance of your salespeople. Research indicates that, at the relevant time, positive feedback about good sales behavior can be a major step toward helping your salespeople to succeed (Rich, 1998).

Companies often underestimate the influence that coaching from a sales manager can have on the team's performance. The best sales manager is one who can coach everyone – top, poor and average – to do better. Ask any cross-section of salespeople what training help is available to them when they hit a gap in their knowledge or skills, and they usually seek advice from their manager. You are their strongest link.

Some managers are wary of coaching; they are concerned that it is too personal and intrusive. But in the very best educational institutions, the power of one-on-one tutorials to accelerate performance and understanding is well known. People need information to keep their efforts on track. Without feedback, people are in the dark.

At the very least, most sales managers will from time to time accompany a salesperson on a customer call. A salesperson might be wary. I have heard salespeople say that they want to keep managers well away from their customers! So some discussion needs to take place beforehand about what you as a manager want to find out from observing the salesperson and from the opportunity to talk to the customer.

The salespeople need to brief you about their experiences with the customers, what is happening with the customers and any concerns they have about how their customer will react to you being there. Perhaps they will see it as an honor, and use the opportunity to introduce you and the salesperson to a higher-level decision-maker. That would be a win–win–win situation. The salespeople might fear that their contacts will use it as an opportunity to undermine them and ask for a concession. There are risks that have to be explored in call preparation as well as opportunities. After the call, make feedback immediate and constructive. Keep your notes for reference, as you need to track each individual's performance over the long term.

For more best practice guidelines on coaching, see Simpkins (2004).

"Having your say" at Britvic

Over two years, 120 sales managers in a division of Britvic Soft Drinks delivered continual revenue growth by developing their coaching skills. Using a 360-degree feedback process called CoachingIndex360, managers gathered anonymous feedback on their coaching.

"It gives people an opportunity to have a say," said a Regional Sales Manager. "We use it to get a more open environment, looking at feedback, problems, and solutions."

The Business Development Manager commented: "I thought I did pre-planning, but feedback was 'no' – I do that very differently now. My problem is to 'keep quiet in front of customers', and allow staff to make mistakes when selling. I learned how to contribute in those meetings in a different way – not just jump in."

The Equipment Supply Controller said: "We have got sustainability in a management development program. It has not 'withered on the vine'. We keep it 'live and fresh', and demonstrate success through the results seen."

Source: Valerie Heritage, The Communication Challenge Ltd (2006)
Used with kind permission

Hopefully, you are spending most of your time with good performers who can be great, or average performers who can be good. Unfortunately, there are also times when you have to deal with salespeople who are not able or are unwilling to improve. It may be just a case of being late with paperwork and causing inconvenience to colleagues in the accounts department, or it may be a customer complaint. Maybe the salesperson is just not working hard enough to succeed. In these cases, you have to work closely with the Human Resources Manager to make sure that all procedures comply with employment law. Counselling about observed problems, backed up by facts, will be the first stage. The person concerned must be given a time limit within which improvement is required, but with a clear indication that dismissal is possible.

Trumpeting

How do you make sure that your people know when they have done the right thing? In the first instance, you can tell them and thank them. If you want them to continue doings things right, a specific reward is very helpful. Symbolic rewards give you an opportunity to exercise leadership. But financial rewards may also be part of the package that your salespeople expect.

Financial reward

Although there is no substantial evidence that it really makes a difference to sales performance, variable pay is part of the culture of selling. Unfortunately, a crudely designed rewards system can concentrate the salesperson on easy pickings rather than strategic sales. Average salespeople do not respond well to high fluctuations in their income and can be seriously demoralized by a bad month. Ironically, the highest earning salespeople can also be the most dissatisfied. The competition inherent in variable pay creates more losers than winners, causes disputes and can even prompt unethical behavior.

Most companies regularly spend time considering or actively trying to change their sales compensation systems. Unfortunately, change is inhibited by a "chicken and egg" situation. If one company changes its compensation scheme and a competitor does not, managers fear that salespeople will defect to the competition.

You may have to live with the pay system that works currently for your organization. Any change to pay systems is very sensitive and may need to be very gradual! The complexity of the customer's purchasing process, the length of sales cycles and the volatility of the market influence the effectiveness of commission. A mix of financial and non-financial elements in performance pay for salespeople, e.g. customer satisfaction as well as sales volume, can help to move from volume-related commission to rewards that help to reinforce the desirable sales behavior.

The pay system itself may not be the issue you inherit, but whether or not it is seen to be fair. Salespeople have a highly attuned sense of fairness, and if they feel that their pay system is fair in its design and fair in its application, salesperson turnover is low and loyalty improves. A high-proportion fixed pay (salary) is more important when results of the salesperson's efforts are only realized over a long period of time. Since sales cycles are lengthening in most industries, many B2B companies are moving toward higher proportions of fixed pay for salespeople, and a variety of metrics for variable pay, including some that influence behavior, such as customer satisfaction.

Status and symbols

Money rewards should be subject to individual confidentiality. To trumpet your approval of good performance publicly, symbols can be more powerful.

Salespeople are known for their concern about very visible status rewards, such as "making the 100% club". Symbolic rewards such as driving a Ferrari for a week, the best parking space, or lunch with the Chief Executive can all be important elements of motivation from a leader who demonstrates what he or she wants followers to do. Symbolic rewards are also an opportunity to reinforce company values. Reward and approval matters. Precise calculation of commission can be left to the accounts department.

Conclusion

Being VP Sales is a tough vocation. You need confidence, and you need to instill confidence. Organizational "shared confidence" operates at four levels.

- Individuals need confidence in themselves, to be equipped with the skills to believe that they can do what needs to be done.
- They need to have confidence in each other.
- They need to have confidence in the systems of the company. To encourage a belief that the structures and routines of the company for accountability and collaboration are truly supportive is often the most difficult thing you have to do.
- Salespeople need to have confidence that shareholders will invest in their success, which is why you need to be close to the Board and have the opportunity to listen to bankers and analysts.

The three fives model incorporating the five tools of sales leadership may help you disentangle all the expectations and demands that are made on you as a leader and help you manage your time so that you can demonstrate leadership. It's entirely your responsibility once you have taken the challenge. You won't find any courses for your salespeople on "followership", no matter how widely you search for one. You have to inspire it.

You won't find any courses for your salespeople on "followership", no matter how widely you search for one.

12

Process management

In a 2006 survey of 1,275 American companies conducted by CSO Insights, only 45% said that they had formal sales processes, and 45% of those that had said that they did not monitor them to make sure that they were helping the company to improve selling performance.

Used with kind permission from CSO Insights
(www.csoinsights.com)

Excellent sales processes are indicators of successful sales organizations. There is a fairly consistent correlation between process sophistication and sales growth, across sectors, across different types of company, and across economies. This correlation is worldwide. In a study of 168 small to medium-sized manufacturing companies in Sri Lanka in 2004, sales volume and sales growth were significantly higher in those with planning and control processes (Wijewardena, De Zoysa, Fonseka and Perera, 2004).

Sales processes are a weakness in many companies, as we can see from the CSO Insights research above. Even if they are good by a quality manager's standards, salespeople can be resistant to making them work as effectively as they could.

Dissatisfaction with processes

In a survey of 426 salespeople in 19 European companies in 2006 by The Communication Challenge Ltd, criticism of sales processes was widespread. "There is a fraught relationship between the sales person and their systems and processes," the authors commented. Salespeople did not find the sales processes in their companies simple or helpful. Some of the scores on the statement "The sales systems and processes are simple and helpful" were extremely low, especially in the larger companies in the study. Many comments were recorded about the need to remove bureaucracy and internal paperwork, and most thought that the solution was to have more "back office" sales administration support.

Source: The Communication Challenge Ltd (2006)
Used with kind permission

In the same study, there was some interest from salespeople in accessing output from the Customer Relationship Management/Sales Force Automation system, such as information about the marketplace or competitors, but they felt that they did not have access to quality information. In reciprocation, they were reluctant to put anything into the system, although they believed that they gathered valuable information about customers. The respondents felt that processes were not robust enough and accountability was unclear.

Does the chicken come before the egg or the egg before the chicken? Clearly there needs to be some compromise. Salespeople deserve the best in terms of processes, but they need to contribute to change and accept their role in processes if that is to happen.

We are part of the problem

When managers at a US company gathered data about the poor quality of order messages that salespeople left for colleagues to follow up, 700 per month were incomplete. Each of the salespeople felt that the problem must be "other people". Each was given their own statistics, so that it was obvious to them that they were part of the problem. The following month, incomplete order messages were down to 259.

Source: Imai (1998)

Compliance

In addition to desirable best practice, sales processes are also necessarily to demonstrate focus on shareholder value. We have already discussed the implications of the Sarbanes–Oxley Act for the sales function.

Sales, as the front door of the company where changes in buying behavior and the economic environment are often first encountered, can also play a critical role in informing business strategy to enable the company to be responsive to market conditions.

All these issues depend on good processes.

How do you know if sales processes are failing?

Is your sales pipeline speculative?

You know that you need to improve your processes if your sales forecasts are poor (many companies would regard 70% accuracy as poor), if the sales pipeline is speculative or if win rates are declining and sales performance is inconsistent. If you cannot identify the barriers and bottlenecks in the process, if handoffs are mis-communicated and if you cannot leverage the success of the best sales team to other sales teams, there are process weaknesses. If the cost of selling is difficult to track, or new sales representatives take a long time to get going, then processes need attention.

Source: Siebel White Paper (2004)
Siebel is now a division of Oracle Corporation

Generally speaking, it is a good idea to design sales processes that fulfill the objectives of your company and meet customer needs before applying technology to them. Many companies have implemented salesforce automation (SFA) systems hoping that the standard process inherent in them will do. A few years ago, IT industry analysts were predicting that companies attempting to implement salesforce automation technology without institutionalized processes would experience very high failure rates.

What are processes?

> **Getting things done**
>
> I have six honest serving men;
> they serve me good and true.
> Their names are what and why and when,
> and where and how and who.
>
> *Source*: Rudyard Kipling

Processes are the means whereby a practice that has proven to be successful is captured as "the way we do things around here". It is how resources work together and interact to deliver value internally and to the customer. Sales processes provide a framework for how the sales organization should work. Processes are designed to enhance efficiency by explaining what should consistently happen in certain situations. They are often represented as linear, but sales processes, unlike processes in many other departments, include external players such as customers, business partners and competitors. It is therefore more difficult to make sales processes entirely standardized and prescriptive; the framework needs to provide parameters for judgment.

Each process is a series of steps involving an action or actions that have inputs and outputs. Each action needs to be allocated to a defined role, and each input and output requires some kind of measure.

Figure 12.1 is an extract from an opportunity management process. The whole process will involve a lot of steps, which will be linked to other steps in a linear or cyclical fashion. Those links may be to other steps owned by sales, or to steps owned by marketing, customer service, logistics or finance. At certain points, the role-holder will have to make decisions. For example, after the first meeting with the prospect, the new business sales representative has to decide whether it is appropriate to follow-up immediately, at a later stage, or to put the lead on hold indefinitely. Each outcome will require different actions. At this junction, the process has what programmers would call "If . . . then" statements. So a full process diagram can become very complicated. If it is written in a list of instructions, it can seem very dry.

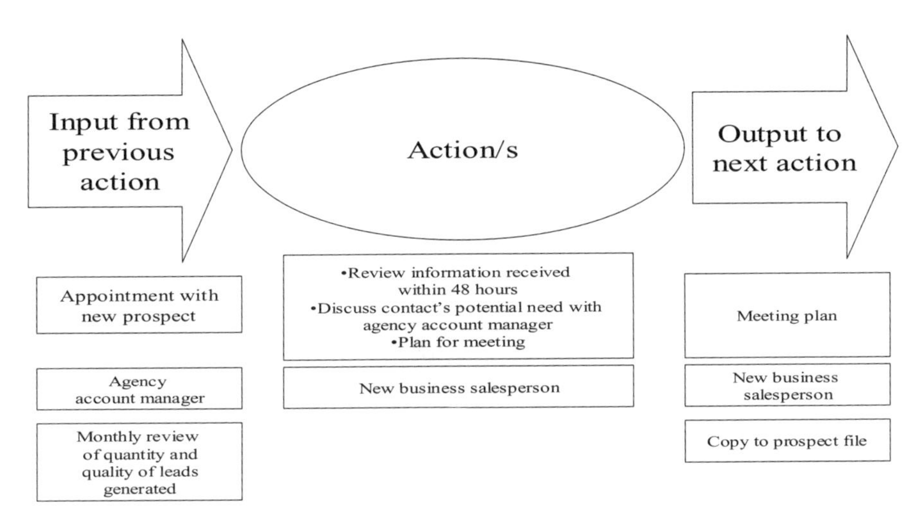

Figure 12.1 *The various steps in a process.*

Having written a sales process manual, I would not necessarily wish to impose it on anyone, but there are specialized consultants who can be hired to help if you are just beginning.

It will come as no surprise to any reader that salespeople regard large sales process manuals with dismay. Salespeople obviously have to take responsibility for knowing and observing key processes, which should form part of their induction training, but as VP Sales you have to be the guardian of the sales process. Since you are very busy with strategy and coaching, employing sales support staff seems sensible. These useful people are rather difficult to find in many companies, but some companies have filled the gap by sub-contracting aspects of their sales processes to agencies.

What processes are needed?

There are a variety of views about benchmarking the sales function, but most that I have seen have recognized the importance of processes. *Harvard Business Review* (Kotler, Rackham and Krishnaswamy, 2006) published a checklist that included six elements of "support systems" alongside sales managers' skills, salespeople's capabilities and sales organizational climate. Figure 12.2 represents the coverage of the UK national occupational standards for sales. The detailed content of those standards focuses on skills rather than processes, but it is a comprehensive and internationally

Figure 12.2 *The sales standards wheel. (Reproduced with kind permission from The Marketing and Sales Standards Setting Body, www.msssb.com.)*

benchmarked description of the sales function. It is therefore very helpful in identifying relevant activities from the clerk keying data into customer records to the director authorizing a budget.

On the basis of this view of the entire sales function, we can identify a number of categories of processes that an auditor on the corporate governance trail might expect to find.

Information management

Managing market knowledge

Salespeople say that they want and need market knowledge. It is difficult to imagine how a company in the 21st century could survive without salespeople having a comprehensive and up-to-date understanding of the markets in which it operates. Nevertheless, marketing knowledge in many companies is gathered, stored and used in an ad hoc way. Intranets can be used to make market information consistently accessible.

Managing customer and contact information

Large companies have huge data warehouses full of customer data that needs maintenance. When you have masses of data it is also apparent that additional software, called "customer analytics", is required to convert the data into actionable information. Some systems are able to provide sophisticated segmentation and can predict when and what customers might buy. The best quality information is needed on the front line to enable salespeople to assist individual customers with useful solutions.

Managing product/service information

Salespeople pride themselves on keeping up to date with product information, but in some companies the pace of change is so rapid that systems have to provide a lot of support. In addition, many customers require direct access to product information via their portal.

Managing price and promotion information

Every accountant has a nagging fear that salespeople are giving away too much discount. Systems are available to ensure that information accessed at the point of sale is the latest pricing, and that only relevant sales promotions are used. This reassures everyone in the process – including the salespeople, who are unlikely to be making deliberate errors that could reduce their bonus.

Opportunity management

How does a "target" relationship become a "suspect" and eventually a "prospect"? Sometimes a sale may span different countries and time zones. Any information gaps or delays at the customer interface are risks. The company needs to pool a lot of information resources to equip salespeople with relevant information to spark insight in front of the customer. You also need a lot of information to make sure that your forecasting is good. The opportunity management process is critical.

Opportunity management

Your process and the Intranet database that supports it needs to reassure you on questions such as:

- Do you have objective, widely understood and widely supported lead qualification criteria?
- Can each qualified lead be linked to a specific marketing or sales activity?
- Which sales or marketing activity is most productive?
- Are reliable lists/directories being purchased?
- If prospects are converted via the website or by phone, are these new contacts systematically reviewed for bigger potential?
- Can salespeople quickly identify who has budget and power in an organization?
- Does every salesperson know the target decision-maker in their prospect?
- Do salespeople make a note of what the customer will get from each call?
- Does the salesperson know how the customer is organized, and the full potential for your product/service across all business units?
- Do salespeople know how to spot potential relationship/strategic customers?
- For each "probable" deal, can the salesperson explain what the "do nothing" scenario is for the customer?
- For each "probable" deal, can the salesperson describe competitor activity in the account?
- Do salespeople have enough proofs to offer prospects, e.g. trial use/visits to reference sites?
- Are your salespeople using the spreadsheet tool to help them to estimate ROI for prospects/customers?
- Are salespeople using the mobile IT devices that can supply them (and customers) with real-time stock and product information?
- By how much does the length of the sales cycle vary per customer?

Business management

Planning and forecasting

The remainder of the company relies on your sales forecast to plan operations and cash flow. Research discussed later in the chapter indicates that even in quite sophisticated companies, sales forecasts skills are poor and the process does not include enough objective analysis. In fact, a CSO Insights survey by Dickie and Trailer (2004) reported "dismal" pipeline analysis. Of course, a sale can only be counted upon when it is signed and delivered, but companies need to choose and make better use of predictive indicators such as salesperson's access to, or influence with, key decision-makers, length of relationship with customer, and urgency of customer need. These should feed from the opportunity management process into your forecasting process.

Budgeting

Sales managers are usually given a budget by finance based on last year's figures. Periodically, sales managers need to sit down with an accountant and work on a zero-sum budget. Starting from zero, how much money is needed to finance each activity? How much return do those activities generate? Activity-based costing is also vital for attributing costs accurately to business relationships.

Are you in control of sales costs?

- Do you budget for and control all costs associated with the salesforce, including salary, bonuses, benefits, expenses and administrative support?
- Do you know the average cost of a sales call?
- Do you know the average number of calls made to close a sale?
- Do you monitor and minimize discount?
- Do you know what proportion of a salesperson's time is spent with customers, preparing, traveling, etc.?
- Are sales measurements coordinated for consistency and relevance?
- Are sales measurements reviewed at least quarterly?

Strategy formulation

Managers are expected to know how to do a plan, but may actually have never been given any training, and there might not be an appropriate entry in the process manual to guide them. Particularly in small companies, I have found that although the need for an objective process is recognized, there is a strong tendency to work with the emergent strategy. There is nothing wrong with an emergent strategy, but having a planned strategy as a comparison can lead to informed decision-making rather than a feeling of drifting. Larger companies have difficulty responding to changes in their business environments. A planning process should incorporate trigger points for reviews and procedures for switching to contingency plans when needed.

Risk management

Risk management is often overlooked, with nerve-wracking consequences for sales managers who find themselves in the thick of "issues" at a later stage. Risks need to be identified, anticipated and managed proactively. (A detailed discussion of risk is presented later in this chapter).

People management

Performance management, including motivation, evaluation, reward and recognition

This is usually the most visible of sales processes, and is also the process that causes most debate. Subprocesses, such as dispute resolution, are often overlooked, leading to perceptions of unfairness. It is also a process that needs to be both simple to understand, and most flexible to adapt to changes in company objectives, both short term and long term.

Recruitment

Recruiting salespeople is a risky process. A wrong decision can be very costly. Therefore, closely working with recruitment process specialists in the human resources function, you need to feel confident that the process is robust.

Minimizing risk in recruitment

- Do you have an objective and transparent process for evaluating CVs?
- Do you have an objective and transparent process for evaluating interviewees?
- Is each candidate interviewed by at least one other manager (as well as HR)?
- Do you follow up references?
- Do you inspect payment slips to validate claimed earnings?
- Do you explain employment conditions in full to candidates?
- Do the evaluation criteria include "soft" factors such as opinions of team members and the customer/s?
- Are their work behavior profiles assessed?
- Are they assessed for their "work ethic"?
- Is there a clear appointment process?
- Does your selection process put the company in a positive light?

Training and development

Many companies have processes for training needs assessment and choosing suppliers. Best practice focus today lies in the long-term evaluation of training interventions and their contribution to improved sales behaviors, customer satisfaction and financial results.

Disciplinary

Things do go wrong, and employment law in most countries requires the process for disciplining employees to be very clear if the employer is to avoid a costly legal action.

Customer interface management

Customer demand planning

A customer demand planning system should enable salespeople, business partners and customers to use relevant information such as three-year trends and currently contracted business to compile quality product and application demand forecasts for a rolling 12-month period. These feed into inventory planning, production planning, revenue planning and services planning systems.

Account planning

Account planning has been discussed in detail in Chapter 4.

Communications protocols

An enormous amount needs to be understood throughout the company about who communicates with customers, when, why and how. Legislation about telephone and e-mail contact in many countries requires "permission-seeking". In other words, the customer defines contact levels, and suppliers must be careful to respect them.

Post-sales support

Previously, post-sales support was largely delegated to operations, but customers now expect sales involvement at this most sensitive stage in their development of attitudes toward you as their chosen supplier.

Customer satisfaction surveys

Some commentators on relationship development regard satisfaction surveys as "old hat". Nevertheless, if they are regularly undertaken, they can identify individual customers' problems and general trends in expectations and needs.

Problem resolution

Effective internal problem resolution improves efficiency and morale. Quality management principles encourage staff to seek out problems for discussion and resolutions so that things can run more smoothly, meaning less stress for them.

Complaints handling

Many of us like to avoid conflict. However, customer loyalty gurus say that complaints should be encouraged, because then the company has an opportunity to put things right. If you put things right for your customers, their loyalty increases. Best practice companies not only have a robust complaints-handling process (see Chapter 8), but publish it and invite contributions.

Process management

Quality management/continuous improvement

Although they are valuable guides, processes cannot be cast in stone, since nothing can be 100% perfect for all time. Continuous improvement itself needs to be a regular process.

Change management, incorporating benefits management

Change process itself should be a defined process in the company manual, because it is always necessary. Minor improvements need to be implemented in a straightforward way, and major changes will require a lot of focus in order to be successful. Culturally, it is quite advantageous to have a process that establishes "this is the way we change things around here", as it helps to reduce the uncertainty and insecurity that change provokes.

Corporate governance and legal compliance procedures

Sales managers need to prove periodically that the process manual is compliant with relevant laws and codes of conduct. This is bread and butter to purchasing managers who are happy to work with rules-based systems, but is stultifying for dynamic sales executives. Having an administrator for this work, or a part of the time of the company quality manager, makes a great deal of sense.

Why are sales processes/sales process improvements needed?

When a company is in its entrepreneurial phase, it is acceptable for everyone to rush around doing everything, because the company needs raw energy to establish itself. Once the volume of customers begins to increase, they expect a certain amount of consistency in the way a supplier operates. Companies that do not develop standardized "business-as-usual" protocols are wasting money in inefficiencies such as:

- sales forecasts being so approximate that inventory levels get too high, operational capacity is wasted and cash flow crises occur;
- new hires taking a long time to become useful members of the team;
- communication gaps leading to information being lost or duplicated;
- out-of-date information leading to customer confusion;
- mistakes causing customer defection;
- poor performance management resulting in salespeople wanting to leave the company.

They are also inviting risks such as:

- legal action from ex-customers;
- legal action from ex-employees;
- corporate governance/other legal infringements;
- wasted resources leading to poor profitability and shareholder defection;
- adverse media coverage.

Using external help to identify productive change

In the mid-1990s, an IT company was concerned because its sales forecasting accuracy of around 60% was considered poor. It commissioned an audit team of academic experts to identify problems and make recommendations for improvements. The audit team spent two days with the customer demand planning team to understand the system at the time, and collected data via teleconferences and interviews with stakeholders in the customer demand planning process from around its global operations.

The analysts identified that stakeholders were using unconnected information systems, forecasting performance was not systematically measured and evaluated, there was minimal use of statistical tools to support forecasting, and sales personnel had limited commitment to the process. They recommended that salespeople were trained in forecasting techniques, including statistical tools, and that some reward or recognition should be linked to forecasting performance that would be measured and evaluated. A core group in marketing was established to develop initial forecasts from statistical analyses, which would be forwarded to salespeople, business partners or, in some cases, direct to customers for adjustment.

Sales forecasting accuracy improved from about 60% to 80–85% in one year, and forecasting accuracy was more consistently accurate across all the sales teams. The knock-on effects of this improvement included meeting customer delivery objectives on-time, and reduced inventory levels.

Source: Moon, Mentzer and Thomas (2000)

How can process improvements be implemented?

Identifying why change is needed

What are the business drivers of change? Is there a need to reduce costs because of global competition? Is there a need to improve traceability because of corporate governance requirements? Sometimes, the people on the receiving end of change assume that it is change for the sake of change, change for the sake of senior managers scoring political points or change to divert attention from something more fundamental. If change cannot be justified to the people expected to implement it, in terms that are relevant to them, then it is going to be a huge waste of time and effort.

Sometimes, the people on the receiving end of change assume that it is change for the sake of change, change for the sake of senior managers scoring political points or change to divert attention from something more fundamental.

Salespeople in particular are notorious for resistance to change, unless it makes their working lives easier or more productive. When you think about it – that is quite reasonable. Sometimes, the cause and effect of "easier" may not be direct, but a case can be made. Compliance with corporate governance does not make life easier today, but it will be a lot easier when the auditor asks questions in 18 months' time. Meanwhile the company is in a position to command trust from customers and investors because it is observing best practice. That should support the salesperson in many situations with their customers in the future.

Objective setting

The setting of objectives and key performance indicators is critical. What will be the main effects of the change? How will that contribute to corporate goals? If you do not know in advance the expected results of a successful change, you will not know that you have achieved it, or notice that you have not achieved it. The benefits sought from an improved sales process might include a shorter sales cycle, reduced sales overhead, reduced administration burden for salespeople or better customer satisfaction.

An assessment or audit of the current process

You need to know with utmost objectivity what is wrong with the current process and why it is failing. Doubtless there are many internal rumblings, but it may take an external analyst to actually pinpoint the root cause of failure.

- Does process *x* add value to the sales team?
- Is it really necessary?
- Has value been communicated and how will it contribute to sales?
- Do they know someone else who uses it, and why?

Who does the best, even with a broken process?

Even with bad processes, some teams do better than others. Perhaps they have found a way to circumvent a problematic or unnecessary process step.

Or perhaps they are applying the process correctly. Internal best practice can inform change as well as external expertise.

Who owns what?

A common reason for processes failing is that no one is taking responsibility for them. Sales managers and their sales team should be involved in deciding the sales processes that are required to fulfill the corporate requirements. Involvement improves ownership.

Process redesign

From an expert point of view, what could achieve the objectives in a simpler way?

Consultation

Generally speaking, a good way to approach salespeople who are going to be affected by process change is to ask them what they would prefer.

A survey of 240 salespeople in 2005 found that "perceived justice" encouraged salespeople to stay with an employer. Having some input into decisions and some control within processes was associated with "perceived justice" (Brashear, Manolis and Brooks, 2005).

The consultation should pose questions such as:

- What would you like the process to do for you?
- How might the process help you to do your job better?
- What benefits might there be for you?
- Does the proposed process cause you problems? If so, how?
- How might the process affect your interactions with other departments?

It is essential to gain insight to make the process improvement worthwhile. Researchers have found that usefulness is the main driver of the adoption of change, and ease-of-use is also important if technology is involved. Usefulness, however, can also be offset by user stress.

Risk discussion

There are risks in any kind of change; some are threats to be avoided, and others may present opportunities. Terry Kendrick of the University of East Anglia identified a number of potential sources of risks inherent in changes undertaken in marketing or sales (Kendrick, 2004).

To begin with, as we have noted earlier, sales processes are often interlinked with the processes of customers, and are indirectly impacted by the processes of competitors. It is possible to consult customers about proposed process changes, but second guessing the reaction of competitors is not an exact science. If you are making your processes easier and your information more accessible, it will probably take your competitors some time to catch up.

Internal risks are just as problematic. Are senior managers aware of the potential for risk? Do they enjoy it, or are they risk-averse? Are they willing to allocate the right amount of resources to deal with the change itself and the knock-on effects that may arise?

Risk may therefore arise from internal or external sources. Kendrick also identified categories of risk that need to be considered:

- *Strategic*: Are we doing the right thing for the right reasons? Could we have misunderstood the need for change? Could we have overestimated our own capabilities?
- *Reputational*: Is there any way that what we are considering would tarnish the company's image? How do we need to amend our business conduct guidelines to reflect that? Do we need to amend our reward system to avoid customer perceptions of inappropriate motivation?
- *Operational*: Is there any supply chain risk that we are either absorbing into our organization or passing up the value chain to suppliers? Teamwork in reviewing and piloting the new process will minimize risks.
- *Compliance*: Is it possible that what we are proposing could be considered inappropriate or even illegal in any of the countries in which we operate?
- *Environmental*: What is the impact on the environment of our new process? If it involves less paper or less traveling, how can we leverage that advantage?

- *Financial*: Any change involves an investment of time and resources, but how confident are we that there will be a financial return in a given timeframe? Can we encourage results – e.g. if a new process is supposed to save costs – through reward or recognition?
- *Information*: Have we considered the protection of our intellectual property and the privacy of customer information?

Any identified risks need to be evaluated for the probability of occurrence and the impact that each might have. For those risks justifying contingency plans, a response should be designed, and monitoring for that particular risk should be formalized in the change management process.

Pessimists (and I know how they feel) say that we should be surprised when things go according to plan, and not be surprised when they go wrong. Successful risk management consists of two principles – being robustly prepared for risk, and having the flexibility to respond to it. Sales managers need to manage the overall risk of change; and salespeople have to be prepared for the day-to-day impact of change.

Align technology if necessary

What is the role of technology in process development?

Companies have to implement technology to speed up processes or risk being uncompetitive on cost of selling, but a perfect technology system to support sales processes is not possible. Incremental change is going to be necessary, so as Ian Corner and I put it in an article in 2005, a "good, slightly imperfect, continually assessed, continually evolving (system) is a much better option".

Companies have to implement technology to speed up processes or risk being uncompetitive on cost of selling, but a perfect technology system to support sales processes is not possible.

A good system should be a factor in achieving business objectives such as reduced selling overheads or customer retention. Qualitative indicators of success listed by Corner and Rogers (2005) include:

1. Senior managers see it as the source of information that is essential for the management of the business.

2. Employees at the interface with prospects and customers like using the system because it makes their jobs easier and they benefit from its use.
3. Staff turnover within the functions that use the system is lower than it was before implementation.
4. The system implementation was managed as an "open" project requiring adjustment and contingencies.
5. Users are involved in identifying more potential benefits from the system.
6. When there is a glitch in the system the staff are more likely to focus on solving it rather than on complaining about it.
7. Users are quite proud of it and pleased with their role within it.

A system that demonstrates less than five of the above characteristics is probably doomed, and it is not helpful to blame the system as it will have been well-designed and coded by competent technicians. It will also have been sold to other companies that have used it successfully. A reasonable response to the risk of technology implementation is to start with limited functionality in a small pilot.

When choosing technology to apply to your sales processes, think carefully about how to decide which technology vendor can best help you with the challenge of changing "the way we do things around here".

Comparing potential suppliers

A commodity distributor invited two vendors to participate in two separate pilot studies: full implementation in limited geographies. This provided a blind test of which solution gave most value. Both pilots were successful, but one vendor differentiated itself by implementing structured change management for the salespeople, working closely and consultatively with them, gaining understanding about what would help them to sell better. The users took ownership of this solution and it was rolled out across the whole company. The distributor achieved better profitability through more accurate pricing, time-savings and better measurability.

Source: A case study by Robert P. Desisto (2006)
Used with kind permission of Gartner Inc. (www.gartner.com)

Training

Learning something new is always at the bottom of everyone's "to do" list. I was recently faced with a new e-mail system, and although I loved some of the instant benefits it delivered, I deeply resented some of the time I had to spend on recreating and/or relearning functions I had become accustomed to on the old system. If you want people to get the most of something new, make sure that you create time for them to learn how to operate it properly. It may take longer than you think.

You also need to ensure that "roll-out" support can be accessed easily, and that it is truly supportive!

Evaluation

Effectiveness of the new process must be evaluated if it is ever to be considered worth the effort of introducing it. For example, in a training process, evaluation would include immediate feedback from attendees after a training event and observation over time about whether their learning was applied and behaviors changed. It is more difficult to link better sales revenue or better customer satisfaction to the training process, but attempts should be made to link cause and effect.

Benefits management

Professor John Ward and his team at the Information Systems Research Centre at Cranfield School of Management worked throughout the 1990s and beyond on a process to identify the benefits from the use of information systems, but found that client companies were using it for all categories of change management. (For more information on their findings, see Ward and Daniel, 2005.)

A benefit is an advantage, or gaining a better position. In the past, the success of IT implementations was a simple matter of whether it was delivered on time and to budget. That might be acceptable for a simple, controllable change such as a network upgrade. Professor Ward identified that the application of technology to strategic systems needed more depth in evaluation, and his benefits management model was successfully used to track cause and effect. Automation is not necessarily a technical issue; technology is not just about saving money, and its functionality alone is not the real benefit.

> *"There are no direct benefits from IT. IT only enables or creates a capability to derive benefits. . . . Things only get better when people start doing things differently."*
>
> Ward and Murray (1997)
> Quoted with kind permission

We must be clear about the difference between an *outcome* and a *benefit*. Because of the application of a new process, a manager might have the opportunity to reduce headcount (outcome), which leads to reduced costs (benefit). Alternatively, he might keep headcount the same to enable staff to spend more time with customers and less on administration (outcome), and thus improve sales and/or customer satisfaction (benefit). Managers have to make decisions to drive benefits; they are not automatically delivered by inputs. In fact, there is probably a more complex cause and effect map at work. Figure 12.3 draws on Professor Ward's Benefits Dependency Model to show how an improvement in a sales process involving automation

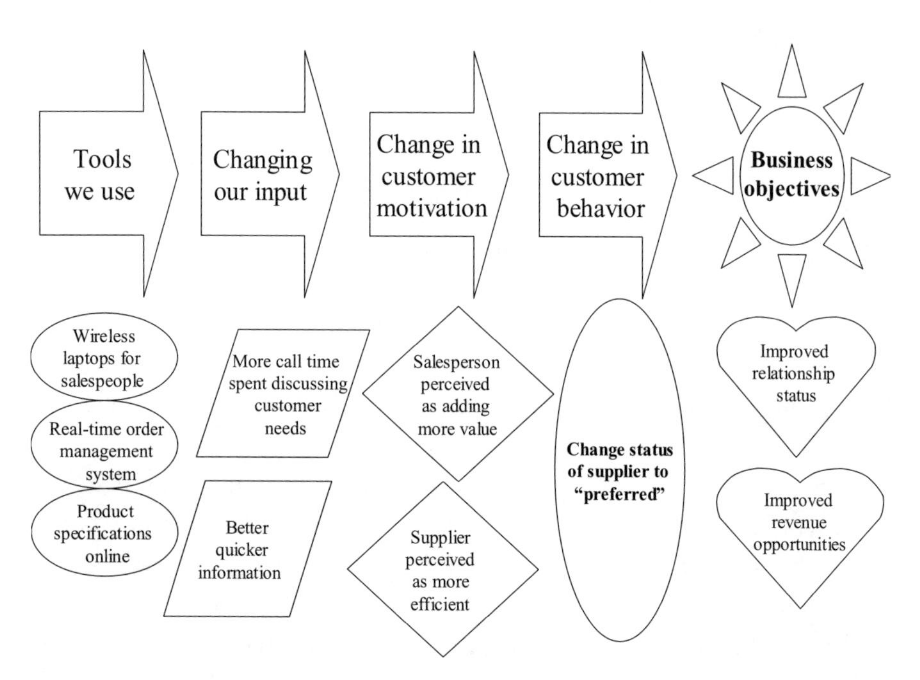

Figure 12.3 *Linking cause and effect. (Adapted with kind permission from Professor John Ward.)*

would lead to achievement of business objectives through incremental changes in other factors.

Feedback

Successful implementation requires a communications plan, support and coaching, monitoring and tracking of the execution, and the communication of the results.

Feedback should include evaluation of such things as ideas generated, the impact on customer satisfaction, and anecdotal evidence of how it helped salespeople to close a sale.

Token rewards such as vacation trips or prizes for exceptional contributions to process improvement can go a long way to convincing people that processes are important and process improvement is worthwhile.

Continuous improvement of sales processes

A Japanese expert in process improvement, Imai, says that we should learn from every mistake, failure or abnormality experienced from day-to-day. Continuous improvement is a concept from the school of Total Quality Management and has been very successful on the factory floor. Market share improvement is positively associated with improvements in a company's reputation for quality (Knouse and Strutton, 1996).

There is no reason that continuous improvement cannot be applied in all processes, including those that involve an interface with customers' systems. It requires those with the closest understanding of customer needs to be trained in problem-solving techniques, such as using an Ishikawa diagram (Figure 12.4) to ask "why" to every "because".

In the diagram, the backbone of the fish represents the problem to be solved – for example, "Why are conversion rates so low?" There may be a number of possible "because" responses, and these can be drawn as bones coming off the spine. The person or group involved in solving the problem must then pose the question "why" to all the possible reasons given. For example, if one of the answers to "why are conversion rates so low?" is "the quality of leads that we work on is poor", then ask why the quality of leads is so poor. A smaller bone coming off the secondary bone represents this line of enquiry, which can go further and into much more detail. The aim

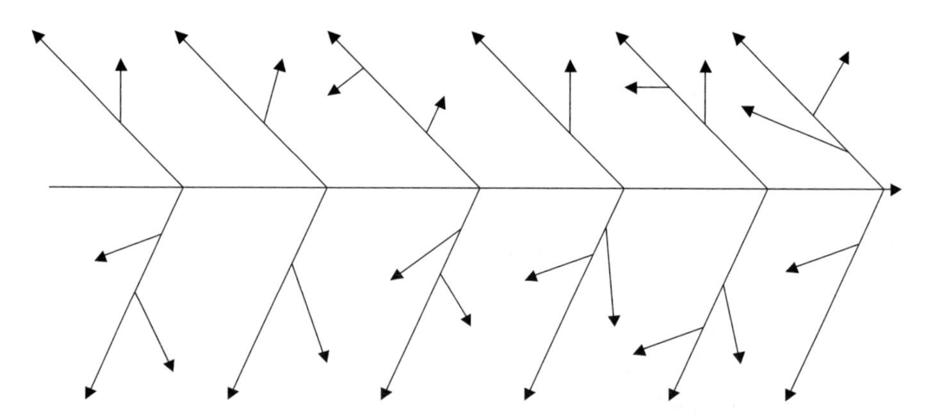

Figure 12.4 *The Ishikawa or fishbone diagram.*

is to establish the genuine root causes of a problem so that solutions are focused on the right activities.

The principles of total quality management are customer orientation, employee empowerment, cross-functional team effort and continuous improvement. All these things are very relevant to a 21st-century salesforce.

For the sales process, Imai (1998) recommends the principles of Gemba Kaizen. Gemba is the point when and where the salesperson meets the customer. The salesperson is an important interpreter of what process improvements would benefit the customer, and you as the sales manager should spend some time at "gemba" too. Kaizen means continuous improvement, based on common sense and lowering costs. The principles of Gemba Kaizen also include the elimination of "muda" – activities that do not add value to the customer. When a problem arises, take temporary counter-measures on the spot, but go back and find the root cause. You must then design a solution and standardize it to prevent a recurrence of that problem.

Gemba is the point when and where the salesperson meets the customer. The salesperson is an important interpreter of what process improvements would benefit the customer, and you as the sales manager should spend some time at "gemba" too.

Day-to-day process improvement is a matter of housekeeping. Sales staff should be encouraged to identify unnecessary steps in sales processes so that they can be eliminated. The remaining steps should be kept in good order.

Another principle of Gemba Kaizen is "gain-sharing". The teams that design particular process improvements are recognized for their contribution to cost reduction, improved customer satisfaction and revenue generation (Imai, 1998).

What's the downside of processes?

A counter-argument to the drive for professional sales processes is that processes kill sales. Purchasers may enjoy rules-based systems, but salespeople are intuitive and creative. Squash that creativity with a personal computer full of step-by-step commands and restrictions, and the salesperson will not be happy. Of course, forecasts are needed for future resource management, and there seems to be no objection to regularizing and automating business for high-volume, low-order-value items. But when considering personal selling, salespeople have a number of pertinent fears about processes.

A waste of time

New forms take time to complete, whether they are on paper or on-line. Without immediate payback, salespeople consider that to be a waste of the time that could have been spent with a customer. So they ignore the new forms or partially fill them in, making the information unusable. When the sales manager then applies threats of discipline, the salesperson becomes demoralized. They feel that "big brother" is watching them. Sales performance decreases and salesperson turnover increases.

Salespeople generally complain about any waste of time at work that affects their time with customers, whether it is paperwork, computer input, writing reports or attending meetings.

Wasted time = Stress

In a study of 400 salespeople in 49 business units of four banks in Ecuador, researchers found that sales representatives' perceptions of wasted time were an important source of stress and emotional exhaustion. These perceptions contributed to role conflict, reducing job satisfaction and commitment to the organization and resulting in a higher intention to leave the company.

Source: Jaramillo, Mulki and Locander (2006)

None of us likes to waste our time. Getting your process experts to focus on simplication will be essential in process change. And the question of who does paperwork also has to be explored.

In the past, salespeople could concentrate on customers as the sales support staff dealt with all the paperwork, phone calls and letters. In this decade I have observed companies trying to recreate the sales support role – certainly in the new business development process – by outsourcing some homework and follow-up activities to the agencies generating leads. Today, sales support staff no longer have to sit at head office inflating headcount.

Role confusion

Some SFA tools may replace some tasks that salespeople have previously done manually. That sounds like a good move, but if things are happening so much more quickly who gets made redundant? The salesperson starts thinking: "It could be me." If the system is intended to help the salespeople to do more complex and interesting work, they have to be convinced of that and shown how.

Technology can be frustrating

In a survey of 454 salespeople from a telecommunications company and a real estate chain, salesforce automation was originally welcomed, but then rejected. Immediately after training the salespeople were positive toward it, but six months later they were frustrated with the technology. Salesforce turnover increased, with SFA being given as a reason in exit interviews. The leavers were going to competitors. The lower morale of those left was highlighted by increased absenteeism. Not surprisingly, sales performance did not increase. Only a small percentage of these salespeople had regarded themselves as "good with technology" or experienced with technology before the SFA implementation. They had been unable to imagine how the technology would impact on their day-to-day jobs.

Source: Speier and Venkatesh (2002)

The salesforce automation (SFA) system had become a driver of dissatisfaction because the tools disrupted the sales process. Salespeople perceived that SFA did not allow them to play to their strengths. They believed that the technology was destroying their competence. They no longer knew what information they owned, and believed that SFA meant that they were not only being monitored more closely but were also losing their autonomy.

Speier and Venkatesh's findings suggest that if SFA creates tasks inconsistent with a sales representative's view of the sales job, it will have unpleasant consequences. This suggests that you must emphasize the role of consultation in making processes relevant and useful.

Information overload

Too much information can reduce selling effectiveness and performance. Humans have limited information-processing capacities (it varies by individual), and when the information available is greater than the amount the individual can process in the time given, information overload occurs, which reduces confidence, makes the individual doubt their abilities, get frustrated and make errors (Hunter, 2004). Salespeople need sophisticated information, but in relevant packages at relevant times. The sheer amount of information processing in the sales job is increasing the educational level required to enter the profession, particularly in business-to-business markets. If you have a problem with process compliance, it could be a development issue.

It won't stick

Change is not always sustainable – individual commitment changes, managerial attention drifts elsewhere, financial benefits are not realized, stakeholder influence changes, and the timing is not right. As new methods do not bed in completely as envisaged, some adjustments and adaptations are necessary. Some salespeople just weather the storm of the process improvements and hope they will be able to revert to normal. Even sales managers have been known for their passive resistance, waiting for the bright young entrants, who are trying to change things, to blunder and lose influence.

Between 2000 and 2003, IT industry analysts were talking about 50–70% failure rates for Customer Relationship Management (CRM) systems. The mistakes that were being made in the early days of CRM included trying to implement the system before formulating the strategy it was supposed to facilitate. Implementing the CRM system before placing the necessary organization infrastructure was also common. The assumption that "more technology was better" led to problems. Some companies bought packages that were too complex. Companies also overexposed customers to their new wizardry, forgetting that the application of technology can be annoying as well as provide convenience (Rigby, Reichheld and Schefter, 2002).

Some companies wasted a lot of money and time trying to implement CRM, and cursed it. Nevertheless, the market for CRM systems grew because companies could not ignore the advantages that the successful 30–50% were achieving.

Conclusion

With all these problems, why take on processes? Because there are win–win scenarios to be explored. Lessons about bad processes should have been learned by now. If you know what not to do, what is stopping you from doing the job better? Pitched against the risk of doing nothing, process improvement is a mountain that sales managers have to climb.

Process-capable sales teams outperform unstructured "lone wolves". Even if your sales processes are not sick, they can get better. It is mainly through neglect that they become a problem. Do nothing, and you can be sure that the burden of "patching up" process breakdowns will always be with you.

Bibliography

ABPI (2006) *Code of Practice for the Pharmaceutical Industry 2006*. Association of the British Pharmaceutical Industry.

Ahonen, P. & Salmi, A. (2003) "Portfolios in supply network management: An analysis of a Finnish company in the electro technical industry". Paper presented at the 19th IMP (Industrial Marketing and Purchasing) Conference, September 4–6, Lugano, Switzerland. Available at http://www.impgroup.org.

AIDA Marketing e Formazione.

Alajoutsijärvi, K., Tikkanen, H. & Skaates, M.A. (2001) "David against Goliath: Coping with adversarial customers: A three-fold relational strategy for SMEs", *The Journal of Selling and Major Account Management*, Vol. 3, No. 4, pp. 33–52.

Alexander, M. & Young, D. (1996) "Strategic outsourcing", *Long Range Planning*, Vol. 29, Issue 1, pp. 116–199.

Alford, H. (2005) *Buyer's Views of Salespeople 2005*, Tack International, Chesham.

Allen, J., Reichheld, F.F. & Hamilton, B. (2005) "The three Ds of customer experience", *Harvard Working Knowledge*, November 7. http://hbswk.hbs.edu.

Allen, J.K., Ebrahim, S.S. & Kelly, G.C. (2006) "Building a top consumer goods sales force", *McKinsey Quarterly*, Web exclusive, February. www.mckinseyquarterly.com.

Ambler, T. (2000) *Marketing and the Bottom Line*, Financial Times/Prentice Hall, Harlow.

www.ameinfo.com (2004) "Is your supply chain ethical as well as efficient?" April 30.

Anderson, J.C. & Narus, J.A. (1998) "Business marketing: Understand what customers value", *Harvard Business Review*, November–December.

Anon. (2000) "M&S sued by supplier", *BBC Business News*, January 11. www.bbc.co.uk.

Anon. (2002) "Astea survey on CEO attitudes towards field services". www.crm2day.com 03/12/2002.

Anon. (2003) "Is process killing sales?", *Boss News*, April. www.documentboss.com.

Anon. (2005a) "Best practices are hard to copy", *Harvard Business Review*, Vol. 83, Issue 5, p. 79, May.

Anon. (2005b) "Reining in outsourcing risk", *Strategy + Business*, November 30.

Anon. (2005c) "Marconi plunges on BT deal news", BBC News, April 28. www.bbc.co.uk.

Anon. (2005d) "Marconi in £1.2 bn Ericsson deal", BBC News, October 25. www.bbc.co.uk.

Anon. (2006a) "Mrs T's sales-marketing link pleases retailers", *Frozen Food Age*, May.

Anon. (2006b) "Olympus medical scopes out the right carrier for its unique needs", *Purchasing*, May 4.

Aranda, G. & Finch, E. (2003) "Using repertory grids to measure changes in risk-taking behavior", *Journal of Construction Research*, Vol. 4, No. 1, pp. 101–114.

Arminas, D. (2003) "CIPS President urges buyers to collect better information", *Supply Management*, p. 10, February 27.

Ashworth, A. (2005) "Accelerating sales performance for Visa by closing the communications gap", *Journal of Financial Services Marketing*, Vol. 9, Issue 4, pp. 318–328.

www.asmnet.com.

Axelrod, R. (1984) *The Evolution of Cooperation*, Basic Books, New York.

Banasiewicz, A. (2004) "Acquiring high value, retainable customers", *Database Marketing and Customer Strategy Management*, Vol. 12, Issue 1, pp. 21–31.

Bannan, K.J. (2005) "10 great websites", *B to B*, September.

Bartholomew, D. (2006) "Supply chains at risk", *Industry Week*, October 1. www.informationweek.com.

Bartol, K.M. (1999) "Reframing salesforce compensation systems: An agency theory-based performance management perspective", *The Journal of Personal Selling and Sales Management*, Vol. 19, Issue 3, pp. 1–16.

Baumgartner, T., John, R.H. & Naucler, T. (2005) "Transforming sales and service – incumbents can serve the whole market without getting stuck in the middle", *McKinsey Quarterly*, No. 4, pp. 80–91.

Beattie, V. & Fearnley, S. (1996) "Auditor changes and tendering", *Accounting, Auditing and Accountability Review*, Vol. 11, No. 1, pp. 72–98.

Beattie, V. & Fearnley, S. (1998) "Audit market competition: Auditor changes and the impact of tendering", *British Accounting Review*, Vol. 30, pp. 261–289.

Bellizzi, J.A. & Hasty, R.W. (2003) "Supervising unethical sales force behavior: How strong is the tendency to treat top sales performers leniently?" *Journal of Business Ethics*, Vol. 43, Issue 4, pp. 337–351.

Bellizzi, J.A. & Bristol, T. (2005) "Supervising the unethical sales force behavior of top sales performers: Assessing the impact of social desirability bias", *Journal of Business Ethics*, Vol. 57, Issue 4, pp. 377–388.

Benson Payne Ltd (2004) *Sales – An Occupational Map*, Produced for the Marketing and Sales Standards Setting Body. Available on www.msssb.org.

Beaujohn, M., Davidson, J. & Stacey, M. (2006) "The 'moment of truth' in customer service", *McKinsey Quarterly*, No. 1, pp. 62–73.

Beverland, M., Farrelly, F. & Woodhatch, Z. (2004) "The role of value change management in relationship dissolution: Hygiene and motivational factors", *Journal of Marketing Management*, Vol. 20, pp. 927–939.

Biederman, D. (2005) "Hazards of outsourcing", *The Journal of Commerce*, November 14.

Blake, R.R. & Mouton, J.S. (1964) *The Managerial Grid*, Gulf, Houston.

Blancero, D. & Ellram, L.M. (1997) "Strategic supplier partnering: A psychological perspective", *International Journal of Physical Distribution and Logistics*, Vol. 27, Issues 9–10, pp. 616–629.

Blattberg, R.C., Getz, G. & Thomas, J.S. (2001) *Customer Equity: Building and Managing Relationships as Valuable Assets*, Harvard Business School Press, Boston.

Bradley, A. (2006) "Halfords supplier terms cause anger among SMEs", *Supply Management*, Vol. 11, Issue 1, p. 8.

Brashear, T.G., Manolis, C. & Brooks, C.M. (2005) "The effects of control, trust, and justice on salesperson turnover", *Journal of Business Research*, Vol. 58, Issue 3, pp. 241–249.

Bristow, D.N., Amyx, D. & Slack, J. (2006) "An empirical look at professional selling from a student perspective", *Journal of Education for Business*, May/June.

Brownlie, D. (1985) "Strategic marketing concepts and models", *Journal of Marketing Management*, Vol. 1, Issue 2, pp. 157–194.

Bryan, L.L. (2002) "Just in time strategy for a turbulent world", *McKinsey Quarterly*, Special Edition – Risk and Resilience.

Campbell, D. (2005) "Farmworkers win historic deal after boycotting Taco Bell", *The Guardian*, March 12.

Campbell, N. & Cunningham, M. (1983) "Customer analysis for strategy development in industrial marketing", *Strategic Management Journal*, Vol. 4, Issue 4, pp. 369–380.

Carbone, J. (2004) "Using TCO to rate suppliers", *Purchasing*, Vol. 133, Issue 3, pp. 30–34.

Carbone, J. (2005) "Reverse auctions become more strategic for buyers", *Purchasing*, December 8.

Carnegy, H. (1995) "Scared of growing fat and lazy?" *Financial Times*, July 10.

Carter, J.R. & Ellram, L. (1994) "The impact of interorganizational alliances in improving supplier quality", *International Journal of Physical Distribution and Logistics*, Vol. 24, No. 5, pp. 15–24.

www.cauxroundtable.org, "Principles for Business".

Cespedes, F.V. (1995) *Concurrent marketing: Integrating product, sales and service*, Harvard Business School Press, Boston.

Chaffey, D. (2000) "Achieving Internet marketing success", *The Marketing Review*, Vol. 1, pp. 35–59.

Chalos, P. & Sung, J. (1998) "Outsourcing decisions and managerial incentives", *Decision Science*, Vol. 29, Issue 4, pp. 901–919.

Christopher, M. & Ryals, L. (1999) "Supply chain strategy: Its impact on shareholder value", *International Journal of Logistics Management*, Vol. 10, No. 1, pp. 1–10.

Christopher, M. & Jüttner, U. (2000) "Supply chain relationships: Making the transition to closer integration", *International Journal of Logistics: Research and Applications*, Vol. 3, No. 1, pp. 5–23.

Chun, R. (2006) "Corporate reputation: Meaning and measures", *International Journal of Management Reviews*, Vol. 7, Issue 2, pp. 91–110.

Clarke, I. & Flaherty, T.B. (2003) "Web-based B2B portals", *Industrial Marketing Management*, Vol. 32, pp. 15–23.

von Clausewitz, C. (1832) *On War*, N. Trübner, London.

Coe, J.M. (2004) "The integration of direct marketing and field sales to form, a new B2B sales coverage model", *Journal of Interactive Marketing*, Vol. 18, No. 2, pp. 62–75.

Colletti, J.A. & Chonko, L.B. (1997) "Change management initiatives: Moving sales organizations from obsolescence to high performance", *Journal of Personal Selling and Sales Management*, Vol. 17, No. 2, pp. 1–30.

Communication Challenge Ltd, The (2006) "Blind faith and the bottom line: What's driving sales performance?". www.communicationchallenge.co.uk.

Corbett, C.J. & Blackburn, J.D. (1999) "Partnerships to improve supply chains", *Sloan Management Review*, Vol. 40, Issue 4, pp. 71–83.

Corner, I. & Rogers, B. (2005) "Monitoring qualitative aspects of CRM implementation: The essential dimension of management responsibility for employee involvement and acceptance", *Journal of Targeting, Measurement and Analysis for Marketing*, Vol. 13, No. 3, pp. 267–274.

Cross, R.G. & Dixit, A. (2005) Customer-centric pricing: The surprising secret for profitability, *Business Horizons*, Vol. 48, Issue 6, pp. 483–491.

Cummings, B. (2006) "Proving the sales process", *Sales and Marketing Management*, Vol. 158, Issue 5, p. 12.

Cummings, B. (2004) "Growing pains", *Sales and Marketing Management*, Vol. 156, Issue 8, pp. 22–29.

Dail, B.S. & West, A.S. (2005) "Building stronger IT vendor relationships", *McKinsey Quarterly*, Web exclusive, June. www.mckinseyquarterly.com.

Daugherty, P.J., Richey, R.G., Roath, A.S., Min, S., Chen, H., Arndt, A.D. & Genchev, S.E. (2006) "Is collaboration paying off for firms?", *Business Horizons*, Vol. 49, pp. 61–70.

Davidson, H. (2000) *Even More Offensive Marketing*, Penguin, UK.

Davis, I. (2005) "How to escape the short-term trap", *The McKinsey Quarterly*, Web exclusive, April. www.mckinseyquarterly.com.

Dawes, P.L. & Massey, G.R. (2005) "Antecedents of conflict in marketing's cross-functional relationship with sales", *European Journal of Marketing*, Vol. 20, No. 11–12, pp. 1327–1344.

Deeter-Schmeltz, D.R. & Sojka, J.Z. (2003) "Developing effective salespeople: Exploring the link between emotional intelligence and sales performance", *The International Journal of Organizational Behavior*, Vol. 11, No. 3, pp. 211–220.

Desisto, R.P. (2006) *Material Distributor Increases Earnings Through Price Optimisation*, Gartner Inc. www.gartner.com.

Dewsnap, B. & Jobber, D. (2000) "The sales-marketing interface in consumer packaged goods companies: A conceptual framework", *Journal of Personal Selling and Sales Management*, Vol. 20, No. 2, Spring, pp. 109–119.

Dickie, J. & Trailer, B. (2004) *Sales Effective Insights: The Top Trends for 2004*, CSO Insights, Boulder. www.csoinsights.com.

Dickie, J. & Trailer, B. (2005) *Benchmarking: Inside Sales and Telesales Performance*, CSO Insights, Boulder. www.csoinsights.com.

Dixon, A.L., Gassenheimer, J.B. & Barr, T.F. (2004) "Identifying the lone wolf: A team perspective", *Journal of Personal Selling and Sales Management*, Vol. 23, No. 3, pp. 205–219.

Donath, B. (2004) "Chief customer officers integrate operations", *Marketing News*, November 1.

Doran, J. (2006) "Hoover is heading for sell-off as Dyson cleans up in America", *The Times*, February 4.

Drucker, P.F. (1955) *The Practice of Management*, Heron, London.

Edwards, C. (2006) "Death of a pushy salesman", *Business Week*, 07/03/2006.

Ellram, L.M. (1991) "A managerial guideline for the development and implementation of purchasing partnerships", *International Journal of Purchasing and Materials Management*, Summer, Vol. 27, No. 3, pp. 2–8.

Ellram, L.M. & Edis, O.R.V. (1996) "A case study of successful partnering implementation", *International Journal of Purchasing and Materials Management*, Vol. 32, No. 4, pp. 20–28.

Ellram, L.M., Zsidisin, G.A., Perrott, S.S. & Stanly, M.J. (2002) "The impact of purchasing and supply activities on corporate success", *Journal of Supply Chain Management*, Vol. 38, No. 1, pp. 4–17.

Eng, T.-Y. (2004) "Does customer portfolio analysis relate to customer performance? An empirical analysis of alternative strategic perspective", *Journal of Business and Industrial Marketing*, Vol. 19, No. 1, pp. 49–67.

Fiedler, F.E. (1967) *A Theory of Leadership Effectiveness*, McGraw-Hill, New York.

Fill, C. (2006) *Marketing Communications: Engagement, Strategies and Practice*, Prentice Hall, Harlow.

Fiocca, R. (1982) "Account portfolio analysis for strategy development", *Industrial Marketing Management*, Vol. 11, Issue 1, pp. 53–62.

Fisher, R., Ury, W. & Patton, B. (1982) *Getting to Yes: Negotiating Agreement Without Giving In*, Random House, New York.

Ford, D. & Hakansson, H. (2006) "IMP: some things achieved: Much more to do", *European Journal of Marketing*, Vol. 40, No. 3–4, pp. 248–258.

Forrest, W. (2005) "Dana takes charge of spend", *Purchasing*, April 7.

Forsyth, J.E., Galante, N. & Guild, T. (2006) "Capitalizing on customer insights", *McKinsey Quarterly*, No. 3.

Forsyth, K. (2004) "Content management: A prerequisite to marketing and sales effectiveness", *International Journal of Medical Marketing*, Vol. 4, Issue 3, pp. 228–234.

Francis, K. (2001) "Telephone account management – a quiet revolution with a big future", *Journal of Selling and Major Account Management*, Vol. 4, Issue 1, pp. 75–81.

Gary, L. (2004) "Dow Corning's push for organic growth", *Strategy & Innovation*, Vol. 2, No. 6, November–December.

Gassenheimer, J.B., Houston, F.S. & Davis, J.C. (1998) "The role of economic value, social value and perceptions of fairness in interorganizational relationship retention decisions", *Academy of Marketing Science*, Vol. 26, No. 4, pp. 322–337.

Genestre, A. & Shao, A.T. (1995) "What does marketing really mean to the Japanese?", *Marketing Intelligence and Planning*, Vol. 13, Issue 9, pp. 16–28.

Gilson, K.A. & Khandelwal, D.K. (2005) "Getting more from call centers", *The McKinsey Quarterly*, April 2005. www.mckinseyquarterly.com.

Goleman, D. (1995) *Emotional Intelligence*, Bloomsbury, London.

Gregory, A. & Rogers, B. (2004) "Take me to your leader!", *Sales and Marketing Professional*, November–December.

Gruber, T., Szmigin, I. & Voss, R. (2006) "The desired qualities of customer contact employees", *Journal of Marketing Management*, Vol. 22, No. 5–6, July.

Gruner, S. (1996) "Outsourcing your sales force", *Inc.*, Vol. 18, Issue 6, pp. 107–108.

Hallen, L. & Johanson, M. (2004) "Sudden death: dissolution of relationships in the Russian transition economy", *Journal of Marketing Management*, Vol. 20, pp. 941–957.

Hancock, M.Q., John, R.H. & Wojcik, P.J. (2005) "Better B2B selling", *The McKinsey Quarterly*, June.

Harrity, C., Higgins, L. & Unizcker, D. (2006) *Performance Benchmarks: Procurement*, American Quality and Productivity Center, Houston.

Harrison, D. (2001) "Network effects following multiple relationship dissolution", Paper presented at 15th IMP (Industrial Marketing and Purchasing) Conference, Oslo, Norway, September.

Hartman, K.B. (2006) "Television and movie representations of salespeople: Beyond Willy Loman", *Journal of Personal Selling and Sales Management*, Vol. 26, No. 3, pp. 283–292.

Hatum, A. & Pettigrew, A.M. (2006) "Determinants of organizational flexibility: A study in an emerging economy", *British Journal of Management*, Vol. 17, No. 2, June, pp. 115–139.

Heide, J.B. & Weiss, A.M. (1995) "Vendor consideration and switching behavior for buyers in high-technology markets", *Journal of Marketing*, Vol. 59, No. 3, pp. 30–43.

Helm, S., Rolfes, L. & Günter, B. (2006) "Suppliers' willingness to end unprofitable relationships", *European Journal of Marketing*, Vol. 40, No. 3–4, pp. 366–383.

Hennig-Thurau, T. & Klee, A. (1997) "The impact of customer satisfaction and relationship quality on customer retention: A critical reassessment and model development", *Psychology and Marketing*, Vol. 14, No. 18, pp. 737–764.

Hersch, W.S. (2002) "Make way for the new C-level exec", *Call Center Magazine*, September.
Hersey, P. & Blanchard, K.H. (1982) *Management of Organizational Behavior*, Prentice Hall, New Jersey.
Heskett, J.L. (2006) "How important is 'executive intelligence' for leaders?", *Harvard Working Knowledge*, July 5. http://hbswk.hbs.edu.
Hess, E.D. & Kazanjian, R.K. (2006) *The Search for Organic Growth*, Cambridge University Press, Cambridge.
Hilson, D. (2006) "Stakeholder risk information needs analysis", *Risk Doctor Network Newsletter*, Risk Doctor Limited.
Holmlund-Rytkönen, M. & Strandvik, T. (2006) "Stress in business relationships", *Journal of Business and Industrial Marketing*, Vol. 20, No. 1, pp. 12–22.
Homburg, C., Koschate, N. & Hoyer, W.D. (2005) "Do satisfied customers really pay more? A study of the relationship between customer satisfaction and willingness to pay", *Journal of Marketing*, Vol. 69, Issue 2, pp. 84–96.
Horn, J.T., Lovallo, D.P. & Viguerie, S.P. (2006) "Learning to let go: Making better exit decisions", *The McKinsey Quarterly*, No. 2.
House, R.J. (1971) "A path–goal theory of leadership effectiveness", *Administrative Science Quarterly*, September.
Hunter, G.L. (2004) "Information overload: guidance for identifying when information becomes detrimental to sales force performance", *Journal of Personal Selling and Sales Management*, Vol. 24, No. 2, pp. 91–100.
Hur, D., Hartley, J.L. & Mabert, V.A. (2005) "Implementing reverse e-auctions: A learning process", *Business Horizons*, Vol. 49, pp. 21–29.
IFC (2005) *Case Studies of Good Corporate Practices*, Companies Circle of the Latin American Corporate Governance Roundtable, International Finance Corporation.
Imai, M. (1998) "Gemba Kaizen as applied to sales management", *Journal of Selling and Major Account Management*, Vol. 1, No. 1, pp. 71–80.
www.ioma.com (2003) "IOMA survey ranks strategic expectations for outsourcing", *Financial Executive's News*, June.
www.ioma.com (2003) "New supplier metrics now include processes along with financials", *Supplier Selection and Management Report*, Issue 2–03, February. (Institute of Management and Administration Inc.)
www.ioma.com (2004) "Supplier performance measurement, a 'must' cost reduction tool", *Supplier Selection and Management Report*, Issue 4–04, April. (Institute of Management and Administration Inc.)
www.ioma.com (2004) "How purchasing at HP builds ethics into supply chain", *Supplier Selection and Management Report*, December.
www.ioma.com (2005) "How purchasing at Yazaki determines when to invest in suppliers", March.
Izzo, G.M. & Vitell, S.J. (2003) "Exploring the effects of professional education on salespeople: The case of autonomous agents", *Journal of Marketing*, Fall.
Jaramillo, F., Mulki, J.P. & Locander, W.B. (2006a) "The role of time wasted in sales force attitudes and intention to quit", *International Journal of Bank Marketing*, Vol. 24, No. 1, pp. 24–36.
Jaramillo, F., Mulki, J.P. & Solomon, P. (2006b) "The role of ethical climate on salesperson's role stress, job attitudes, turnover intention and job performance", *Journal of Personal Selling and Sales Management*, Vol. 26, No. 3, pp. 271–282.
Jelassi, T. & Enders, A. (2005) *Strategies for E-business: Creating Value through Electronic and Mobile Commerce – Concepts and Cases*, Prentice Hall, Harlow.

Jelinek, R. & Ahearne, M. (2006) "The ABCs of ACB: Unveiling, a clear and present danger in the sales force", *Industrial Marketing Management*, Vol. 35, pp. 457–467.

Johnsen, T. & Ford, D. (2005) "At the receiving end of supply network intervention: The view from an automotive first tier supplier", *Journal of Purchasing and Supply Management*, Vol. 11, pp. 183–192.

Johnson, G. (2000) "Strategy through a cultural lens: Learning from managers' experience", *Management Learning*, Vol. 31, No. 4, pp. 403–426.

Johnson, C.R. & Schultz, D.E. (2004) "A focus on customers", *Marketing Management*, Vol. 13, Issue 5, pp. 20–27.

Johnson, J.T., Barksdale, H.C. & Boles, J.S. (2001) "The strategic role of the salesperson in reducing customer defection in business relationships", *Journal of Personal Selling and Sales Management*, Vol. 21, No. 2, pp. 123–134.

Johnson, M.D., Herrmann, A. & Huber, F. (2006) "The evolution of loyalty intentions", *Journal of Marketing*, Vol. 70, pp. 122–132.

Kahn, K.B. & Mentzer, J.T. (1998) "Marketing's integration with other departments", *Journal of Business Research*, Vol. 42, pp. 53–62.

Kakabadse, A. & Kakabadse, N. (2000) "Outsourcing, a paradigm shift", *Journal of Management Development*, Vol. 7, No. 2, pp. 107–118.

Kakabadse, A. & Kakabadse, N. (2002) *Smart Sourcing: International Best Practice*, Palgrave, Basingstoke.

Kalyanam, K. & Zweben, M. (2005) "The perfect message at the perfect moment," *Harvard Business Review*, Vol. 83, No. 11, November.

Kalwani, M.U. & Narayandas, N. (1995) "Long-term manufacturer–supplier relationships: Do they pay off for supplier firms?" *Journal of Marketing*, Vol. 59, Issue 1, pp. 1–16.

Kellough, R.D. & Kellough, N.G. (1999) *Secondary School Teaching: A Guide to Methods and Resources; Planning for Competence*. Prentice Hall, Upper Saddle River, New Jersey.

Kendrick, T. (2004) *Strategic Marketing Risk Management*, Thomson Gee, London.

Kim, C.W. & Maubourgne, R. (1997) "Value innovation: The strategic logic of high growth", *Harvard Business Review*, Vol. 75, Issue 1, January/February, pp. 40–48.

Knouse, S.B. & Strutton, D. (1996) "Molding a total quality salesforce through managing empowerment, evaluation, and reward and recognition processes", *Journal of Marketing Theory and Practice*, Summer 1996.

Kolb, D.A. (1984) *Experiential Learning*, Prentice Hall, Harlow.

Kotler, P., Rackham, N. & Krishnaswamy, S. (2006) "Ending the war between sales and marketing", *Harvard Business Review*, July/August 2006.

Krol, C. (2005) "Telemarketing team rings up sales for Avaya", *B to B*, Vol. 90, Issue 12, pp. 34–37.

Kraljic, P. (1984) "From purchasing to supply management", *The McKinsey Quarterly*, Spring.

Kwak, M. (2002) "Smart ideas on reverse auctions", *Harvard Working Knowledge*. Excerpt published on http://hbswk.hbs.edu.

Lagace, M. (2005) "The Zen of management maintenance: Leadership starts with self-discovery", *Harvard Working Knowledge*, May 9. http://hbswk.hbs.edu.

Lagace, M. (2006) "Negotiating in three dimensions" (Q&A with James Sebenius), *Harvard Working Knowledge*. http://hbswk.hbs.edu, downloaded October 2.

Lambert, D.M. & Pohlen, T.L. (2001) "Supply chain metrics", *International Journal of Logistics Management*, Vol. 12, No. 1, pp. 1–19.

Lambert, D.M., Emmelhainz, M.A. & Gardner, J.T. (1996) "So you think you want a partner?" *Marketing Management*, Vol. 5, No. 2, pp. 24–41.

Lamming, R. & Cousins, P. (1999) "For richer or poorer", *Supply Management*, p. 26, April 15.

Lamons, B. (2005) "Dow targets segment to keep market share", *Marketing News*, June 15.

Landry, E. & Pandrangi, J. (2005) "Making the most of 'feet on the street'", *Strategy + Business*, June 16.

Lax, D. & Sebenius, J.K. (2006) *3–D Negotiation*, Harvard Business School Press, Boston.

Lay, P. (2003) "Who should be accountable for the sales pipeline: The VP sales or CEO/COO"? *Under the Buzz*, Vol. 4, No. 5, May (electronic "viewsletter" from The Chasm Group).

Lewis, M. (2006) "Customer acquisition promotions and customer asset value", *Journal of Marketing Research*, Vol. 43, pp. 195–203.

Liataud, B. (2004) "The littlest sales force", *Harvard Business Review*, Vol. 82, Issue 10, October.

Litsky, B.E., Eddleston, K.A. & Kidder, D.L. (2006) "The good, the bad and the misguided: How managers inadvertently encourage deviant behaviors", *Academy of Management Perspectives*, February.

Liu, A.H. (2006) "Customer value and switching costs in business services: Developing exit barriers through strategic value management", *Journal of Business and Industrial Management*, Vol. 21, No. 1, pp. 30–37.

Lock, D. & Meimoun, E. (1999) *International Purchasing: Selecting, Engaging and Managing the World's Best Suppliers*, American Quality and Productivity Center, Houston.

Lorange, P. (1975) "Divisional planning: Setting effective direction", *Sloan Management Review*, Vol. 17, Issue 1, pp. 77–91.

Lynch, J. & de Chernatony, L. (2004) "The power of emotion: Brand communication in business-to-business markets", *Brand Management*, Vol. 11, No. 5, pp. 403–419.

Martilla, J.A. & James, J.C. (1977) "Importance-performance analysis", *Journal of Marketing*, January, pp. 77–79.

Maslow, A.H. (1993) *The Farther Reaches of Human Nature*, Arkana, New York.

McDonald, M. (1984) *Marketing Plans: How to Prepare Them: How to Use Them*, Butterworth Heinemann, Oxford.

McDonald, M., Millman, A. & Rogers, B. (1996) *Key Account Management: Learning from Supplier and Customer Perspectives*, Cranfield School of Management in association with the Chartered Institute of Marketing, United Kingdom.

McDonald, M., Millman, A. & Rogers, B. (1997) "Key account management: Theory, practice and challenges", *Journal of Marketing Management*, Vol. 13, pp. 737–757.

McDonald, M. & Woodburn, D. (1999) *Key Account Management – Building on Supplier and Buyer Perspectives*, Cranfield School of Management/Financial Times.

McDonald, M., Rogers, B. & Woodburn, D. (2000) *Key Customers – How to Manage Them Profitably*, Butterworth Heinemann, Oxford.

McDougall, P. (2005) "The importance of an outsourcing prenup", *Information Week*, May 23. www.informationweek.com.

McLean, E. (2006) "A major role", *Winning Edge*, July/August.

Menkes, J. (2005) *Executive Intelligence: What All Great Leaders Have*, Collins, New York.

Mentzer, J.T., Blenstock, C.C. & Kahn, K.B. (1999) "Benchmarking sales forecasting management", *Business Horizons*, May–June.

Meredith, L. (1993) "A customer evaluation system", *Journal of Business and Industrial Marketing*, Vol. 8, No. 1, pp. 58–72.

Millman, A.F. (1994) "Relational aspects of key account management", *Fourth Seminar of the European Network for Project Marketing and Systems Selling*, University of Pisa, Italy, April 22–23.

Millman, A.F. & Wilson, K.J. (1994) "From key account selling to key account management", *Tenth Annual Conference on Industrial Marketing and Purchasing*, University of Groningen, The Netherlands, September 1994.

Millman, A.F. & Wilson, K.J. (1995) "Developing key account managers", *Eleventh Annual Conference on Industrial Marketing and Purchasing*, Manchester Business School, United Kingdom, September 1995.

Minahan, T.A. & Vigoroso, M.W. (2002) *The Supplier Measurement Benchmarking Report*, Aberdeen Group and iSource, December 2002.

Moon, M.A., Mentzer, J.T. & Thomas, D.E. (2000) "Customer demand planning at Lucent Technologies", *Industrial Marketing Management*, Vol. 29, pp. 19–26.

Morgan, J. (1998) "Just how good a customer are you?", *Purchasing*, November 19, Vol. 125, No. 8, p. 53.

Mota, J. & de Castro, L.M. (2005) "Relationship portfolios and capability development: Cases from the moulds industry", *Journal of Purchasing and Supply Management*, Vol. 11, pp. 42–54.

www.msssb.org, Sales National Occupational Standards.

Myers, J.B., Pickersgill, A.D. & Van Metre, E.S. (2004) "Steering customers to the right channels", *The McKinsey Quarterly*, No. 4. www.mckinseyquarterly.com.

Myron, D. (2002) "Analysts feud over CRM Failure", *Line56.com*, May 2002.

Nichols-Manning, C. (1978) "Sales to marketing: the crucial transition", *Management Review*, July (published by the American Management Association).

Olsen, R.F. & Ellram, L.M. (1997) "A portfolio approach to supplier relationships", *Industrial Marketing Management*, Vol. 26, pp. 101–113.

Pacetta, F. (1995) "*Don't Fire Them, Fire Them Up: Motivate Yourself and Your Team*", Simon & Schuster, London.

Paladino, M., Bates, H. & da Silveira, G.J.C. (2002) "Using a customer-focused approach to improve quality across the supply chain: The case of Siderar", *Total Quality Management*, Vol. 15, No. 5, pp. 671–683.

Parikh, J. (2005) "The Zen of management maintenance: Leadership starts with self-discovery", *Harvard Working Knowledge*, 5/9/2005. http://hbswk.hbs.edu.

Pardo, C. (1997) "Key account management in the business to business field: The key account's point of view", *The Journal of Personal Selling and Sales Management*, Vol. 17, No. 4, pp. 17–26.

Perrin, R.A. & Conway, K. (2005) "How to achieve the promise of e-commerce", *Healthcare Purchasing*, July 2005.

Persaud, R. (1997) *Staying Sane: How to Make Your Mind Work for You*, Metro Books, London.

Pesta, J. & Ramakrishnan, V. (2001) "Indian software firm Wipro wins praise for reducing its reliance on sales to GE", *Wall Street Journal*, January 4.

Piercy, N.F. & Lane, N. (2003) "Transformation of the traditional salesforce: Imperatives for intelligence, interface and integration", *Journal of Marketing Management*, Vol. 19, pp. 563–582.

Piercy, N.F. & Lane, N. (2005) "Strategic imperatives for transformation in the conventional sales organization", *Journal of Change Management*, Vol. 5, No. 3, September, pp. 249–266.

Piercy, N.F. & Lane, N. (2006) "The hidden risks in strategic account management strategy", *Journal of Business Strategy*, Vol. 27, No. 1, pp. 18–26.

Piercy, N.F. & Lane, N. (2007) "Ethical and moral dilemmas associated with strategic relationships between business-to-business buyers and sellers", *Journal of Business Ethics* Vol. 72, pp. 87–102.

www.pimsonline.com.

Porter, M. (1985) *Competitive Advantage*, The Free Press, New York.

Pressey, A.D. & Mathews, B.P. (2003) "Jumped, pushed or forgotten? Approaches to dissolution", *Journal of Marketing Management*, Vol. 19, pp. 131–155.

Rackham, N. (1989) *Major Account Sales Strategy*, McGraw-Hill, New York.

Rackham, N. & Ruff, R. (1991) *Managing Major Sales: Practical Strategies for Improving Sales Effectiveness*, McGraw-Hill, New York.

Rackham, N., Friedman, L. & Ruff, R. (1996) *Getting Partnering Right*, McGraw-Hill, New York.

Rackham, N. & de Vincentis, J. (1998) *Rethinking the Salesforce*, McGraw-Hill, New York.

Rackham, N. (2000) column in *Sales and Marketing Management*, Spring 2000.

Rask, M. & Kragh, H. (2004) "Motives for e-marketplace participation: Differences and similarities between buyers and sellers", *Electronic Markets*, Vol. 14, Issue 4, pp. 270–283.

Reinartz, W., Thomas, J.S. & Kumar, V. (2005) "Balancing acquisition and retention resources to maximize customer profitability", *Journal of Marketing*, Vol. 69, pp. 63–79.

Rich, G.A. (1998) "The constructs of sales coaching: supervisory feedback, role modelling and trust", *Journal of Personal Selling and Sales Management*, Vol. 18, No. 1, pp. 53–63.

Richard, S. & Wilson, K. (2000) "Developing organisational commitment to global strategic account management programmes – the Marriott experience", *The Journal of Selling and Major Account Management*, Vol. 2, No. 4, pp. 66–77.

Rigby, D.K., Reichheld, F.F. & Schefter, P. (2002) "Avoid the four perils of CRM", *Harvard Business Review*, February.

The Risk Newsletter, supplied by Risk Doctor and Partners. www.risk-doctor.com.

Robbins, S.P. (1991) *Organizational Behavior*, London: Prentice Hall.

Robinson, S.J.Q., Hitchens, R.E. & Wade, D.P. (1978) "The directional policy matrix: Tool for strategic planning", *Long Range Planning*, Vol. 11, Issue 3, pp. 8–15.

Rock, D. & Schwartz, J. (2006) "The neuroscience of leadership", *Strategy + Business*, June.

Rogers, B. (1999) "The key account manager as leader", *Journal of Sales and Major Account Management*, Vol. 1, No. 3, February.

Rogers, B. (2003a) "Seven steps to stunning account plans", *USP Magazine*, October.

Rogers, B. (2003b) "Security and privacy – Legislative burden or commercial opportunity?", *Interactive Marketing*, Vol. 5, No. 2, October/December.

Rogers, B. (2004) "Lending a hand", *Sales and Marketing Professional*, May/June.

Rogers, B. (2005a) "Raising the bar for sales professionalism", *The Marketing Yearbook*.

Rogers, B. (2005b) "Mediate or mandate? How should sales and marketing integrate?" (Unpublished).

Rogers, B. & Stone, M. (2004) "Quick win strategy for the era of the 500-day CEO". www.wnim.com.

Roman, S. & Ruiz, S. (2005) "Relationship outcomes of perceived ethical behavior: The customer's perspective", *Journal of Business Research*, Vol. 58, pp. 439–445.

Roman, S. (2003) "The impact of ethical sales behavior on customer satisfaction, trust and loyalty to the company: An empirical study in the financial services industry", *Journal of Marketing Management*, Vol. 19, pp. 915–939.

Ross, W.T. Jr, Dalsace, F. & Anderson, E. (2005) "Should you set up your own sales force or should you outsource it? Pitfalls in the standard analysis", *Business Horizons*, Vol. 48, pp. 23–36.

Rouzies, D., Anderson, E., Kohli, A.K., Michaels, R.E., Weitz, B.A. & Zoltners, A.A. (2005) "Sales and marketing integration: A proposed framework", *Journal of Personal Selling and Sales Management*, Vol. 25, No. 2, pp. 113–122.

Ruokolainen, J. & Igel, B. (2004) "The factors of making the first successful customer reference to leverage the business of start-up software company – multiple case study in Thai software industry", *Technovation*, Vol. 24, pp. 673–681.

Ryals, L. & Rogers, B. (2005) "Sales compensation plans – one size does not fit all", *Journal of Targeting, Measurement and Analysis for Marketing*, Vol. 13, Issue 4, pp. 354–362.

Ryals, L. & Rogers, B. (2006) "Holding up the mirror: The impact of strategic procurement practice on account management", *Business Horizons*, Vol. 49, Issue 1, pp. 41–50.

Ryals, L. & Rogers, B. (2007) "Key account planning: Benefits, barriers and best practice", *Journal of Strategic Marketing* (forthcoming).

Sa Vinhas, A. & Anderson, E. (2005) "How potential channel conflict drives channel structure: Concurrent (direct and indirect) channels", *Journal of Marketing Research*, Vol. 42, pp. 507–515.

Sargeant, A. & West, D.C. (2001) *Direct and Interactive Marketing*, Oxford University Press, Oxford.

Sant, T. (2004) *Persuasive Business Proposals*, Amacom, New York.

Schultze, A. (2004) "Taking channel performance to the next level", October 18. www.destinationCRM.com.

Seely Brown, J.S. (2005) "Innovation blowback: Disruptive management practices from Asia", *The McKinsey Quarterly*, No. 1, pp. 34–45.

Sengupta, S., Krapfel, R.E. & Puserati, M.A. (1997) "Switching costs in key account relationships", *The Journal of Personal Selling and Sales Management*, Vol. 17, No. 4, Fall, pp. 9–16.

Senn, C. (2006) "The executive growth factor: How Siemens invigorated its customer relationships", *Journal of Business Strategy*, Vol. 27, No. 1, pp. 27–34.

Shapiro, B. (2002) "Want a happy customer? Co-ordinate sales and marketing", *Harvard Working Knowledge*, October 28. http://hbswk.hbs.edu.

Sharma, A. (1997) "Who prefers key account management programs? An investigation of business buying behavior and buying firm characteristics", *The Journal of Personnel Selling and Sales Management*, Vol. 17, No. 4, Fall, pp. 27–39.

Sharma, A. (2000) "Do salespeople and customers understand each other? Surprising results from extant research", *Journal of Selling and Major Account Management*, Vol. 3, Issue 1, pp. 29–39.

Shaw, R. (1998) *Improving Marketing Effectiveness*, The Economist Books, London.

Siebel White Paper (2004) "Developing an effective sales process for the enterprise". www.siebel.com.

Simpkins, R.A. (2004) *The Secrets of Great Sales Management*, AMACOM, New York.

Slavens, R. (2006) "SAS wins MLB account, uses testimonial ads to land clients", *B to B*, Vol. 91, Issue 4, p. 22, March 4.

Smith, A. (1776) *Wealth of Nations*.

Smithers, C. (2006) "Improving communication to boost sales at BT", *Strategic Communication Management*, Vol. 10, Issue 1, pp. 18–21.

So, S.L.M. (2005) "What matters most in advertising agency performance to clients: implications and issues on their relationship in Hong Kong", *Journal of Current Issues and Research in Advertising*, Vol. 27, No. 2, pp. 83–97.

Speier, C. & Venkatesh, V. (2002) "The hidden minefields in the adoption of sales force automation technology", *Journal of Marketing*, Vol. 66, Issue 3, pp. 98–113.

Sweet, C., Sweet, T., Heritage, V. & Turner, M. (2006) *Blind Faith and the Bottom Line: What's Driving Sales Performance?*, The Communication Challenge Ltd. Available via www.ismm.co.uk.

Sweet, C., Sweet, T., Rogers, B., Heritage, V. & Turner, M. (2007) "Developing a company-wide sales capability", *Industrial and Commercial Training*, Vol. 39, No. 1.

Sweet, T. (2003) *The Manager's Story: A Simple Approach to Coaching Makes a Difference at Britvic*, The Communication Challenge Ltd.

Swinder, J. & Seshadri, S. (2001) "The influence of purchasing strategies on performance", *Journal of Business & Industrial Marketing*, Vol. 16, Issue 4, pp. 294–308.

www.tennyson.uk.com.

Tjosvold, D. (1984) "Co-operation theory and organizations", *Human Relations*, Vol. 37, No. 9, pp. 743–767.

www.uic.com, *Dover Corporation Code of Business Conduct and Ethics.*

www.upsa-intl.org, *The UPSA Professional Selling Ethics Framework.*

Ulaga, W. & Eggert, A. (2006) "Relationship value and relationship quality: Broadening the nomological network of business-to-business relationships", *European Journal of Marketing*, Vol. 40, No. 3–4, pp. 311–327.

Van Hoek, R. & Evans, D. (2005) "When good customers are bad", *Harvard Business Review*, Vol. 83, Issue 9, p. 19.

Walter, A. & Gemünden, H.G. (2000) "Bridging the gap between suppliers and customers through relationship promoters: Theoretical considerations and empirical results", *Journal of Business and Industrial Marketing*, Vol. 15, No. 2/3, pp. 86–105.

Ward, J. & Murray, P. (1997) *Benefits Management: Best Practice Guidelines*, Cranfield School of Management, Cranfield.

Ward, J. & Daniel, E. (2005) *Benefits Management: Delivering Value from IS and IT Investments*, John Wiley & Sons Ltd, Chichester.

Wengler, S., Ehret, M. & Samy, S. (2006) "Implementation of key account management: Who, why and how? An exploratory study on the current implementation of key account management programs", *Industrial Marketing Management*, Vol. 35, pp. 103–112.

White, P.D. (1994) "9 common mistakes in customer acquisition strategies", *Bank Marketing*, Vol. 26, Issue 6, pp. 32–36.

Wijewardena, H., De Zoysa, A., Fonseka, T. & Perera, B. (2004) "The impact of planning and control sophistication on performance of small and medium-sized enterprises: Evidence from Sri Lanka", *Journal of Small Business Management*, Vol. 42, Issue 2, pp. 209–217.

Wilkinson, J.W. (2006) "Leadership support received by Australian business-to-business salespeople", *Proceedings of the Academy of Marketing Conference, London, Middlesex University Business School*, CD-ROM.

Wilson, H. (2004) *Channel Combining for Wealth*, Cranfield Management Update. www.Winthrop.edu.

Witchells, C. (2006) "Case study: London Stock Exchange", *Computing Business*, June 22.

Wood, G. (1995) "Ethics at the purchasing/sales interface: An international perspective", *International Marketing Review*, Vol. 12, No. 4, pp. 7–19.

Woodburn, D. (2005) *Teaching Notes*. www.marketingbp.com.

Workman, J.P., Homburg, C. & Jensen, O. (2003) "Intraorganizational determinants of key account management effectiveness", *Journal of the Academy of Marketing Science*, Vol. 31, No. 1, pp. 3–21.

Wright, R.F. & Lundstrom, W.J. (2004) "Physicians' perceptions of pharmaceutical sales representatives: A model for analysing the customer relationship", *International Journal of Medical Marketing*, Vol. 4, No. 1, pp. 29–38.

Yanamandram, V. & White, L. (2006) "Switching barriers in business-to business services: A qualitative study", *International Journal of Service Industry Management*, Vol. 17, Issue 2, pp. 158–192.

Yorke, D.A. & Droussiotis, G. (1993) "The use of customer portfolio theory – an empirical survey", *Annual Conference on Industrial Marketing and Purchasing*, Bath, UK, September.

Zsidisin, G.A. & Ellram, L.M. (2001) "Activities related to purchasing and supply management involvement in supplier alliances", *International Journal of Physical Distribution and Logistics Management*, Vol. 31, No. 9–10, pp. 617–634.

Index

Note: Figures and Tables are indicated by *italic page numbers*

Index compiled by Paul Nash